D0500081

Through Divided Minds

Dr. Robert Mayer

Through Divided

MINDS

Probing the Mysteries
of Multiple Personalities
—A Doctor's Story

DOUBLEDAY

New York   London   Toronto   Sydney   Auckland

Excerpt from "Vicious Pleasure."
Reprinted from *My Voice Will Go with You: The Teaching Tales of Milton H. Erickson, M.D.*; edited by Sidney Rosen, M.D., by permission of W. W. Norton & Company, Inc. Copyright © 1982 by Sidney Rosen, M.D.

Excerpt from "Learning to Stand Up."
Reprinted from *My Voice Will Go with You: The Teaching Tales of Milton H. Erickson, M.D.*; edited by Sidney Rosen, M.D., by permission of W. W. Norton & Company, Inc. Copyright © 1982 by Sidney Rosen, M.D.

Excerpt reprinted with permission from J. K. Zweig (ed.), *A Teaching Seminar with Milton H. Erickson*, pp. 211–16. Copyright © 1980 by the Milton H. Erickson Foundation. New York: Brunner/Mazel.

Published by Doubleday, a division of
Bantam Doubleday Dell Publishing Group, Inc.
666 Fifth Avenue, New York, New York 10103

Doubleday and the portrayal of an anchor
with a dolphin are trademarks of Doubleday,
a division of Bantam Doubleday Dell
Publishing Group, Inc.

Library of Congress Cataloging-in-Publication Data
Mayer, Robert
Through divided minds: a doctor's exploration of multiple
personalities / Robert Mayer. —1st ed.
p.   cm.
1. Multiple personality—Case studies.   I. Title.
RC569.5.M8M39   1988
616.85'236—dc19   88-15676
                                                              CIP

Book Design by Claire M. Naylon

ISBN 0-385-24396-0

First Edition
BG

TO LAURA

*In deep appreciation
for the help, support,
understanding, and love*

Acknowledgments

I would like to thank Arlene Levine, Ph.D., clinical director of Odyssey House; Pat Weltman, M.S.W.; Sidney Rosen, M.D.; Beth Garmat; Mildred Gelfond; and Laura Lubin, all of whom read the manuscript and gave me many valuable suggestions. I am also indebted to Lisa Wager, who heard me speak at a conference on multiple personality disorder and suggested that I write this book; Jim Fitzgerald, my editor at Doubleday; and Richard Levine. And, of course, I am most grateful to my patients, who consented to let me tell their stories so that others might be helped.

Contents

And philosophers of old have said,
"As a man thinketh, he is."

And all philosophers say,
"Reality is all in the head."

MILTON H. ERICKSON, M.D.

Through Divided Minds

Introduction

As the grandson of immigrants who could barely speak English and the son of a father who couldn't read or write it and a mother who had to quit high school to work, I have often thought about the unlikely path that led me to become a college professor and, eventually, a psychotherapist specializing in the treatment of multiple personality disorder. But in retrospect, it sometimes seems as if my unconscious mind had a career picked out for me all along.

As a child I wanted to be a professor, living a cloistered life. Unfortunately, my family was quite poor and I soon found myself accepting a scholarship to the Rutgers College of Pharmacy, which I hoped would enable me to emulate three uncles who were making a good living as pharmacists. In 1956 I was licensed to practice pharmacy, and within a few years I owned two stores in New Jersey. But although I was financially successful, I was intellectually unfulfilled. I found myself taking courses in subjects my scientific training had left out—philosophy, literature, history, art history, comparative religion, sociology, and psychology. In 1962 I sold the stores and used the proceeds to support my family, which now included a son, Wayne, while I went back to Rutgers, this time for a doctorate in history. By the late sixties, I had my degree and an appointment as assistant professor at Kean College in Union, New Jersey.

I liked teaching, and I liked my students. But I still felt something was missing. I came to believe I was ignoring an entire dimension of my field. I was teaching my students about economic, political, and sociological influences, but not about the psychological underpinnings of events. Once again I decided to go back to school, this time to become a psychohistorian, someone who is aware of the psychological dimensions of history as well as the history of psychology. I envisioned myself teaching such courses as psychobiography, the history of the family, psychology of warfare, the history of psychology, and other such subjects.

I enrolled in the American Institute for Psychotherapy and Psychoanalysis in New York City. Although it was a training institute for psychotherapists, I remember telling Ross Thalheimer, the institute's director, that I was not interested in practicing but had a more academic end in mind. He was agreeable, and soon I was taking courses with psychiatrists, psychologists, and social workers in the evenings while I taught at the college during the day. I was also analyzed, which was a requirement of the program. Thinking I would someday write about the history of the profession to supplement my course work, which was classically oriented, I traveled all over the country to study different methods and approaches—gestalt therapy with Fritz Perls, psychosynthesis training with Harry Sloan, behavioral therapy, bioenergetics, psychodrama with James Sacks, rational emotive therapy with Albert Ellis, hypnosis with Elliot Podel, family systems theory with Gregory Bateson and Jay Haley, mythology with Joseph Campbell, and so on.

After my second year at the institute, Dr. Thalheimer called me in for a chat. He told me he was aware that I had no intention of practicing psychotherapy but asked me to reconsider. Apparently, some of my teachers thought I would be good at it.

I reminded him of my unorthodox background, but he insisted that my medical and pharmacological knowledge and my knowledge of history would be assets, not liabilities. He noted that Freud himself had argued that people with varied backgrounds make the best analysts. He also argued that if I was going to write about the profession, I should have firsthand knowledge of it.

After much soul searching, I accepted my first patient from the institute's clinic, the Community Guidance Service. By the mid-seventies, I had a fellowship from the institute and a small, private psychotherapeutic practice. Four years later, Toby, the central character in this book, was referred to me and I had a new specialty as well—multiple personality disorder.

Toby and the other patients you will meet are real. However, I have changed their names as well as the names of their alter personalities to insure their privacy. I have also taken other liberties, in some cases exchanging incidents of similar psychological significance among patients, also in the interests of privacy, and in other cases compressing episodes for the sake of clarity. Many of the conversations and episodes you will read about happened years ago, at a time when I had no intention of writing about them, but I have tried to recollect them as accurately as I could.

T O B Y

I was reclining in my new chair, obtained after a long search and at great expense to comfort my ailing back. The patient was lying on my new, official, imitation leather analytic couch. The sun was streaming through the blinds, and I was feeling very much like a Greenwich Village Analyst.

My patient, Toby, had been in treatment for about a year, and from the very beginning she had been one great pain. She had tested my analytic skills as well as my patience, which quite frankly was starting to run out. Now, in addition to complaining about lying on the couch, she was refusing to talk, eliminating the only tools I had. I work with words. Without them I have nothing.

Toby had been referred to me by one of my other patients, who was Toby's coworker at a New York City publishing house. She was twenty-eight, short, grossly overweight, not even a little attractive, and very needy, both emotionally and financially. Since I was young, relatively new in my profession, and trying to build a practice, I took her case at a reduced fee and scheduled her for two sessions a week.

Toby had moved to New York from Akron, Ohio, a few years earlier and appeared to be having trouble adjusting—to the city, to her colleagues, and to men. When I first began seeing her, my instant analysis was that she was a garden variety neurotic who, after a few years of talking about how hard life was and how poorly she had been treated by her parents and friends, would get bored with our sessions and, with some attention from me, would grow up and face what we all have to face. (I was a little more cynical early in my career than I am now.)

Still, I couldn't help feeling there might be something more to this case, something beneath the surface. Just two days after my first session with Toby, she phoned me, nearly hysterical. I was on a weekend retreat in upstate New York with some other patients, but I took time out from the group therapy session and managed to ease her anxiety.

By Monday she had calmed down, and during the next few weeks she settled into treatment so smoothly that I returned to my initial hypothesis that hers was a relatively straightforward case. Slowly, she grew comfortable with me and I tried to learn more about her and why she was willing to pay money to talk to me.

Apart from the fact that her father had died six months after she was born, she seemed to have had an extraordinary childhood, at least what she could remember of it. Bright and talented, she could read classical Greek at the age of ten. She painted, selling some oils to a local museum while she was still in high school and going on to major in art history at college. She was also very well read, usually devouring four to five books a week. Her life had been full, she told me, with many girlfriends and at least one boyfriend. When I pressed her for details, however, I noticed that she had little memory of events in her life before the age of fifteen.

Things changed for the worse shortly after she finished college and moved to New York. After a fight with a lover—he tried to force himself on her sexually, she said—she started gaining weight. Although she had three older sisters, Toby had virtually no contact with them, nor with her mother or any other members of the family. She had no friends, constantly fought with her colleagues, and was not at all interested in men, much less dating, marriage, or children. When she started therapy, she was living an asexual life. She hated her job, hated New York, and wanted nothing more than to move to a small cabin in the woods where she could live alone, paint, read, and play with her cats, which seemed about the only things she did like.

After a few months the case took a turn that gave me pause. Toby arrived at my office quite upset, complaining that nightmares had kept her up all night. All she could remember was that one of her dreams was about a person placing a precious object in a box, which was dark and closed. It could have meant anything.

I followed classic dream interpretation procedure, which goes like this: First, I ask the patient to tell me about the dream. Next I suggest that she think of what she did the day before to see what might have triggered it. Dreams usually take some real event for their canvas. Finally, I ask the patient to think about possible symbols that might be lurking in the dream. I try to get her to let her mind wander—a process Freud termed "free association"—to see what hidden meanings a dream may have. When it works, this technique allows a patient to uncover long-buried memories and feelings.

Freud, who originated this approach, believed the mind is divided between the conscious and the unconscious, which is the hidden reservoir of all that happens to us along with all of our primitive instincts and drives. Whenever troublesome information bubbles up, the mind disguises it with symbols, repressing these unpleasant thoughts and feelings, keeping them beyond the range of our awareness. This process protects us, but at a cost. Freud believed it consumes a tremendous amount of psychic energy to keep troubling memories locked away. Free association can dislodge the secrets of the unconscious, releasing blocked emotions and freeing this energy, which patients can use to better face life.

I like to think of the unconscious as a computer that stores everything placed into it but can display only a fraction of the information on the screen at any time. The trick to using a computer is learning how to access the information you want. Similarly, free association is the way to access information buried deep in the memory banks of the mind.

The day before Toby's dream appeared to be normal. She went to work, which she hated. She ate lunch in the company dining room with some colleagues. She went home, stopping first at the safe deposit box at her bank—she had gained so much weight that her ring no longer fit, and, fearful that it would be stolen or lost, she wanted to put it in the bank's vault for safekeeping—and then went to a local Chinese takeout to pick up dinner. After dinner, she turned on the television to watch the remake of *Invasion of the Body Snatchers*, a clue I missed at the time.

When Toby started to associate about the box in her dream, a frightening thing happened. She suddenly went back in time and relived an apparently unrelated childhood experience. Not just remembered it, relived it. She was being taken into the cellar by her mother, who placed her on the stairs, turned the light off, closed the door and locked it. Lying there before me, Toby started screaming that there was a monster in the cellar, a horrible creature with a big red eye that was going to devour her. The woman before me was in abject terror. Or rather, the child, since I realized that she was talking and behaving like a five-year-old, describing in detail events that had happened more than twenty years before and in a youthful voice. Tears were streaming down her cheeks, and her body was shaking with fear.

Freud had his patients lie on a couch because he could not stand them staring at him all day. I thanked God Toby was on a couch so that she could not see my amazement.

My shock then turned to excitement when I realized I was witnessing a psychological phenomenon called an abreaction, the reliving of an original, tension-evoking experience that has long been buried in the unconscious. This is an extension and even a goal of the dream interpretation process that allows a patient to release an emotional burden by acting it out anew. Patients do not usually reach this stage for a long time, if they reach it at all. In fact, although I had read about abreactions, I had never before witnessed one of these magical events, either in my fledgling practice or in my own analysis, which had taken place four times a week for five years.

I decided to let the process continue and then to try to calm Toby and bring her back to reality. Dealing with an abreaction is much like lancing a psychic boil. Allow it to come to a head, pierce it, clean it out, and then let the body heal it. At least, that was what Freud advised in *Studies on Hysteria*.

On and on went Toby's abreaction. She was shaking like a child, her head alternately between her arms and her knees, screaming that it was dark, that she was alone, and that a red-eyed monster was approaching. She reminded me of patients in hypnotic states who actually regress, talking—sounding—like children. Our minds are vaults of information that include memories of how we behaved at various ages. By plugging into those memories, hypnotists can take subjects back to different stages in their lives. Older people often regress, too, due to senility, and surgeons can make patients feel as though they are reliving a past experience by stimulating parts of the brain during operations. And now Toby was doing it, abreacting like crazy on the couch before me.

The problem was, there was nothing I could do to stop her. I could not get her out of the cellar or even out of 1958, much less out of the Midwest and into New York City. And my next patient was already in my waiting room. What was I going to do? I hoped my office soundproofing was working.

For a moment, I nearly panicked. Then out of *my* unconscious popped an idea it had tagged away from the famed hypnotherapist Milton Erickson, whose writings I had devoured. Encountering a patient who was having difficulty talking, Erickson instructed him to change chairs, suggesting that the problem that prevented him from talking would remain behind in the empty seat. The patient moved and immediately began to speak. Erickson believed we all have many avenues of consciousness, just as a television set has many channels. If one doesn't work, he reasoned, simply switch to another, which was what he was making his patient do when he moved to another chair.

"Toby, you are in the cellar. The couch you are lying on is the cellar. Get up off the couch and move to the chair. The chair is in my office. Not in the cellar. Get up and move. *Now.*"

She got off the couch, moved to the chair, and, to my amazement and relief, was transported back to New York City and the present. I knew this because she straightened up and stopped crying and shaking. She looked and sounded normal, although she was clearly confused about what had just happened.

Borrowing another psychological technique, this time from that noted amateur practitioner, Scarlett O'Hara, I told her we would talk about it tomorrow. This was mostly because I did not understand the amazing scene I had just witnessed or know quite how to explain it to Toby. And, of course, I had to get on to my next patient, who thankfully behaved like a proper therapeutic subject, reclining on the couch and musing about how hard it was for her to meet men in New York City, since they all were either gay, married, or jerks.

I spent much of that evening thinking about Toby. Clearly, she had a problem for which I had not been trained. I decided to schedule her for the last session of the day, so that if she regressed again I would at least have time to bring her out of it —assuming I could bring her out of it—without having to worry about running out of chairs in my waiting room.

Then again, I wondered whether it wasn't a mistake to put too much time and thought into one patient, lest the others suffer. By giving her more than her hour on the couch, was I giving her a false impression of what she was entitled to from her analyst? Was I diminishing her resolve to get better and reinforcing her illness? Perhaps Toby's abreaction was a ruse to get more attention from me.

I didn't know how to answer those questions, but I really didn't have any choice. I wasn't experienced enough to take the chance that Toby's abreactions would get out of control. So she started coming in the evening. And, as I had feared, her episodes happened again and again and again. One moment, she would be lying on my couch, a model if somewhat resistant psychoanalytic patient. Then she would spontaneously regress to an earlier period of her life and relive some truly awful event. To make matters worse, Toby's episodes seemed progressively more horrible. As a five-year-old, she told me in a quivering five-year-old voice, she had wandered into a neighbor's garage to look around. The neighbor happened to be the town pathologist—Toby was lucky that way—and she became engrossed by the various specimens he had stored on the shelves. She didn't realize that he had sneaked up behind her and, after yelling at her for trespassing, proceeded to rape her. He told her that if she told anyone about the incident he would put *her* in one of the jars.

I had read various accounts of pedophiles and was aware that sexual abuse of children was far more common than we all would have suspected just a few years ago. My first reaction was not to believe her, though. She was a psychiatric patient, and who believes them? No, she was trying to make me feel sorry for her and thus give her more attention and couch time than she was entitled to.

But if it was an act, it was a polished one. And the tales Toby related were grotesque. In one grisly episode Toby was abused —no, tortured is more like it—by her mother, who, without warning, picked up a pot of boiling water and poured it over her daughter's arms and shoulders while she was playing on the floor, scalding her severely.

Then there was a time when Toby was playing in the yard and accidentally disturbed a bees' nest. As the insects started to swarm around her, she ran for the house, only to have her mother slam the door in her face.

On two other occasions her mother broke her arm and stabbed her in the hand. The old lady also had a nasty habit of putting her cigarettes out on her daughter's arms, sometimes while telling her she loved her. And if after any of these atrocities Toby told the family doctor or anyone else what had really happened, her mother warned, there would be further punishment.

I didn't know what to think. Where were her sisters or other relatives? Where were the authorities?

Toby told me she had tried to run away many times, but the police had always brought her back with instructions to be a good girl and listen to her mother. Adults rarely believed children in such cases then. If I questioned her, much less asked her to show me her scars, she would accuse me of treating her the same way. Anyway, I had been trained not to confront a patient, especially so early in treatment. Just as a carpenter does not knock down the walls of a house without first shoring up the ceiling, a psychoanalyst should not tear down a patient's defenses until some internal supports have been built to replace them. Better to accept the patient's version of reality, no matter how unreal. Better to engage in a process my profession calls "joining."

Whether Toby's stories were true or not, she was clearly very disturbed—and very fragile. So I proceeded as if the events had really happened and had been walled off by some childhood defense mechanism. She could not cope with the repeated trauma, could not even tell anyone about it for fear of further violence, so she dissociated—she simply forgot the experiences. But of course they were not really forgotten, just locked away in her unconscious. And my sessions with her were somehow starting to stir them up.

I stuck to my plan, which was to let her talk, encouraging her to free-associate, knowing it would trigger her episodes. I hoped she would exhaust her repertoire of horror stories, reliving them and through her abreactions gradually releasing the tension. Then she would get better. And if they weren't real? Then at some point she would get bored by our sessions— or at least become drained by the expense—and give it up. Or so I kept telling myself.

For a few months it seemed to work. I became skilled at containing her spontaneous eruptions within the therapeutic hour. I would let them run their course, even accentuating the gruesome details. I would also carefully watch the clock, allowing enough emotional recycling time. Put the rest of the pain away, I would tell her. We will come back to it another day. If Toby was very upset after a session, I would let her sit in the waiting room until she felt strong enough to go home.

Before I had much of a chance to congratulate myself on my skill, however, the case took a distressing new turn. Toby started to have the episodes at home, while she was watching television, listening to a radio, trying to draw. Anything, it seemed, could set her off.

I began getting phone calls at all hours of the night from a panicky, childlike woman in the midst of reliving some almost unspeakably terrible experience that had happened to her years before. Dealing with these episodes while she was on my couch was hard enough, but coping with them over the phone was another matter. I had been taught not to respond to patients out of the office unless it was an emergency—by my definition, not theirs. There were two good reasons for this. Without being able to observe them, I couldn't really be sure how to respond. More important, patients should not get the sense the therapist is always available. It can become a crutch. But given my inexperience and the fact that I was not sure what was happening, I decided I had to give Toby some extra emotional support, even over the telephone.

Fortunately, the same method I used to calm her down in the office seemed to be equally effective over a phone line. I would ask her where she was sitting, then tell her that was the place where the trauma was happening and ask her to move to another spot. Then she would come out of it. Thanks again, Milton Erickson.

Still, I was getting more and more worried, and so was Toby. According to the theory, the abreactions were supposed to stop as the patient relived an experience. Then the patient and the analyst could talk about it, put it into proper perspective, and move on. But far from unburdening her, these horrible and continuing episodes, relived with nearly the same intensity as when they had happened, were making her terribly anxious and hardly making me sleep better at night, either. The only party to the case who was not concerned was my psychiatric supervisor, Arnold, whom I, as a relatively new analyst, would go to once a week. Together we would discuss my cases, and he would give me the benefit of his knowledge and experience, which was vast and varied. The psychoanalytic profession is structured sort of like the Catholic Church— the priest talks to the bishop, who talks to the cardinal, who talks to the Pope, who talks to God. I always wondered whom Arnold talked to. Freud, perhaps.

Arnold was a classical analyst with a Ph.D. in clinical psychology. He was also a full professor of psychology at a major university and a senior professor at an analytic school, where people with degrees in medicine, psychology, and social work are trained in the techniques of psychoanalysis and psychotherapy. While he felt I was generally proceeding properly, Arnold was concerned that I was overstimulating Toby's unconscious. My treatment, he believed, had worn down her defenses, allowing the memories to flood in so fast that Toby did not have time to integrate them and thus benefit from the episodes. He suggested that I switch the focus of therapy from investigating her past to helping her with problems in the present, such as her dissatisfaction with her job and her coworkers.

His advice didn't make all that much sense to me, I'm afraid. It really didn't take any prodding on my part to trigger one of her episodes. Certainly I could not be accused of stimulating her unconscious while Toby was at home, watching television.

Having failed with my superior, I tried sending Toby to a psychiatrist. Maurice had a medical degree, so he could prescribe medication if it turned out she needed it. He also worked in a psychiatric hospital, so I felt he might be more familiar with more severe forms of illness than either Arnold or I.

Maurice is an abrupt man, and it didn't take him long to formulate his diagnosis: Toby was a dissociative hysteric, a pathological overreactor. And with that he put her on Atavan, an antianxiety medication. Maurice told me that my job was to do what I could to keep Toby out of a hospital. Obviously, this was not a very positive prognosis, nor a very helpful one. Just how was I supposed to keep her out of the hospital? I could hardly control her abreactions.

The Atavan was only mildly effective. It made Toby a tad calmer but did little else to make the case more manageable, much less solve it. Indeed, the case soon took yet another twist: Toby began coming to my office and claiming she was unable to talk, and according to Maurice it wasn't due to the Atavan. Week after week, she would sit on the couch facing me, mute. By this point, enough of her defenses had fallen that she felt so vulnerable she feared someone might sneak up and attack her if she reclined. She would say she had things to tell me but was unable to. She was resisting, the classical analyst inside me said. We needed to work through it. But how?

"Talk about it," I asked her.

"I can't talk about it."

"You don't have to talk about the things that you can't talk about. But can you talk about why you cannot talk?" I said, knowing I was sounding a bit like Chico Marx.

"No."

"Do you know why you can't talk about it?"

"No."

After a few minutes of quiet, I said: "Are you comfortable with the silence?"

"No," she emphatically replied.

"Shall I talk?" I asked, trying to get her to see how difficult this situation was becoming and at least start her talking to me about how we should proceed.

"Yes."

"What shall I talk about?"

"I don't know."

"If you don't know, how am I supposed to know?"

"You're the shrink."

Obviously, this technique did little to resolve her resistance. Her phone calls in the evening continued. Traumas that were supposed to be relived in the office were now being relived exclusively at home, while during her therapeutic sessions Toby sat silently before me. She seemed to be deteriorating rapidly. What the hell was going on? And what was I going to do?

Once again I found myself suspecting that it was all an act to get more of my time. Perhaps it was in my interest to think that way. Then again, if she really were regressing to childhood, how could she have the presence of mind to use the telephone or remember my number? One thing I was sure of was that she was wearing me out. I would have referred her to another therapist with more experience than I, but this was impossible. The fee that I was charging was so low that no well-trained analyst would take her. Anyway, if I had suggested that she seek help elsewhere, she would have felt rejected, and there was no telling what she might have done. Nor did I have the courage to begin cutting back on the attention I was lavishing on her, even though the midnight phone calls were becoming too much.

There was no choice. All I could do was to hang on.

Almost in desperation, I decided to teach Toby self-hypnosis, in the hope that she could use the technique to bring herself out of her memory cycles, as she called them. It would also shift some of the responsibility for the case from the thera-pist to the patient, a beneficial side effect. Hypnosis would not be totally alien to her. In dissociating from traumas as a child, she intuitively relied on self-hypnotic technique. I would sim-ply be using her natural defense toward a healthy end. The more I thought about it, the more reasonable it seemed.

For a few sessions it was Hypnosis 101. Then, as a test, I gave my pupil a posthypnotic suggestion: Whenever these ab-reactions occurred at home, I told her, she was to consider herself already in a trance and simply bring herself back to reality.

Toby proved to be a hypnotic virtuoso. Sometimes she would have to call me for help or just to hear my voice, but by and large she became less dependent on the telephone and more comfortable on her own. And our sessions were becom-ing more productive as well, as she began to talk about some of the episodes.

Then, just as I was beginning to feel more confident, Toby abruptly stopped talking again. I didn't know whether she was doing this to annoy me, but it certainly had that effect. I tried my best to let it roll over me, since hostile thoughts from the analyst can destroy therapy. I had to assume that through our sessions we were reaching some traumatic lodestone that was stimulating this new resistance.

One of my teachers used to say that if a patient comes, pays, and talks, he or she will be cured. Of the three, showing up is most important, paying comes next, and talking ranks third, because you can always get the patient to talk. Well, Toby was showing up, all right, and she was paying for the privilege, but nothing I could do would get her to utter more than a few stilted words at a time.

"I notice that you are having trouble talking to me today," our sessions would typically begin, after a long silence. (In theory, one is supposed to let the patient start the session.)

"I can't talk."

"Do you know what is preventing you from talking?"

"Something is constricting my throat and not letting the words out."

After a few weeks of this, I got an inspiration from Fritz Perls, the father of a technique called gestalt, with whom I had worked at the Esalen Institute in California. As a young man Perls was enamored with Freud, undergoing analysis, becoming a psychiatrist, and traveling to Vienna to meet the master. When Freud would not receive him, Perls became unhappy with his idol, with Freudian theory, with Freudian technique—with anything remotely Freudian. Instead, he came to believe that people had various parts to their personalities—a part that wants them to grow and a part that doesn't, a part that encourages them and a part that tears them down. This is why we sometimes talk to ourselves in internal debates, he reasoned.

To cure this potentially destructive duality, Perls developed a technique to further "split" his patients, making their internal dialogues more conscious to them by asking one part to speak to the other. He believed that making patients more aware of these dialogues would lead them to examine—and reconcile—the differences.

Perhaps Toby was split, I thought, with one part trying to communicate with me and another stopping her cold. So I tried Perls's technique.

"Toby, let yourself experience trying to talk and feel the thing that is preventing you from talking."

There was a pause.

"I see by your expression that you are experiencing it. Where is it located in your body?"

"In my throat. It feels like there are hands around my throat preventing me from talking."

"Now, imagine that those hands have a voice and can talk, and let them talk to me. Here, I'll help you. Start with this sentence: 'I am the part of me that is preventing me from talking.'"

"Okay. 'I am the part of me that is preventing me from talking.'"

I tried to get a conversation going with this voice. "Where are you located?" I asked it.

I was not prepared for the response.

Toby shut her eyes for a second or two, and when she opened them her posture—no, her whole person—had changed. Her body wiggled and fidgeted like that of a child who just couldn't get comfortable.

"Hi. I'm Beth. I thought you would never get around to talking to me."

A chill started at my toes and rose up my spine. I felt like I had as a kid, hanging around the haunted houses down on the Jersey shore. Toby's voice was that of a small child. But not the five-year-old Toby I had heard during her episodes. This was a different voice. A different child.

In her earlier episodes, Toby had regressed in age but stayed Toby. Now she wasn't Toby, she was Beth, or so she insisted. If this was an act, it was worthy of an Oscar. Still, I was trained not to be thrown by such maneuvers, to accept what my patients tell me, not to challenge them. At first, anyway. So I retained my outward cool and introduced myself.

"I'm Dr. Mayer, Toby's doctor."

"We don't like doctors," she replied. "Doctors give shots. Are you going to give us a shot? We don't like shots. Are we sick?"

As I tried to explain to a five-year-old the difference between a Ph.D. and an M.D., an almost futile task that I was to come back to time and time again, I tried to be friendly.

"Beth, where did you come from?"

"Inside. I live inside."

"What do you mean inside? Inside Toby?"

"Yes."

"Well, why did you come out now?"

"We were waiting to talk to you. We wanted you to call us. We were waiting for you to call us."

I did my best to ignore her use of the first-person plural. "Why didn't you just talk to me?"

"We were brought up to be polite. We were waiting for you to ask us."

With that, she put her thumb into her mouth, then scrunched up her face in juvenile revulsion.

"Yuk. Tastes terrible," she said. Then she started to wail.

I'm not good with children, and I don't know the first thing about child psychiatry, but I did my best to calm her. Then I remembered that Toby used a lot of hand lotion, often putting it on during our sessions. I figured this was what Toby—or Beth—was complaining about. So I took her to the bathroom to wash her hands, since she was too frightened to go by herself. It was like dealing with a profoundly retarded adult. If she was inventing all this, she was a better actress than I could have guessed.

When we got back into the office, she asked if she could have a cookie, a chocolate one. Fortunately, I had some in the kitchen. Once she was pacified, I asked some very basic questions. Beth was a precocious child, who knew she should be well behaved but was not. Nearly all of her answers were interspersed with demands, often for more cookies. I knew my supply would not last much longer.

I was still wondering about her use of "we" and "us." Not wanting to hear the wrong answer, I asked, "Are there any more like you in there?"

"Oh, yes, there's Anna."

"Can I meet her?"

"I don't know. I'll ask. Be right back."

Her eyes rolled up to the ceiling, and I could see her going "internal" again, as she had when she first switched identities. Then Beth came back and said Anna was willing to meet me.

"But you'll talk to me again, won't you?"

"Absolutely. But how will I reach you?"

"Just call me, silly, and I'll come. Okay?"

"Okay."

She closed her eyes for a second or two. Her posture changed again, becoming almost rigid. Her voice deepened. To my relief, I realized that Anna was an adult. Whatever was going on here, I knew that it would be easier for me to talk to an adult than a child.

Indeed, Anna was brilliant. All her words seemed chosen in advance, and she spoke in perfect sentences that said exactly what she wanted them to say, no more, no less. It was also reassuring that Anna said she was twenty-eight, the same age as Toby. She told me that she lived "inside" with Beth, who she called "that arm waver," a fairly accurate description as far as I could tell.

"You mean you don't like her?"

"I'd like to kill her. She's a real pain in the ass, always getting into trouble. And I'm the one who has to take care of her."

"You don't mean you *really* want to kill her?"

"Yes, I do."

My instincts told me I didn't want anybody dying.

"Listen, Anna, I don't think you ought to talk that way. Everybody is valuable, everybody is important."

She sat silently. I tried another tack.

"Anna, do you know who I am?"

"Yes, you're Dr. Mayer."

"Do you know why you are here?"

"Therapy."

Like Beth, Anna said she had been watching me and listening to me for a long time, but she could at least understand my relationship with Toby. Anna, bless her, was cognitive, aware —adult. I told myself that if this behavior continued—if it were real—Anna could be very useful.

Because Toby had the last appointment of the day, I could go beyond the therapeutic hour if I had to. Even so, it was now time for her to leave. I wanted to end the session before things got further out of control and give myself a chance to think it all through.

"We have to stop, Anna. Is it okay if we bring Toby back? I really should say good-bye to her."

"Yes, okay, I'll get her."

It seemed almost too easy. Once again, her eyes went to the ceiling and she faded away. A moment later her body language told me Toby had returned. She looked startled. She knew something had gone on but not exactly what. She said she was exhausted and wanted to go home to bed. I decided that would be best, reminding her that I would see her again in two days. And with that we said our good nights.

After she left, I made a quick call to Arnold and scheduled an appointment for myself for the following day. Then I sat down and thought about what had just occurred.

2

Questions

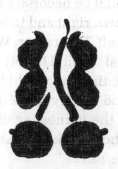

I went to bed thinking I would figure something out in the morning, but I couldn't sleep. All I could think of was Toby, Beth, and Anna.

By 1 A.M., I was searching through the shelves where I keep psychiatric reference books, looking for something that might help. There were references to multiple personality disorder in some of the more encyclopedic works, but nothing with any meat to it. That hardly surprised me. I had spent eight years training at the American Institute for Psychotherapy and Psychoanalysis, and not once had the subject of multiple personality come up. Nor had any of my colleagues ever mentioned it in the years since.

It seemed the stuff fiction was made of, or at any rate bestsellers, for among the high-minded tomes I had diligently collected was a slightly battered paperback copy of Flora Rhea Schreiber's *Sybil,* the story of a woman with sixteen personalities. After seven years of therapy, her psychiatrist, Cornelia Wilbur, had merged them into one person. I had read *Sybil* years ago but, like many in my line of work, had not taken it altogether seriously. It was a popular book, not an academic study. Professionals, myself included, did not fully trust such works.

Rereading the paperback that night, I found that Sybil, too, had been physically and sexually abused at an early age. Wilbur did not know what to do when her patient began to reveal her multiplicity. Apparently as confused as I was, she searched the literature and came up with eleven reported cases of multiple personality, eight women and three men. But she could find almost nothing about the origin of the illness or how to treat it. She decided to use psychoanalysis, which if successful would lead her to the roots of the disorder, and braced herself for a long ordeal. "She knew that it would be necessary to treat each of the selves as a persona in her own right and to winnow away the reserve of Sybil, the waking self," Schreiber, Wilbur's Boswell, wrote. "Otherwise the total Sybil Dorsett would never get well. The doctor knew, too, that she would have to make tremendous sacrifices of time and modify her usual consulting-room Freudian techniques to the harnessing of every shred of spontaneity that would help her break through to the truth that lay concealed behind these selves."

Wilbur started treating Sybil by meeting her various personalities and building relationships with each of them. Sometimes they would appear spontaneously during the therapeutic sessions. Other times, she would use hypnosis to draw them out. Wilbur eventually uncovered the abuse in her patient's past and made Sybil understand what had happened to her. She also enabled Sybil to release emotions she had long bottled up, which helped heal her. I realized as I read the book that Wilbur was far more active in treating Sybil than the usual classical psychoanalyst, and far more sympathetic as well. She would hold Sybil and take her on picnics and day trips. She even visited Sybil's hometown to interview people from her past. Was this what Toby needed?

It was almost dawn when I finished the book, all 450 pages of it. I was feeling more than a little relieved. I was young and ambitious. I felt that I was onto something. Perhaps I would be the new Wilbur. Or even the new Freud.

I woke up much closer to reality. Was I really so sure Toby was a multiple? Perhaps she was manipulating me? And how could I base my treatment on a paperback account of a case written for popular consumption, rather than a case published in a medical journal?

Once again I sought out my supervisor, Arnold. I was convinced I had solved the mystery of Toby's overwhelming abreactions. It wasn't a matter of my overstimulating her at all. The patient had multiple personalities. I expected my learned colleague to congratulate me on a job well done, then tell me how to proceed with the case. I had a lot of faith in Arnold. He was wise. He would have the answer.

After I recounted the events of the last incredible session with Toby I paused, waiting for the praise I felt I justly deserved. I was totally unprepared for Arnold's succinct response.

"There is no such thing as multiple personality."

"Arnold, the woman switches into different personalities in front of me." I didn't suppose it would help to remind him that multiplicity was listed in the second edition of *The Diagnostic and Statistical Manual of Mental Disorders*, the official list of diagnoses for the profession published by the American Psychiatric Association. (It was listed under hysterical neurosis. "In the dissociative type, alterations may occur in the patient's state of consciousness or in his identity to produce such symptoms as amnesia, somnambulism, fugue, and multiple personality.")

"I know what I saw. If it isn't multiple personality, what is it?"

"If there is such a thing as multiple personality, it is very rare. More likely what you saw is a resistance to treatment."

Arnold was an expert on resistance, that perplexing, frustrating, and distressingly common phenomenon in which a patient comes to therapy and then, consciously or unconsciously, rejects help, all toward the end of keeping painful memories locked away out of conscious awareness. Working through a patient's resistance is one of the major steps toward helping him.

There were two views on how this might be accomplished: One could confront resistance, or one could circumvent it. Arnold generally took the latter approach, believing that if you attacked the problem head on you only made it stronger. Force, after all, opposes force. So he would appear to give in to his patient's behavior—to "join it"—until his patient was compelled to examine his lack of cooperation and give it up. Even if a patient always came late to a session, for example, Arnold would refrain from pointing out that the tardiness was costing them both valuable time. Instead, he might say something like "I'm very glad you were able to get here today, but perhaps this time is not good for you." Next would come a gracious offer of some alternate times. Getting no opposition, the patient would be forced to think about his tardiness and eventually see it for what it was.

I thought over what Arnold had said. If it was resistance, then the proper therapeutic response would be to accept the multiplicity and proceed from there. But I wanted to hear him say it, just to make sure. "So, what do I do now about this resistance, Arnold?"

"Tell it to go away."

He had stunned me again.

"Are you serious? Tell it to go away? Did *you* ever do that?"

"I had a similar case years ago. I told it to go away, and it did."

"Was the case successful?"

"I think so. She stayed a while, got a little better, then terminated treatment."

"Have you heard from her since then?"

"No."

This wasn't helping me. Arnold, it seemed to me, had a resistance to the idea of a multiple personality, and I was not financially in a position to join it, at least at the rates he charged.

Of course, when you are in supervision you are treated like

a patient, and I'm sure Arnold thought I was the one who was resisting. It was an argument I could not win and that would cost me more than a buck a minute to lose.

I left his office shaken. I had lost a pillar I had been planning to lean on.

I sought out a few of my colleagues later that day and got pretty much the same response. Either they didn't believe multiplicity existed or, if it did, that it was like the purple cow they had never seen and never hoped to see. Had they ever learned anything about it in graduate school? No. In analytic school? No. Had they ever treated a multiple? No. Did they think they would be able to diagnose one? Maybe.

My next stop was Kean College in Union, New Jersey, where I am an associate professor of history, specializing in psychohistory. The library had just installed a computer to make searches of the professional literature. I asked the librarian to check for multiple personality disorder.

"Sorry, Dr. Mayer. We don't have the funds. It costs money to go on line, and the college did not budget for it."

"You mean we spent thousands of dollars to buy the computer but there isn't any money to use it?"

She just looked at me.

"How much does a search cost, anyway?"

"Oh, about five dollars."

"Well, I would certainly be glad to pay for it."

"Sorry again. There isn't a provision for us to accept money from people, except for late or lost books."

I headed for the office of the college president, an eminently reasonable man, and soon the computer spat out a list of about twenty-five citations since 1967. Now I knew how Wilbur had felt. In a profession that regularly fills more journals than it probably has any right to or need for, twenty-five articles was nothing more than a collective clearing of throats. On top of that, Kean College is an undergraduate institution, and most of the journals on the list were not in its modest library. I live four blocks from New York University and its extensive medical library, but professors from other schools are not allowed to use it. That meant a trip uptown to the New York Public Library or the New York Academy of Medicine.

Then I had an idea—why not send Toby? It was not exactly orthodox, but I felt it would do her good. She could use the money I would pay her, and besides, she liked doing work for me, since it made her feel needed. Our relationship was the only one she really had during those years, to the point where I sometimes viewed myself as a rent-a-friend. Maybe being my research assistant would also encourage her to assume some responsibility for solving her problem. (I knew she wouldn't read the journals—they would probably be far too threatening.)

Predictably, some of the articles merely questioned whether multiple personality disorder existed or whether the patient—or the therapist—concocted it, for whatever reason. But other studies concluded that multiplicity was very real indeed. They noted that component personalities may be of different ages or sexes than the "host"; may or may not know each other; may or may not like each other; may be of different faiths, ethnic origins, parentage, politics, professions, right- or left-handedness or sexual orientation; may have different IQs, brain waves, allergies; may speak different languages and dream different dreams; may possess banks of different memories; may have different ambitions and outlooks—may even claim to be spirits, ghosts, angels, devils, or other supernatural beings. These personalities could be demonstrated to be physically, chemically, and psychologically different, almost as if they indeed were different people encased in the same body.

The bizarreness of the disorder would challenge anyone's assumptions of what was real and unreal. What does a therapist do when confronted with this? Dissociate? Deny it? That was what Arnold and most of the profession seemed to be doing— and were advising me to do.

Just how common is multiplicity? According to another of the articles, a survey of the professional literature on this subject, 160 cases of multiple personality had been reported since 1816—more cases than Wilbur had found when she searched the literature. Still, as someone trained as a historian before I was trained as a psychoanalyst—which I suppose is really only personal history—the numbers seemed absurdly low. Multiple personality means one or more individuals living inside another person. When conditions are right, one of these entities takes charge of the body, and the host is transformed. Now isn't this what might have happened to the poor souls who were supposed to have been possessed by the Devil, or those more fortunate individuals who claimed to have conversed with the gods? Weren't such transformations of personality reported in every century from which we have written records?

Fortunately, I found *The Discovery of the Unconscious* by Henri F. Ellenberger, a 930-page study of the evolution of modern psychiatry that noted that multiple personality had a long, well-documented history. In fact, it was one of the first psychiatric disorders to be thoroughly studied and, Ellenberger observed, was hailed as the royal path to understand the workings of the mind.

But even the researchers who accepted multiplicity did not agree with each other on how the syndrome developed, although there seemed to be a consensus that early trauma was a factor.

One author argued that the "inability to express anger toward important figures caused the splitting of the personality." In Freud's time, it was the inability to express sexual needs that was believed to cause the forgetting. In contrast, my patients do not have much trouble talking about their sexual worries but often have great difficulty even being aware of their anger, much less expressing it. And it seemed logical that an abused child would have difficulty expressing anger toward a guilty parent likely to inflict more pain at the slightest provocation.

What happens to this unreleased anger? Perhaps another personality is formed to express it, or to be the "keeper of the rage." Or perhaps the system becomes overloaded with trauma and pain and creates another personality to share the burden. Either way, the benefits of extra personalities can be enormous. "I didn't break the window, Johnny did" . . . "I am a good girl, Sally isn't" . . . "I didn't spend all that money, Harry did." Another personality can behave in a way that is unacceptable to the primary personality, allowing someone, for example, to fulfill homosexual urges even if the host feels it is unacceptable to be gay.

But, of course, not everyone reacts to trauma by forming other personalities, and none of the researchers seemed to know why those who did, did. Some suggested that the parents might have been multiples and genetically or behaviorally passed the mechanism on to their offspring. Or even if not actually a multiple, a parent might behave so inconsistently toward the child—a good mommy one moment and a bad one the next—that it appears she is a multiple, and the child picks up on the cues. Other professionals argued that if parents set standards that are so high as to be unreachable, a child might have to change identity to escape from the anxiety of not being able to meet the standards—or from the resulting punishment. Which is really just another way of saying that dissociation is a way of maintaining psychological (or emotional) survival in the face of great stress.

Still others thought multiplicity might be a return to some primitive or infantile state. Most researchers believe that the ego, like an embryo, starts as a single "cell" and gradually becomes more complex. That is why a baby, with an immature ego, can't handle conflicting messages, such as a mother who sometimes feeds it promptly and sometimes lets it cry. So it forms internal representations of "good mommy" and "bad mommy" to keep them separate. The machinery that can do this, the theory goes, may be the same mechanism that multiples use to create their alters. But it is virtually impossible to prove this hypothesis. Psychic structures cannot be physically identified—where is the ego?—but rather are theoretical constructs, based on observation.

Only a few of the researchers hazarded a discussion of how to conduct therapy with multiples. Not surprisingly, hypnosis figured prominently. Also not surprisingly, there were almost as many opponents as proponents. Some researchers argued that a suggestible patient might pick up the wrong signals and create new personalities to please the therapist. A trance state is an altered state—push a little further and, presto, a multiple. For example, a person in a trance might invent an imaginary playmate to absorb the pain. The more experiences one assigns to the imaginary playmate, the richer the playmate's personality.

This kind of confusion is part and parcel of hypnosis. Few terms in the psychological lexicon are so thoroughly bewildering. The problems arise from the tendency that dates back to the discoverer of hypnotism, by Franz Anton Mesmer, to regard the process as one that transports the subject to a different mental state. We now believe that such a state does exist but seems somewhat less dramatic than Mesmer theorized. In this sleeplike state, normal planning functions are reduced, attention becomes selective, role playing is readily accomplished, posthypnotic suggestion is observed, and frequently there is amnesia.

Toward the end of the eighteenth century, when priests were curing the seemingly possessed using the power of Christ, Mesmer, an Austrian and an ex-Jesuit, began to perform secular exorcisms. Mesmer, from whom we derive the word mesmerize, believed that "possession" was caused by the presence in the victim of a magnetic fluid. To cure him, he would have the patient drink an iron solution, then place magnets on his body to draw out the "evil spirit." His technique also seemed to heal physical ailments.

Mesmer and his followers were soon "magnetizing" vats of water and having patients hold rods in them, so their diseases could pass into the fluid. They magnetized trees and hung ropes from them, which patients wrapped around their afflicted parts. A showman at heart, Mesmer took to working in darkened, music-filled rooms, dressed in a long purple robe and carrying a wand that he would pass over his patients with a flourish. And it seemed to work, demonstrating that there were other powers to relieve "possessed" states than those of Christ.

Eventually, the magnets and other paraphernalia were discarded and it became clear that what was at work here was the power of words on the mind. Words could free a person from an altered state, and they could also move a person into a trance state, an altered state. This concept is in fact the root of modern psychiatry—that words, which are but symbols of ideas, not only can cause mental problems but also, when wielded by hypnotists and psychotherapists, can cure them. Indeed, the mesmerists were already starting to treat states of "lucid possession," in which the subject felt two souls striving against each other, and "somnambulistic possession," in which the subject lost consciousness of himself while an intruder took over his body.

In 1791 the German physician Eberhardt Gmelin reported a case of "exchanged personality." It was during the French revolutionary wars, when Gallic troops were overrunning Germany. As aristocratic refugees arrived in Stuttgart, a twenty-eight-year-old German woman suddenly adopted "the manners and speech of a French lady" and even began to speak German with a French accent. Moreover, she appeared to have complete memory of being a French person. (Obviously, this was a useful ability in a time when territory often changed hands.)

Gmelin could not cure her but was eventually able to make her shift from one personality to the other with a motion of his hand. When she changed back to her German personality, she did not remember her "French" state, but she had complete "German" memory.

Around 1815, a case of "dual personality" was reported in Pennsylvania by Dr. John Kearsley Mitchell. His patient, Mary Reynolds, had suffered an attack of blindness when she was eighteen, after which she fell into a deep sleep for twenty hours. When she awoke she could not remember anything, had a marked change in personality, and had lost her hearing as well as her sight. Five weeks later she woke up to find her hearing restored and her vision improving. Eventually she fully recovered her sight, but for the next fifteen years she had periodic episodes in which she would find herself in that second sightless, soundless state.

During the next decades more such cases were published —two British, three French, one German, and two American. What's more, "possession" was being studied seriously, scientifically. In 1840, for example, a French clinician in Aix-en-Savoie reported the successful treatment of a young Swiss girl named Estelle who suffered from dual personality—she was paralyzed when she was herself but able to move normally while in a "magnetic" or hypnotized state. She traveled to Aix by coach for five days, lying flat on her back in a large flat willow basket padded with eiderdown. Perhaps fortunately, she was also absorbed by daydreams and hallucinations and forgot from one moment to the next what was happening to her.

After a few hypnotic sessions, the physician noted, "a comforting angel appeared to her in her magnetic sleep whom she named Angeline and with whom she engaged in lively conversation." After a few months, Estelle predicted that she would visualize a big ball that would burst, upon which a great improvement would follow. This prophecy came true two weeks later, after which the patient was able to take a few steps in her waking state. There was also an improvement in her magnetic state. Over the next few months the gradual fusion of her normal and magnetic states slowly took place, and Estelle was discharged from treatment. Thus, it was a case both discovered and successfully treated by hypnotism.

During the last third of the nineteenth century, interest in multiplicity, hypnosis, and altered states accelerated. Some of the greatest psychological minds of the United States and Europe became caught up in the field. One of them was Jean-Martin Charcot, chief physician at the Salpêtrière, a huge hospital in Paris. A brilliant doctor who had already made contributions to the understanding of pulmonary and kidney diseases, geriatric medicine, and neurology, Charcot turned his attention to hysteria, a complex disorder in which uncontrollable emotional states such as fits of rage or anger are accompanied by epileptic-like physical symptoms, including paralysis and tremors without discernable organic cause. The term is not used much today, having been broken down into a wide variety of emotional disorders such as phobic reactions and anxiety neurosis. But the syndrome had been around for centuries. Since it occurred mostly in women, the Greeks thought it was caused by a "wandering uterus." In the Middle Ages, when scientific interest shifted from the physical universe to the spiritual, hysterical symptoms were thought to be the result of possession by an evil spirit. And as psychological theories started to parallel cultural development and science displaced mysticism in the eighteenth century, physicians thought the symptoms were caused by a lesion of the nervous system, even though they rarely could find one. Later in the century, some began to believe that erotic cravings or frustrations were the root of the syndrome, a theory that picked up adherents until a French physician, Paul Briquet, found that hysteria was almost absent among nuns but common among Parisian prostitutes.

When Charcot, trying to distinguish between organic and psychological convulsions, put his patients into a hypnotic state, he found that he could relieve a physical symptom of hysteria merely by issuing a command that it go away. And he was also able to demonstrate the reverse, creating a symptom where none had existed, also by using hypnosis. The problem was that the changes were not permanent. Within a short while arms that were freed would refreeze, coughs and tics that were quieted would return. Still, Charcot proved that the syndrome was psychological, not physical, and that words could cure it—or for that matter cause it.

What was happening in these cases of hysteria? Was another personality causing the symptoms? Was there a personality that could stiffen an arm, tighten a throat, make one blind? Charcot's scientific mind rejected possession as an explanation. Instead, he theorized that a person's consciousness can break up into diverse streams. In other words, the mind can have more than one center of consciousness, or personality, each with its own characteristics or symptoms.

It was, of course, an idea that dated to the magnetizers, who were struck by the fact that their hypnotized patients seemed to manifest new lives of which the host personality was unaware.

Another French physician, Pierre Janet, continued Charcot's research into hysteria. One of his patients, Lucie, had fits of terror for no apparent reason. Under hypnosis, Janet discovered a forgotten unconscious experience that generated the symptom—when she was seven two men had jumped out from behind a curtain as a practical joke and terrified her.

Another patient, Marie, suffered depression, pains, nervous spasms, and a compulsion to take an icy bath each month before her menstrual period. Under hypnosis, she revealed that when she had first menstruated at the age of thirteen she had become profoundly ashamed and in desperation plunged herself into a bucket of freezing water. This stopped the menses but caused her to become delirious. Although she thought she had purged this experience from her memory, she felt compelled to repeat it every month, without knowing why.

These cases may not have been classical examples of multiple personality, but they were close. They demonstrated that there was another part of a person's consciousness that was controlling behavior. Janet was so convinced of this view that he took Charcot's theory one step further, suggesting that independent centers of personality existed outside the area of normal consciousness, and that in certain circumstances they could seize a person and disrupt normal behavior. It was the first scientific explanation for possession.

The next step in the field would be taken by Josef Breuer, a Viennese physician who was treating a woman he called Anna O. (Her real name was Bertha Papenheim, and she later became Germany's first social worker.) Anna had come to Breuer with an unusual problem: She had suddenly found it impossible to drink water. She also suffered from a myriad of other symptoms that phased in and out, including paralysis of the arms and legs, hallucinations, a nervous cough, loss of memory, and tangled speech. Since there was nothing wrong with her physically, Breuer concluded that she was suffering from hysteria and attempted to treat her hypnotically.

One day while in a trance Anna recalled a forgotten memory. She recounted with anger and disgust how a friend's little dog—a "horrid creature," she said—had once drunk out of a glass in front of her. She had said nothing at the time out of politeness but was deeply horrified. After she finally expressed her anger to Breuer during the therapeutic session, a remarkable thing happened—she suddenly found that she could again drink water. "I was greatly surprised," Breuer wrote with more than a little understatement of what was the first recorded abreaction.

The case led Breuer to theorize that a person adept at self-hypnosis could use the talent to create a mental reservoir cut off from normal consciousness in which unpleasant memories could be deposited, and thus the original unpleasant experiences would be buffered or even avoided. But although the experience is forgotten, it does not go away. It lurks in the back of the mind, a haunting presence.

Breuer could have been talking about multiple personality. He could have been discussing my patient as well as his.

To cure these patients, all one had to do was reverse the process, excavating the memories by summoning up the dreaded experiences—which was what happened with Anna O. and all of her afflictions. "Each individual hysterical symptom immediately and permanently disappeared when we had succeeded in bringing clearly to light the memory of the event by which it was provoked and in arousing its accompanying affect, and when the patient had described that event in the greatest possible detail and had put the affect into words," Breuer wrote of the case. But, he added, "Recollections without affect almost invariably produce no result. The psychical process which originally took place must be repeated as vividly as possible; it must be brought back to its status nascendi and then given verbal utterance."

From a finicky brat's reaction to the antics of a puppy dog, a door to a discipline opens. Breuer was able to see beyond a trivial incident to its psychological significance. He had made a major discovery, but he was not the one to get credit for it. No, that was reserved for a young friend and colleague of his named Sigmund Freud.

As a student, Freud had heard about Charcot's work and had gone to Paris to study with him. He also studied with Hippolyte-Marie Bernheim, a leading hypnotherapist. When he started his own medical practice, Freud was referred several hysterical patients. At first he treated them in accordance with the accepted methods—rest, hand holding, hydrotherapy, massage—without success. Gradually, he started to use the techniques of Breuer and Janet, hypnotizing his patients, investigating their symptoms, and abreacting them, after which the symptoms would generally clear up.

Freud eventually came to the conclusion that the early trauma that caused the initial dissociation almost always had a sexual component. (That meant that something other than the dog was bothering Anna O.) These painful experiences, he further believed, were always threatening to bubble up to the surface and caused patients to expend more energy to keep the traumatic memory bottled up. Like a watermelon seed squeezed between two fingers, out popped a symptom—a frozen arm, a constricted throat, or some other otherwise inexplicable malady.

These novel ideas, which came from observable phenomena, were taking root outside of Breuer and Freud's Vienna as well, leading to the promulgation and acceptance of the theory of multiple consciousness among the practitioners of the fledgling field of psychology on two continents. In England, Frederick Myers proposed a theory of the subliminal self—a second personality. And in America, Morton Prince, a professor of psychiatry at Tufts Medical School in Boston, published the case of Miss Beauchamps, a Radcliffe student who had what he termed a "disintegrated personality," with two secondary personalities. Although his terminology was different, it was nonetheless significant that a well-respected American psychiatrist at a prestigious university accepted the concept of multiplicity. In fact, Prince wrote a book on the case, *The Dissociation of a Personality,* and devoted a good part of his professional career to the study of dissociated states.

But just when it seemed the concept of multiple personality was gaining worldwide acceptance, it fell into disrepute. This was mostly because of Freud and his followers, who became the dominant psychiatrists of the age but who, for all their contributions, did the field a couple of disservices as well.

First, Freud, an admittedly poor hypnotist who could not get many of his patients into a trance, abandoned the technique in favor of free association. He discovered that if his patients talked spontaneously about a symptom, without censoring their thoughts or feelings, the chain of association would lead to the original trauma. By defining his new method as "nondirective," he gave credence to the charge already circulating that hypnotherapists, who are directive, were actually inducing multiplicity in their patients.

An even stranger change in course by Freud would push the concept of multiplicity further from favor. In two works published in 1895–96, *Studies on Hysteria* and "The Aetiology of Hysteria," Freud argued that early sexual abuse caused neurosis. Such abuse was also linked with multiple personalities, since in all the cases reported there was early abuse, mostly sexual. However, later in his career Freud abandoned the sexual origin of neurosis, arguing that so many young women were neurotic that it would have been impossible for all of them to have been sexually abused. Instead, he asserted, they *imagined* it. It was a wish on their part to have sex with their father—in other words, the Oedipus complex.

Freud changed either because he could not believe there was so much sexual abuse in so civilized a society as Vienna or because he could not stand the hostility of his colleagues. When he read the "The Aetiology of Hysteria" to the Society for Psychiatry and Neurology, he was met by silence. The professionals did not want to even think about the possibility that children could be sexually abused on so large a scale. (In his provocative book *The Assault on Truth*, Jeffrey Masson suggests that some of these very same physicians were abusing their children, including Dr. Wilhelm Fliess, a close friend and advisor of Freud. Masson was thrown out of the Freudian Society and lost his position as director of the Freud Archives for his trouble.)

While Freud and his followers were discrediting the existence of multiple personality disorder and hypnosis, the hypnotists were virtually committing professional suicide by taking their trade to the stage. Who can take anyone seriously when they make people imagine that there is a dead chicken on their laps? And then there were the spiritualists and mediums, who supposedly contacted a dead person, speaking in the voice of the deceased. If they were honest, then another personality had certainly taken them over.

Some of the leading scientific investigators of the nineteenth century, among them the American psychologist William James, were interested in these supposedly mystical phenomena. But science likes mysticism even less than it likes show business. Most psychologists dismissed spiritualists and mediums as fakes.

Many of those researching multiple personality were also knee deep in parapsychology, further discrediting the syndrome. And then there was Walter Franklin Prince, a Methodist minister who was a member of the American Society for Psychical Research and the editor of their journal. Prince apparently successfully treated a woman who suffered from multiple personality, then committed the cardinal sin of living with her. It only provided more ammunition for the skeptics.

The academic and training institutes did not include multiple personality or dissociated states in their curricula, and the number of cases being reported in the literature started to decline. Concurrently, there was a rapid increase in the reported cases of a new diagnostic category, schizophrenia, which was literally defined as a splitting of the mind. The term was chosen by Eugen Bleuler, a prominent Swiss physician, because the disorder reflected a cleavage between the functions of feeling or emotion and those of cognition. Today, schizophrenia has become a catchall category for a number of psychotic disorders such as delusions, hallucinations, severe regressive behaviors, wildly inappropriate moods, and incoherent speech.

Multiple personality disorder may seem to fit into this category, but it doesn't. A person with multiple personality disorder is in touch with reality. There is no thought disorder. Still, most of the practitioners seemed content to sweep it under the schizophrenic rug.

The public, at least, was curious. In the 1950s, readers and moviegoers were fascinated with Corbett Thigpen and Hervey Checkley's famous case of Eve, a woman with three personalities. It was a role for which Joanne Woodward won an

Academy Award. Twenty years later, it was Dr. Wilbur's even more famous case of Sybil, played by Sally Field.

Sybil was published as a popular book because, the author Flora Schreiber wrote in the introduction, "in addition to great medical significance, the case had broad psychological and philosophical implications for the general public." However, Cornelia Wilbur later told me there wasn't any choice, since the medical journals had refused to publish it. Not that it stopped some of her colleagues from criticizing her after the fact for not publishing the case in the professional journals.

Wilbur treated her many-sided patient with hypnosis, which had once again become a respectable therapeutic tool, thanks largely to the work of Milton Erickson, perhaps its most prominent and skilled practitioner.

Toby had been coming in three times a week, and I was doing the best I could to keep her calm. I was pretty sure that she was a multiple, though I still had some doubts. If I understood all that I had read, her condition was caused by early trauma—the rape by the pathologist who lived next door, the beatings and abuse by her mother, and God knows what else—which caused her to dissociate and create the personalities. It was akin to self-hypnosis, therefore hypnosis should be the method of treatment. I would use it to access Beth and Anna, find the episodes that had led to their creation, and, like Breuer, Freud, and Wilbur before me, abreact them.

I had a little hypnotic training, but not enough for a case this challenging. So I wrote to Erickson, explaining my problem and requesting a consultation and further training. As it happened, he was about to conduct a study group and had a space left for me. If his health allowed, he said, he would even set aside some time to discuss Toby's case in private. He suggested a motel in the area where his students customarily stay. I made the reservation and booked my flight.

3

Lessons

When I checked into my Phoenix
motel I found a message that Dr.
Erickson was too ill to work. I
knew the rules. To study with Erickson, one had to be prepared
for an extended stay in Arizona. If
on a given morning he was well,
you went to his office on Hayward
Avenue. If not, you sat and
waited.

As it turned out, I only had to wait the one day. The next
morning I drove from my motel to Dr. Erickson's home, which
was located in a suburban development on the outskirts of
town. The houses had low, flat roofs and green lawns that stood
out against the desert. My destination was an inexpensive
ranch house with a semidetached guest cottage.

The group had already gathered in a room furnished in
Salvation Army modern—an old table here, an old couch
there, five or six mismatched uncomfortable chairs scattered
around. A weary air conditioner rumbled in a window, and I
feared it would make it hard to hear the master's voice. At one
end was a smaller room with a bed I later learned was for
visiting scholars and dignitaries who slept over. At the opposite
end an open door led to Erickson's private office. It contained a
wooden kneehole desk that looked about fifty years old and
two battered green filing cabinets, one of which featured a
poster of a rabbit smoking a cigarette with a caption, "This is a

dumb bunny." Homemade bookshelves filled two walls, and on a third was the usual assortment of degrees and honorary awards. A sampling of knickknacks and ironwood carvings of animals made by the Seri Indians reinforced the folksy mood. I also noticed a picture of Erickson's mother and father, Clara and Albert, in the American Gothic pose, along with a picture of Sigmund Freud in an Army general's uniform. He looked like the General of Psychoanalysis.

Erickson's fees were as unpretentious as the surroundings. I paid forty dollars for each of the five- to seven-hour days, in contrast to the seventy-five dollars per hour I paid Arnold. It was a bargain considering Erickson's status in the profession. He was arguably the world's foremost hypnotherapist as well as the founder of the American Society of Clinical Hypnosis and its journal, which he edited for a decade. In the 1950s, he had written the entry on hypnosis for the Encyclopaedia Britannica. The list of professionals and nonprofessionals who had consulted him included Margaret Mead, who was a student of Erickson's for forty years. He had hypnotized Aldous Huxley and collaborated on Huxley's study of altered states of consciousness. He had been singularly responsible for hypnosis's return to respectability. And he had done all this against fearsome odds.

Born in 1901 in Nevada and raised in Wisconsin, Erickson suffered a crippling attack of polio at the age of seventeen. The doctors said he would be dead by morning, but he overheard them and decided not to comply. "Our country doctor had called in two Chicago men as consultants," he later told me, "and they told my mother, 'The boy will be dead by morning.' I was infuriated. The idea of telling a mother that. Outrageous."

Erickson obviously did not die that night, although he came very close. After three days in a coma, he awoke to find all but his mouth, eyes, and half his diaphragm paralyzed. To amuse himself during his long recuperation, he honed his skills of observation to the point where he could tell who was entering his room—and even their mood—by the sound of their feet on the floor. He laboriously retaught himself to move, muscle by muscle, by watching his baby sister learn to walk. By the time he was twenty he was able to complete a 1,200-mile trek across Wisconsin's lake country, managing to transport his canoe over dams and through woods by himself.

At fifty-one, Erickson suffered a rare second attack of polio, which was later compounded by crippling arthritis that left him in a wheelchair, in constant, terrible pain. Then he suffered a stroke that immobilized all but his left arm, the left side of his mouth, and his left eye.

As if this wasn't enough, Erickson was tone deaf, which led to his intense interest in the effects of alterations in breathing patterns associated with the "yelling" that others called singing. He was also dyslexic and suffered from a peculiar form of color blindness that enabled him to perceive the color purple but few others.

At about eleven that morning, an hour later than usual because it took Erickson a bit longer to hypnotically block out his pain—something he did every day in order to work—his wife, Betty, wheeled him into the room, where I waited along with eight other professionals. Despite his infirmities, Erickson was a rugged-looking man, part American Indian, part Norwegian Viking, with white hair and moustache and dark eyes that seemed to see you even when they were looking elsewhere. He was dressed in a purple leisure suit with a string tie that featured a huge turquoise clasp. Although I knew why he wore the color, his outfit made me think of Mesmer—no doubt a sign of some lingering, covert resistance to hypnosis on my part.

Erickson, by now adorned with a number of lapel microphones pinned on by various students taping the proceedings, passed out yellow paper and asked us to write our names, degrees, specialties, and whether we were from the city or the country. Not much of a workup, I thought to myself, while he glanced at our brief resumes. Then, looking straight at me, he launched into a long discourse in which he berated psychoanalysis in general and Freud—General Freud—in particular. His thesis was that Freud, in moving away from hypnosis, had set psychiatry back seventy-five years.

At first I thought he was staring at me merely because his wheelchair happened to be pointing in my direction. But it soon became horrifyingly apparent that—since I was the only card-carrying, classically trained Freudian analyst in the room —the attack was directed at me. As he continued to berate Freud and his followers, I started to get angry. I felt I was being judged solely by my degrees. Didn't he know that I had parted company with the traditionalists, who subscribed to Freud's belief that the therapist should be passive and that a directive technique such as hypnosis was in error? Why else was I here? But Erickson kept at it. His words all but made me flinch.

"Freud was wrong. He started with hypnosis. He used hypnosis successfully to treat patients and then threw it away. He preached and taught a doctrine that doesn't work. By abandoning hypnosis he did the field of psychology a disfavor. The analysts who came after Freud miss the whole point of treatment. Psychoanalysis is like a cult, with people following blindly without thinking about the patient, without even knowing the patient. It takes too long, it's inefficient, it doesn't work. There is no need to keep a patient in therapy that long."

On and on he went. I started to identify more strongly with the group he was attacking. I began to think that maybe the classicists were right. After all, they had helped me. They had given me insight into myself. I had spent eight years at a training institute, where I had been taught by some of the finest psychological minds in New York City. What was I doing in Phoenix, anyway? This was hostile territory. Perhaps this old man, this presumed master, had lost it. Perhaps he was senile.

And what was he doing in a purple robe, anyway? All he was missing was a magic wand.

Meanwhile, Erickson droned on and on about the Freudians. At some point, I noticed that I wasn't even listening to him. I was thinking about other things. Then a curious thing happened. Erickson took a break from the diatribe and, reaching over to me, lifted my left arm, which obediently extended itself out from my body and somehow stayed there, rigid, *of its own accord.* I looked at my arm, which remained parallel to the floor and motionless without any effort on my part. It didn't feel tired. It didn't hurt. I felt that I could move it if I wanted to. I just didn't want to. It just stayed there.

Then I experienced what could only be described as a moment of pure clarity. *I realized I was in a trance.*

All the while, Erickson hadn't been criticizing me, he had been teaching me, I suddenly felt, and moreover he had put me in a trance. While he undoubtedly meant what he said about Freud, his withering attack was also intended to demonstrate to me the process of dissociation—the same process my patient Toby had intuitively used to shield herself from her childhood attackers.

When I thought about it later, it seemed so logical. What choice did I have? I could not criticize Erickson. It would not have been polite. Anyway, I knew he would certainly win any confrontation. I couldn't leave, either, since I had only just arrived and had not gotten the help I had come across three quarters of a continent for. Erickson had maneuvered me into a double bind. The only way to escape the attack was to go into a trance. If you can't beat them, join them—but if you can't join them, dissociate.

It was a magnificent example of Ericksonian technique. He had taught me about trauma and dissociation in the most vivid way possible—by example. I realized that just as I had ducked into a trance to escape his blistering words, a multiple creates other personalities to escape from his or her personal childhood Auschwitz. As I had fled from Erickson, Toby had fled from her attackers, going into a trance and creating other personalities to absorb her pain. Multiplicity was a self-hypnotized state, albeit an extreme one.

I had come to the right place, after all.

Just to make sure the message was clear, he then told the following parable from his childhood: "One day my father was trying to get a stubborn heifer into the barn. The old cow just planted her feet and refused to move in, no matter how hard my father pulled at her head. I started to laugh at the scene. My father said, 'If you are so smart, you get the cow into the barn.' I simply went to the rear of the cow and pulled hard at its tail, while my father pulled at its head. The cow proceeded into the barn, following the path of least resistance."

That was exactly how I had gotten into the trance, by following the path of least resistance.

Once I realized what was going on, I was quite comfortable. I listened as Erickson, shifting his attention to the others in the room, told stories about his family, his childhood, and his patients. He would start a story, perhaps in response to a question, chuckle, fix his eyes on some spot on the floor, watching the people in the class through his peripheral vision, and wend his way through his tale. Even though he must have told these stories a thousand times, they seemed fresh, almost improvisational. This was the way he taught, with tales cunningly designed to put his listeners into a trance and give him access to their unconscious. Although some of the stories seemed aimed at particular students, they were designed to have a meaning and significance to the others as well. They seemed to follow archetypal patterns like fairy tales, biblical tales, and folk myths. Many were built around the theme of a quest, giving them a peculiarly American quality. Once he started a story, Erickson would monitor the room, changing course according to the reactions of his audience. He would present an idea, switch to another subject, come back to the original thought and build upon it, and then move off again. It was all very complicated, since he was working on about four levels at one time with eight different people. It was remarkable how, despite his mostly paralyzed body, he could communicate with a look here or a gesture there.

What seemed to happen during the session was that the participants, myself included, identified with the characters and learned from them. Erickson introduced us to new possibilities. We felt a sense of accomplishment when his heros prevailed—a feeling, I suspected, that was engineered to allow us to approach a situation, whether new or old, with greater confidence. One of his favorite stories, which he liked to tell his study groups during the first session, was about Joe, the town delinquent while Erickson was growing up, and his sudden change:

"I was ten years old and living on a farm in Wisconsin," the tale began. "One summer morning my father sent me to the nearby village on an errand. As I approached the village, some of my schoolmates saw me and came and told me, 'Joe is back.' I didn't know who Joe was. They told me what their parents had told them.

"The story of Joe was not very good. He had been expelled from every school because he was combative, aggressive, and destructive. He would soak a cat or dog with kerosene and set it on fire. He tried to burn down his father's barn and home twice. He had stabbed the pigs, the calves, the cows, and the horses with pitchforks.

"His father and mother, when he was twelve years old, acknowledged that they couldn't handle their son. They went to court and had him committed to the Boy's Industrial School, which is a permanent home for delinquent children who cannot be handled in an ordinary home for delinquents. After three years of school, they paroled him to visit his parents. He committed some felonies on the way home. The police arrested him and returned him to the industrial school, where he had to stay until he was twenty-one years old.

"At age twenty-one, he had to be discharged by law. He had a prison-made suit and prison-made shoes and a ten-dollar bill when he was discharged. His parents were dead. Their property had otherwise been disposed of, so that was all he had —ten dollars, a prison suit, and prison shoes.

"He went to Milwaukee and promptly committed armed robbery and burglary. He was arrested by the police and sent to the young men's reformatory in Green Bay. At the reformatory, they tried to treat him like the other inmates. But Joe preferred to fight everybody. He would have riots and fights in the dining room, smash up the tables, and that sort of thing. So they locked him in a cell and fed him in the cell. Once or twice a week, two or three guards as large as he was took him for a walk as exercise, after dark. And Joe spent the entire term at the young men's reformatory without any time off for good behavior.

"When he was discharged, he went into the town of Green Bay and committed burglaries and other felonies and was promptly sent to the state prison. At the state prison they tried to treat him like the other convicts and Joe would have nothing of that. He just wanted to beat up the other convicts and break windows and cause trouble. So they sent him to the dungeon.

"The dungeon is in the basement, eight feet by eight feet, and the floor was concrete and sloped toward a gutter in front of the dungeon. No sanitation provisions were made. He was locked in that dungeon, with or without clothes. I've been in that dungeon, and it is lightproof and soundproof. And once a day, usually 1 or 2 A.M., a tray of food is slipped through a hole in the doorway. The tray might be bread and water or the usual prison fare. And two prison guards his size—he was six foot three—one standing ten feet to his right and the other ten feet to his left, took him out for exercise after dark so he wouldn't beat up on any of the inmates.

"He spent the term in prison in the dungeon. One term in the dungeon is usually enough to tame anybody—lightproof, soundproof, and no sanitation. After his first term of thirty days he came out fighting mad, so he went back. In fact, he spent his entire first term in the state prison in that dungeon. Usually two stays in that dungeon are likely to cause you to become psychotic or stir bugs. And Joe spent a couple of years there.

"When he was released, he went into a local village and committed some more felonies. He was promptly arrested and sent back to the state prison for another sentence, which he also spent in that dungeon.

"After completing his second sentence in the state prison, he was discharged. He returned to the village of Lowell, where his parents used to shop. There were three stores in that village. He spent his first three days standing beside the cash registers mentally adding up the day's income.

"All three stores were burglarized. A motorboat on the river that passed through the village disappeared. Everybody knew that Joe had burglarized the stores and stolen the motorboat.

"I came into the village on the fourth day. Joe was sitting on a bench unwaveringly staring into space. My playmates and I formed a semicircle around him, staring bug-eyed at a real live convict. Joe paid no attention to us.

"A little over two miles from the village was a farmer, his wife, and his daughter. He had two hundred acres of rich Dodge County farmland, all paid for. In other words, he was a very rich farmer.

"Well, the farmer had a daughter, age twenty-three, and a very attractive girl. She had what was considered an excellent education. She was an eighth-grade graduate. She was five foot ten, very strong. She could butcher a hog alone, plow a field, pitch hay, cultivate corn, and do any work that a hired man could do. She was also an excellent dressmaker. She usually made the bridal dresses for the young girls that got married, and the baby dresses. She was an excellent cook and was recognized as the best cook, the best pie maker, and the best cake maker in the community.

"On that morning when I went to the village at 8:10 A.M., Edye, the farmer's daughter, was sent to town on an errand by her father. Edye tied up her horse and buggy and came walking down the street. Joe stood up and barred her way. Joe looked her up and down very thoroughly, and Edye stood her ground and looked up and down Joe. Finally, Joe said, 'Can I take you to the Friday night dance?' In that community, the village of Lowell, a Friday night dance was held in the town hall and everybody attended. Edye said, 'You can, if you are a gentleman.' Joe stepped aside and Edye went on her errand.

"On Friday night, Edye came in to attend the dance, tied up her horse and buggy, and then went into town hall. There was Joe, waiting. They danced every dance that evening, even though it made the other young men very envious and resentful.

"Now, Joe was six foot three, a very powerfully built young man and good-looking. The next morning, all three merchants found their stolen goods returned and the powerboat was returned to the owner's pier. Joe was seen walking down the road toward Edye's father's farm. Joe asked Edye's father for a job as one of his hired men. Edye's father said to him that being a hired man was hard work. It begins at sunrise and you work until long after sundown. You go to church on Sunday morning, but you work the rest of the day. There are no holidays, no days free of work, and the pay is fifteen dollars a month. 'I'll fix you up a room in the barn; you can eat with the family.' Joe took the job.

"Within three months every farmer wished that he had a hired man like Joe, because Joe was, in country talk, 'a working fool.' He just worked and worked and worked. After a day's work for his boss, he would go help out the neighbor with the broken leg and did the neighbor's work, too. Joe became very popular. Joe was not very talkative, but he was friendly.

"After a year, a wave of gossip went over the community. Joe was seen taking Edye out for a ride in the horse and buggy on Saturday night. That was standard procedure for courting a girl, or 'sparking,' as it was called.

"The next morning there was yet another wave of gossip because Joe took Edye to church. That meant only one thing. A

few months later Joe and Edye were married and he moved
out of the barn into the main house. Joe became her father's
permanent hired man, very much respected by everyone. Joe
and Edye had no children, but Joe became interested in the
community.

"When the Erickson kid announced that he was going to
high school, the entire community felt very bad because the
Erickson kid seemed to be a promising young farmer. They all
knew that a high school education ruined a man. Joe looked me
up and encouraged me to go to high school and encouraged a
lot of others to go to high school. When I announced my desire
to go to the university, Joe encouraged me and he encouraged
a lot of others.

"So someone, as a joke, put Joe's name on the ballot for the
school board. Everybody voted for Joe, which gave him the
largest number of votes, and that automatically made him
president of the school board. Everybody attended that first
meeting of the school board. Every parent, in fact every citi-
zen, was there to see what Joe would say.

"Joe said, 'You folks elected me president of the school
board by giving me the most votes. Now I don't know nothin'
about schooling. I know all you folks want your kids to grow up
and be decent and the best way to do that is to send them to
school. You hire the best teachers and you buy the best stuff for
the schools, and you don't yell about taxes.' Joe was reelected
many times to the school board.

"When Edye's parents died, she inherited the farm and Joe
began looking for a hired man. He went to the reformatory
and asked for the names of promising ex-convicts. Some lasted
a day, some a week, some a month, some worked a considerable period of time before they felt ready to go out and make
good in society.

"Joe died in his seventies, and Edye died a few months
later. The entire area was interested in their will. The will
provided that the farm could be sold in small farms and the
additional land sold to anybody interested. All the money was

to go into a trust fund administered by a bank and the superintendent of the reformatory to aid promising young ex-convicts.

"Now all the psychotherapy he had was, 'You can, if you are a gentleman.'

"When I got the job as state psychologist, I had to examine all the inmates of the correctional and penal institutions. Joe congratulated me and said, 'There is an old record at Waukesha you ought to read.' There is an old record at Green Bay. I knew he meant *his* record. So I read them. It was the blackest kind of record. He was a troublemaker for the first twenty-nine years of his life. Then a pretty girl said, 'You can take me to the dance if you are a gentleman.' No other change was made in Joe. He made the changes. The therapist doesn't do it, the patient does."

The story of "Joe" was a motivating tale that laid the groundwork for some of his basic principles. Erickson used it to demonstrate that people can change quickly and dramatically, that no one is locked into patterns of behavior.

Another of his stories, with a typically Ericksonian message but conveyed in a vastly different style, was called "Learning to Stand Up."

"We learn so much at a conscious level," the story began, "and then we forget what we learn and use the skill. You see, I had a terrific advantage over others. I had polio, and I was totally paralyzed, and the inflammation was so great that I had a sensory paralysis, too. I could move my eyes, and my hearing was undisturbed. I got very lonesome lying in bed, unable to move anything except my eyeballs. I was quarantined on a farm with seven sisters, one brother, two parents, and a practical nurse. How did I entertain myself? I started watching people and my environment. I soon learned that my sisters could say 'no' when they meant 'yes.' And they could say 'yes' and mean 'no' at the same time. They could offer another sister an apple and hold it back. I began studying nonverbal language and body language.

"I had a baby sister who had begun to learn to crawl. *I* would have to learn to stand up and walk. And you can imagine the intensity with which I watched as my baby sister grew from crawling to learning how to stand up. And you don't know how *you* learned how to stand up. You don't even know how you walked. You can *think* that you can walk in a straight line six blocks—with no pedestrian or vehicular traffic. You don't know that you *couldn't* walk in a straight line at a steady pace!"

"You don't know what you did when you learned to walk. You don't know how you learned to stand up, even. You learned by reaching up your hand and pulling yourself up. That put pressure on your hands—and, by accident, you discovered that you could put weight on your *feet.* That's an awfully complicated thing because your knees would give way —and when your knees would keep straight, your hips would give way. Then you got your feet crossed. And you couldn't stand up because both your knees and your hips would give way. Your feet were crossed—and you soon learned to get a wide brace—and you pull yourself up and you have the job of learning how to keep your knees straight—one at a time—and as soon as you learn that, you have to learn how to give your attention to keep your hips straight. Then you found out that you had to learn to give your attention to keep your hips straight and knees straight at the same time *and* feet far apart! Now finally you could stand having your feet far apart, resting on your hands.

"Then came the lesson in three stages. You distribute your weight on your one hand and your two feet, this hand not supporting you at all. (At this point, Erickson raised his left hand.) Honestly hard work—allowing you to learn to stand up straight, your hips straight, knees straight, feet far apart, this hand pressing down hard. Then you discover how to alter your body balance. You alter your body balance by turning your head, turning your body. You have to learn to coordinate all alterations of your body balance when you move your hand, your head, your shoulder, your body—and then you have to learn it all over again with the other hand. Then comes the terribly hard job of learning to have *both* hands up and moving your hands in all directions and to depend upon the two solid bases of your feet, far apart. And keeping your hips straight— your knees straight and keeping your mind's attention so divided that you can attend to your knees, your hips, your left arm, your right arm, your head, your body. And finally, when you had enough skill, you tried balancing on one foot. That was a hell of a job!

"*How* do you hold your entire body up, keeping your hips straight, your knees straight and feeling hand movement, head movement, and body movement? Then you put your one foot ahead of the other and alter your body's center of gravity! Your knees bent—and you sat down! You got up again and tried it again. Finally you learned how to move one foot ahead and took a step and it seemed to be good. So you repeated it—it seemed so good. Then the third step—with the same foot—and you toppled! It took you a long time to alternate right, left, right, left, right, left. Now you could swing your arms, turn your head, look right and left, and walk along, never paying a bit of attention to keeping your knees straight, hips straight."

This story suggests that learning anything new, hypnosis included, may be difficult to begin with but gets easier with persistence and practice. After all, we all now can perform that complicated task called walking without any thought or effort. By talking about his own paralysis, Erickson was demonstrating how a negative can be turned into a positive. That much was obvious, but the story worked in more subtle ways. Recited in an incantatory style, it had a relaxing, soothing quality that edged listeners toward the trance state or encouraged them to remain there. And its emphasis on infantile kinetic experience subtly programmed them to regress.

There is much more to be plumbed in the tale. For example, the metaphor of the "apple," which underscores the essential ambiguity of language, also summons up images of the garden of Eden, of forbidden fruit and of Genesis, the beginning. A child brings an apple to the teacher, who then is pleased. But an apple can contain a worm.

By now the other students, professional therapists of many varieties, were also drifting in and out of trances and reacting to his stories. I felt that at any time I could have taken control of myself or even gotten up and walked out of the room. But I was so comfortable, I just didn't want to. Sometimes Erickson's tales went into my mind like a beam from a laser. But at other times his words were off in the distance, and my mind was occupied with thoughts about my life and my patients.

Sometimes I would come out of a trance and watch Erickson work with a particular person. Other times I would notice someone crying softly, or laughing. But it was hard to focus on the others for long, because I was so self-absorbed.

Erickson showed us that hypnosis is nothing more than a state of extreme concentration in which the external environment fades, the attention mechanism focuses inward, and the body becomes relaxed and motionless, like an animal that, when frightened, will freeze. It is a natural defense, Erickson reminded us, since other animals will not kill an animal that appears dead.

The ability to go into a trance is a natural skill, although some are more talented than others and children are generally the most talented of all. A hypnotist does not actually hypnotize anyone, just gives a subject directions on how to achieve a state that the subject could reach by himself if he knew how. "I am only going to ask you to do things that you can do even though you don't know that you know how to do them," is the way Erickson presented this paradox. "Which muscle, which part of the body moves first when you stand up? You don't know, but you can stand up." By this he was also demonstrating that much of our lives is unconsciously controlled, governed by the existence of a vast body of knowledge that we have collected in our unconscious. Erickson believed in using the unconscious. He believed that the unconscious should be trusted, as opposed to Freud, who believed that the unconscious was the repository of our primitive, socially unacceptable drives.

We are in a natural trance when we become so engrossed in a book that we don't hear someone call our name. Or when we become so caught up in a movie that we are oblivious not only to the people seated around us but also to time itself. Time is relative and can be manipulated by the mind, which is why two hours spent in the darkened theater can seem like fifteen minutes.

Similarly, the mind can blunt pain. Around the time I went to Phoenix, I had been having bad backaches, and I dreaded a day in Erickson's uncomfortable chairs. But I found that when I focused on Erickson and his stories the pain disappeared. (Unfortunately, when I came out of the trance the pain returned.)

It can be demonstrated that all neocortical functions—focal, motor, sensory, mental, or emotional—can be manipulated with complete realism in a hypnotic state. They can be diminished, enhanced, distorted, or even obliterated.

My classmates and I were constantly drifting in and out of trances all week. The sessions seemed to merge together. At one point, Erickson used a young woman to demonstrate age regression. He helped her enter a trance by having her focus on a figurine of a white horse on top of a chest on the other side of the room. Then he asked her to close her eyes and visualize the object in her mind. She was not to pay attention to outside sounds unless she wanted to. (Erickson left her this option to eliminate any possible control battle that would have prohibited her from going into a trance. It is a subtle way of circumventing a patient's resistance.)

He then suggested she go back to a younger period in her

life. "I want you to choose some time in the past when you were a very little girl," he said. "And my voice will go with you. And my voice will change into that of your parents, your neighbors, your friends, your schoolmates, your playmates. And I want you to find yourself playing someplace, a little girl feeling happy about something, something that happened a long time ago, that you forgot a long time ago."

Her body relaxed and her facial muscles flattened. I noticed that she was staring without blinking, almost completely immobile.

"Where are you, Stephanie?" Erickson asked, using her name for the first time to get her attention and establish rapport.

"I'm in the schoolyard." Although Stephanie was thirty years old, she talked and acted like a child. Her voice, her language, and her posture were childlike. In the trance state, she was able to access a memory bank of youthful experience— to become youthful.

"What are you doing?" Erickson asked.

"I am playing horse with Sally."

"Are you having fun?"

"Yes," she giggled. "Sally is my best friend."

"How old are you?"

"Six."

What Erickson had done with Stephanie, I realized, was similar to what Toby had done when she relived the experience in the cellar. In both cases, their consciousness was experiencing the past as present. But while Toby's age regression had led to the abreaction of a horrible event, Stephanie relived an utterly pleasant experience. Still, hypnosis had been used to access the unconscious and divulge memories. Erickson also believed that patients in a trance state might be most open to change because they accept the hypnotist's suggestions more readily.

After a few more questions, Erickson brought Stephanie back to her real age. Then he chose another subject, a very pretty woman with long, dark hair. He put her into a trance and after a few introductory questions instructed her to take off all of her clothes. She refused and immediately came out of the trance. Thus, he demonstrated the limits of hypnosis: A person will not do anything in a trance that he or she would not normally do in his or her waking life.

As my week with Erickson progressed, I began to wonder what psychiatric theory he was following. But that, as I later found out, was futile. Erickson was a technician, not a theoretician. He was opposed to theory, any theory, on practical grounds, insisting that none could explain or describe the variety and complexity of individual functioning. It was reductionistic, like summarizing Homer's *Odyssey* in a paragraph. He contended that people who held tenaciously to a theory were lazy and insecure. "Did you ever notice that every blade of grass is a different color?" he would say. Translation: Every patient is different. Look, study, notice, observe, then treat.

His results, at least in cases reported in journals and books, appeared miraculous. In only a few hours he seemed to be able to cure problems that took other professionals years. He had relieved one patient's claustrophobia in a single session by giving her the feeling of being closed in while in a trance state, thus showing her that she could experience her worst fear and still survive. A case of bed wetting was cured by giving a twenty-year-old patient a suggestion in a trance to simply walk into the bathroom when he felt the urge to urinate. After three sessions, no more bed wetting.

Once, a twenty-five-year-old man consulted Erickson after a two-week honeymoon, during which he had been impotent. He was depressed and already contemplating a divorce. Erickson put him into a trance and in that state created for him not only the feeling of having an erection but also that of a very pleasing sensual experience with his wife. "The marriage was consummated that night," the doctor reported proudly.

Best of all was a story he told of a young woman who was happily married but afraid of having children. Brought up by governesses and sent to boarding schools, she was frightened that, since her mother had been absent and she had not had a normal childhood, she would not know how to be a mother herself. Over a few months Erickson would hypnotize her, take her back to a younger age, and give her the experiences she had missed as a child, in effect redoing her childhood and filling it with positive memories. Erickson learned years later that the woman had had three children, all psychologically healthy, and had enjoyed the experience of raising them. I believe it would have taken a conventional therapist at least five years to obtain the same result.

Erickson held that if a person could get sick quickly, he could also get well quickly. I can remember him saying over and over, "Look, see, observe, listen, study your patient. Learn their language, learn to speak it, enter their reality, join them. Determine what the problem is, solve it, and send your patient on his way."

Naturally, he had a story to illustrate his approach. One day during his youth on the family farm, he and his father found a horse in their barn that didn't belong there. They had no idea who owned it. "I'll take him home," young Milton volunteered. He returned a few hours later and told his father he had succeeded. When his father asked him how, he replied, "I simply got on the horse's back and took him to the road and gave him his head. I only intervened when the horse went off the road or stopped to graze. The horse took himself home." The point was that the job of the therapist is simply to get the patient back on the path. With the proper encouragement, the patient's unconscious will find the way to mental health.

Erickson's was a permissive, humanistic, heuristic approach to hypnosis. It assumed a healthy, positive unconscious, rather than the dark Freudian unconscious filled with primitive drives, anger, repressed desires to have sex with one's parents, and other such things. It assumed an unconscious that protected an organism, an unconscious that wanted to help rather than hinder.

On the last day of the seminar, I had a chance to talk to Erickson about Toby. The consultation came late in the day, and he was tired. I described the case, and he quickly confirmed my tentative diagnosis of multiplicity. He told me he believed that multiple personality was a self-hypnotizable state, a creative way in which the patient handled childhood problems, and that hypnosis was the way to cure it. I asked him how I should proceed and prepared for a story. In fact, he told me three.

The first took place when he was a medical intern, and it involved two patients. One was a career criminal who was in the hospital because he had been severely beaten. Erickson examined him and concluded he would recover. Then he went into the next room and visited a young and charming woman who was suffering from an incurable disease and would be dead within the month. Why should the criminal live and the nice woman die? Erickson went into a room and sat by himself for a while, but could find no answer. After that, he realized that he had better reconcile himself to the unfairness of life.

Erickson's second story also occurred when he was a young doctor at a medical center. A senior physician suddenly asked him to take over a class for him, catching Erickson with no time to prepare. He was insecure and frightened, until he reminded himself that he, too, was a teacher, and that teachers can teach.

Story number three involved a woman in her thirties who had been sexually molested by her father several times a week from the time she was six until she turned seventeen, when she left home. She still managed to finish high school and even went on to college and graduate school. But she often had periods where she lost her self-respect, especially when men "propositioned" her, as she put it.

"All through college and graduate school I was propositioned," she told Erickson. "And that proved I didn't deserve self-respect. And I thought I would enroll for a doctorate, but men kept propositioning me. I just gave up altogether and became a prostitute. But that's not very nice. And some man offered to let me live with him. Well, a girl needs food, clothing, and shelter, so I agreed to it.

"Sex was a horrible experience. A penis is so hard and looks so threatening. I just became fear-stricken and passive. It was a painful, horrible experience for me. This man got tired of me, and I began living with another man. The same thing happened over and over, and now I have come to you. I feel like filth. An erect penis just terrifies me, and I just get helpless and weak and passive. I am so glad when a man finishes.

"But I still have to live. I have to have clothes, I have to have shelter, and essentially I am not worth anything else."

"That's an unhappy story," Erickson told her, "and the really unhappy part is—you're stupid! You tell me that you are afraid of a bold, erect, hard penis—and that's stupid! *You* know you have a vagina. A vagina can take the biggest, boldest, most assertive penis and turn it into a dangling, helpless object. And your vagina can take a vicious pleasure in reducing it to a helpless dangling object."

Erickson noticed a wonderful change on her face as he finished. A month later, when the woman returned for her next appointment, she was beaming. "You're right!" she told him. "I went to bed with a man and I took a vicious pleasure in reducing him to helplessness. It didn't take long, and I enjoyed it. And I tried another man. Same thing. And another. And it's pleasurable! Now I am going to get my Ph.D. and go into counseling, and I am going to wait until I meet a man that I really want to live with."

Erickson slumped in his chair, his head sagging more than usual. He called for his wife to take him back to the house, but she was out. So he asked me to wheel him into his quarters and put him to bed, which I did. After chatting for about half an hour, he proudly showed me some mementos of his life. At what I deemed to be the appropriate moment, I thanked him and took my leave.

Later that night, after dinner in my motel room, I thought about the three stories, trying to wring from them their meaning. With the first story, Erickson was telling me that bad things happen to good people, and that I should not get too emotionally involved with Toby at the possible expense of my other patients. I had to detach myself, even though life had been so horribly unfair to her. The second story, about the last-minute teaching assignment, gave me the conviction that my unconscious would know how to solve my patient's problem, even if my conscious state seemed to be foundering. Remembering the horse that knew its way home, I felt a surge of confidence about helping Toby.

The third story was more difficult to interpret. He was telling me that she could convert her passivity and helplessness to action. He was also pointing out that her hatred and resentment of men could be converted to pleasure. But how? Taking a cue from Erickson, I decided I would start by telling Toby the story.

The next day, as my flight to New York was boarding, I found myself with an irresistible urge to stay on in town. To my amazement, I found myself changing my ticket for one for the next day, reclaiming the rental car that I had just turned in, and driving back into my motel, wondering what the hell I was doing. After I checked back in and got a strange look from the motel keeper, I drove around Phoenix looking at the sights, came to Squaw Peak, a small mountain near the city, and started a leisurely climb.

Later I would learn that my "spontaneous" hike was the result of posthypnotic suggestion from Erickson, a trick he played on many of his students.

When the master was just shy of his seventy-ninth birthday,

it was said that he had ordered that his body be cremated and the ashes spread from the same summit. So Erickson finally climbed Squaw Peak, too, doing in death what his body would not allow him to do in life.

4

T O B Y

Toby was upset over my absence from New York. She had put her trust in me, telling me things she had not told anyone else. She had let her defenses down, and in her mind I had abandoned her. It did not seem to matter to her that I had gone to Phoenix to learn how to help her. Just as a toddler mourns when a parent leaves the room, Toby interpreted departure as demise, and it triggered unresolved, festering feelings of childhood neglect and cruelty that she had not let herself experience for years.

Just before I left she had complained that the work we had done so far only seemed to make her condition worse. Other people were living in her body, and I was forcing her to think about that horrendous fact. Moreover, she was still reliving the memories of the abuses she had suffered as a child. I tried to assure her that her problem could be solved, but I had to tell her that it would take long-term therapy—and that she might get still worse before she got better.

While I was in Arizona, Toby left emergency messages on my answering machine several times a day, every day, without fail. In what became a nightly ritual, I would check the machine from my Phoenix motel room, listen to her panicky calls, and try to decide whether or not to respond. More often than not, I would phone her, if only to remind her that I was still alive and would be back in a few days.

Although Erickson had confirmed the diagnosis of multiplicity, I am not sure that Toby fully accepted it. I had not been able to convince her to listen to tape recordings of our sessions, during which she switched from Beth to Anna to herself. And she was far too terrified to watch the movie of *Sybil* when it was shown on late-night television.

To tell the truth, even after all my research and all my sessions with Erickson, I, too, still had some doubts about multiplicity. I guess part of me was still under the sway of the Freudians.

Even if there were people with more than one personality, was Toby really one of them? Or was she faking, acting her several parts as a way to manipulate me into giving her more attention? There is no denying that there is great secondary gain for such a patient. Anyone with such a rare and fascinating disorder would surely become a therapist's favorite. In fact, even Dr. Wilbur was accused of creating multiplicity in her patient Sybil.

If all these terrible things really had happened to her, she deserved all the support I could give her. But if Toby was guilty of manipulation, it was important that I draw the line with her, and soon. Too much attention from me would reinforce her behavior and prevent her from developing healthier ways to deal with the anxieties of life.

There was also the problem of my countertransference— how my own needs, drives, and ambitions affected the way I treated Toby. I knew my desire to take care of birds with broken wings had not been resolved during my own analysis and training. Perhaps my male rage at hearing about the horrors suffered by her as a little girl was making me unprofessionally sympathetic to Toby. Or was my undeniable desire for fame and fortune tempting me into thinking that Toby would be the next Sybil and I the next Dr. Wilbur? These were the needs that I was in touch with and could try to control. God only knows what, despite years of analysis and supervision, was still buried in *my* unconscious.

In the back of my mind, I knew I really didn't have much of a choice. If I did not go along at least a little with Toby—if I followed Arnold's advice and simply commanded her symptoms to go away—I would lose Toby as a patient. No, I knew I had to try to treat Toby as a multiple, even though there was a possibility her multiplicity was feigned. Through a titrated dose of attention, I would try to establish a balance between frustration and satisfaction—just enough nurturance to soothe her and prevent overtly destructive behavior, but not so much as to relieve all her anxiety, since anxiety is necessary to motivate any patient. I was hoping all this would buy me some time to figure out how to put this Humpty-Dumpty of a patient back together again.

While I was ruminating about these theoretical issues, I was discovering a host of practical problems in treating a patient who insisted that she was really three patients. Toby, Anna, and Beth were all quite different. In fact, they did not even like each other, although like many unhappy families they would rally round each other when faced with a common threat.

Toby was quiet, friendly, shy, serious, insecure, confused, always trying to be the good girl, almost eager to take the blame, self-effacing, sensitive, but quick to fly into a rage or break down in tears if her feelings were hurt. She was also Jewish and very interested in the mystical side of that religion, having studied the Cabala, a religious philosophy based on a mystical interpretation of the Scriptures. At least in her case, Marx may have been right about religion being a narcotic.

Anna was serious, humorless, intellectual, and depressed. She could think—and argue—like a computer with volition. She was also versed in philosophy. Anna claimed to be an unbaptized Catholic who was very concerned about dying before she received the last rites. Her goal was to take charge of

Toby's body, get rid of the others, enter a convent, take her vows, and live a life of peaceful contemplation. (Score another one for Marx.)

Anna described herself as tall, thin, and beautiful, with long, straight blond hair—the exact opposite of Toby. Her posture was rigid, and she held herself almost as if her body were encased in plaster. When we talked, she always sat cross-legged on precisely the same spot on my couch. She would hold her hands in front of her in prayerlike fashion, the tips of her fingers gently touching, palms apart, as if it helped her maintain absolute control.

Then there was Beth, a precocious little girl, friendly, loving, and bright. She described herself as slightly roly-poly, with unruly brown hair and short, spindly legs. Aside from the fact that she was enclosed in Toby's obese twenty-nine-year-old body, she seemed to me the type of child you want to pick up and hug.

Beth had no concept that she was in a psychotherapist's office, much less that she was undergoing psychotherapy. She had met only three doctors in her life. One was the pathologist who had lived next door and had raped her. (Actually, he had raped Toby, or so Toby claimed, but during the act Toby had called on Beth and Anna to come out to help deal with the pain, so on some level they were all raped.) Another doctor, who must have been the family physician—and, if Toby's abreactions were accurate, remarkably insensitive to his young patient—gave her shots that hurt and vile-tasting medicine and recommended she have a tonsillectomy, something for which she never forgave him. The third doctor in Beth's life had been the kindly man who lived nearby and let her (and Toby, Anna, and the others, of course) sit on his lap, read her stories, and gave her chocolate cookies. Beth referred to him as "Mr. Carter." In a burst of curiosity, Toby went back to her hometown, looked him up at the local newspaper, and learned from his obituary that he had, in fact, been a psychiatrist. Why this Dr. Carter had failed to report the beatings and mistreatment that Toby was suffering—and that he must have known about—is a mystery. Anyway, Beth seemed to associate me with Dr. Carter, whom I supposedly resembled, dark hair, beard, and all. She regarded me as a nice man who could amuse her and make her feel better.

Beth was happy to be "out" in charge of the body and was always eager to play. Fidgety and uncoordinated, she would frequently wander around the office. Sometimes, especially when she was frightened, she would hide under the couch. When she lost her temper, which was not infrequent, her whole body would shake with rage.

Anna hated children in general and Beth in particular. But she said she had no other choice but to take care of her younger soulmate. Anna didn't like Toby either, chiefly because she felt Toby was too wishy-washy. Anna said she resented having to come out and take over the body whenever Toby encountered a situation she couldn't handle.

Anna, in fact, claimed that she had been born before Toby and that *she* was actually the host personality—an assertion that, thinking back on it, should have thrown me but didn't, since I was already dealing with three people in one body and had become pretty much unflappable about this sort of thing. Patients typically get unnerved when analysts start to question inconsistencies in their stories, but from what I could gather, Anna had created Toby much the way a normal child might create an imaginary playmate, but for a much more desperate reason. Anna's first recollections of Toby dated back to the times when they would sit on the cellar stairs after her mother had locked her in the basement as punishment. Given a bowl of food, some water, and a bucket to use as a toilet, the child would just sit there, afraid to move, because in the dreadful dark the furnace appeared to her like a monster. Once she had stayed there for two days, only to be carried out unconscious. During these times, Anna said, Toby would keep her company and comfort her, providing her encouragement to face an increasingly bewildering and brutal life. Later, when her mother began hitting her, Toby would be there to absorb some of the pain. One of them would endure the first half of a beating and the other the rest.

Normal children eventually abandon their imaginary play-mates, but Toby had become more and more important to Anna, which was understandable, given the awful circum-stances of her life. She had become as real as Pinocchio was to Giuseppe.

When I pressed Anna under hypnosis about her relation-ship with Toby, she recalled a particularly awful episode. She was at the dinner table and accidentally spilled her milk. Her mother became enraged, charged around the table, and pulled her out of her chair by the arm, yanking it so hard that it was badly broken. The pain was excruciating, and Anna called Toby to come out and help her handle it. For a while they took turns absorbing the pain, but at some point Anna refused to endure it anymore. She had had enough pain. Toby screamed (internally, of course) that if Anna didn't come back right away and take her share she would lose control of the body forever and Toby would be in charge. Anna refused, and Toby took over. To use Toby's words, Anna had "abrogated her birth-right."

Although Anna claimed to be the eldest, only Toby admit-ted to having a mother. When I questioned Anna about it, she said she didn't know how she had been born and gave me an uncharacteristically blank look. Beth said the stork had brought her—she was probably teasing me—in 1954, but ex-plained that her growth had stopped after five years. "And how is it that a five-year-old has breasts?" I asked her. She felt them, looked confused for a moment and then said, "But it's *her* body."

Even when they were inside, both Anna and Beth said, they could see what was happening outside, in the real world, through Toby's eyes.

"And is that how you hear?" I asked.

"Naturally," Beth answered. "We do it all the time, when

we go to the movies, when we watch television, and when she is in here, talking to you.

"The best time is when we go to dinner. Toby orders the appetizer, Anna the main course, and I get to order dessert. But Toby's been trying to diet, and so I never get to have chocolate cake." She smiled her sly smile. "But sometimes I eat when she goes to sleep. She doesn't understand why she can't lose weight."

Anna and Beth described their internal world as a beautiful, Tolkien-like Shangri-La with mountains, rivers, streams, valleys, wooded paths, caves, trees, and flowers. Most of the time it was sunny and pleasant, and the rain was always gentle and warm.

The two alter personalities internally romped, lay in the sun, climbed trees, took walks. When they wanted to "come out," they walked to one end of this paradise, where there was a gate to the real world.

Curiously, Toby entered and left reality through a different gate. I always wondered what would happen if one went in and another did not come out. Would there be a body without a person?

While Anna or Beth were out, Toby would linger in the back of the internal world, usually hiding behind a bush with her eyes closed and her back to the others. She did not see or hear her alter egos, either when they were out or in. I took this as a sign Toby was not ready to face her multiplicity, much less begin resolving it. Then again, I wondered if I was up to dealing with the problem. Here I was just starting out, and I had a patient who insisted she had two extra personalities inside of her, one belonging to a five-year-old child and the other to a person who wanted to be a nun.

At least I didn't have to worry about Toby keeping her appointments with me. She was so upset with the way her life was unraveling that I had become her mainstay. But the more I saw her, the worse she seemed to get. I began to think that I was treating Hydra. Cut off one head, and two more would grow in its place.

On top of switching from one personality to another, Toby was now experiencing abreactions at an alarming rate. They were like bubbles in a glass of seltzer that slowly rise to the top and then burst. Typically, these "memory cycles," as she termed them, would be preceded by a couple of weeks of relentlessly increasing anxiety. I would try to keep Toby calm, but after a while her emotional pain would become unmanageable. She would lose her sense of reason and telephone me repeatedly, demanding that I make the pain go away and that I hold her. Then she would call and be unable to talk. She just wanted me to ramble on. My voice, she said, made her feel safe, like a parent cooing to a baby. It didn't seem to matter what I said.

Finally, she would arrive at my office for what I came to call a "psychic operation." (Toby, like many people, always felt more comfortable if she had some term, however vague, to label things.) I would hypnotize her to find out what the event was that was troubling her and guide her through its reenactment. Usually the experience was so wearing I would let her rest in a trance for an hour or so in the waiting room after the session before gently waking her and sending her home. If she was still upset, I would bring out Anna to take the body home, with posthypnotic instructions to sleep and rest.

Invariably, though, the phone calls would start up again, sometimes as soon as the next day. There would be more yelling and screaming. I wasn't taking care of her. I wouldn't hold her. I would then suggest that she come in for another session. Sometimes she would say she could not afford it, implying that I should treat her for free.

What had happened to Toby in the past had enraged her, and those emotions, which she had been unable to express as a child, were now being directed at the only person available to her—me. Classical analysts call this transference. It is supposed to be all in a day's work, but my patience was being tried. It would have been easier for both of us had I realized that multiples characteristically test their therapists to see if they will stick with them no matter what. After all, these are people who as children were abused and abandoned by adults. Absent proof to the contrary, they continue to expect the worst from all adults. The problem is, they must learn to trust in order to be treated. It wasn't until years later that I realized how difficult a problem this could be. A multiple I had been treating gave my name to a coworker and I agreed to see her, thinking that if my patient had sent her it would be all right for me to treat her. As it turned out, another of my patient's personalities could not abide it. She was too angry for words. In her mind—or a portion of it, anyway—I had failed a loyalty test by accepting the referral. After a rational discussion of the matter failed, and faced with an extremely distraught patient who wanted to leave therapy over the issue, I sent the second patient to a colleague, knowing full well that by doing so I was allowing myself to be manipulated but agreeing to allow myself to be manipulated rather than lose the patient.

About this time, I made a false step with Toby that was to teach me another lesson about treating multiples—there are no shortcuts. I had been reading a book called *Frogs into Princes,* by Richard Bandler and John Grinder. Although they, too, had studied with Erickson, they did not believe in multiple personalities. Or more precisely, they believed the syndrome was actually created by therapists. In every case they encountered, they said, they used what they called their "visual squash" technique to integrate the patient in minutes.

It seemed worth a try. I began by putting Toby into a trance.

"Visualize Beth in your right hand and Anna in your left hand," I said, when she was under. "Okay. Now bring your two hands together, watch Anna merge with Beth, then bring your two hands onto your stomach."

She started to bring her hands together. Then, just as her palms met and started to clasp, she suddenly became Beth. The child immediately started to scream at me, crying and rubbing her head.

"You bad person. You tried to squish me. It hurts. I am not an orange. Oh my God, my head is all lopsided."

At Beth's insistence, I promised I would never try the "visual squash" technique again. So much for Bandler and Grinder. I have often wondered why techniques work like magic for one therapist and fail miserably in the hands of another. Does anyone ever check the data?

After that, I decided to proceed more slowly, concentrating on Toby's internal communication skills. Anna and Beth could converse, but Toby could not hear or talk to either of them, at least not since the fight with Anna. Because of this, she was now in constant chaos, feeling as if she was being pulled in many different directions. She must have been switching before she started to see me, but therapy seemed to be making her switch more often. During one session, for example, she complained that she had gone to her hairdresser for a simple wash and set and had come home with an extremely short cut that she hated, evidently because either Anna or Beth preferred it.

I suggested that Toby go into a hypnotic trance and asked her if she would like to talk to Anna. Using me as an intermediary, the two women tearfully reconciled. Then I asked if they wanted to have permanent communication. They said they did, but that there was a glass wall between them. I suggested that we put in an intercom system, and after Toby was in a trance I used imagery to go through the motions of installing it. But as we began to drill through the wall, Toby screamed, pulling her head back and grimacing in pain. It was as if a sadistic dentist had suddenly started to drill a tooth without novocaine. The trance broke, and a higher-pitched, adolescent voice addressed me. It was different from Toby's, I realized with a chill.

"Hullo. I'm Morgan."

Another personality? Apparently. But why had she taken so long to make herself known?

Morgan didn't know how old she was, but from the pitch of her voice, her language, and her interests, which revolved around baseball and boys, I judged her to be eleven or twelve, or just about to enter puberty. She seemed to be a happy young woman, friendly but tough and not easily frightened. She was more extroverted than the others, of whom she was aware. She also knew who I was and even had a vague idea of why we were in my office. She had been anxious to talk to me for a long time, she said. Like Beth, she saw me as someone who could amuse her. When I asked why it had taken her so long to introduce herself, she said she simply hadn't been ready until now.

The session was at an end, and I welcomed the chance to think about this latest twist. I told Morgan that I was happy to have met her and that we would assuredly talk again. Then I asked her to return inside and bring Toby back. She said good-bye and closed her eyes. The body before me slackened, then stiffened slightly, a sign that Toby had reemerged, allowing me to end the session. Early on I had instituted a rule that whoever walks into the office is also the one who walks out.

That evening, as I was making some notes on the case, the phone rang. I recognized Toby's voice through her panic.

"Dr. Mayer, I'm in trouble. I'm in some man's house, I don't know where, and he's angry with me because I won't go to bed with him. But I don't know him, and I don't know how I got here. I ran into the next room, locked the door, and called you, but he's banging on it. He is screaming that he is going to get me. I am afraid that he will break the door down. He is going to kill me."

The classical position is that therapists are not supposed to intervene directly in their patients' lives. We are not even supposed to give advice. But this situation clearly was not covered by the psychoanalytic rule book. Was it real? Was it a test? Could she get out of there by herself? There is an analytic commandment that says, "Never do for a patient what a patient can do for herself." If I intervened now, would I be giving her the wrong message? Did I really have a choice?

I told her to tell the man that she was a psychiatric patient, and that she had just talked to her therapist and given me his phone number, so there was someone who knew where she was. That was insurance that she would not be harmed. After that, she was to ask him to point her to the nearest subway station and lend her a token, since as usual Toby was walking around with virtually no money.

She came back to the phone a few moments later and said the man didn't believe her and wanted to talk to me. Then he was on the phone.

"What goes on?" he said in a voice more confused than angry. "This woman picks me up in a bar on Broadway and Eleventh Street. I ask her if she wants to come home with me. She agrees. We get to my place in Brooklyn, I put some music on, we listen for a while, we dance, everything is fine. Then we sit on the couch and I go to kiss her and she freaks out. Her voice changes and she starts pretending that she doesn't know me."

"What did she call herself?" I asked.

"Morgan."

Hoping he wouldn't think I was as batty as his newfound friend, I tried to explain the situation. To my relief, he seemed to understand and, in fact, welcomed the chance to get rid of Morgan or whoever she was. He would call her a cab and pay for it right away, he assured me.

An hour later my phone rang again. It was Morgan, now safely home. She was guilt-ridden and terribly apologetic. It seemed that after Toby had left my office, Morgan had come out, taken charge of the body, and started to wander around my neighborhood. She said she hadn't been out in a long time and wanted to meet some people and have some fun. She wandered into a place on Broadway with a few pool tables in the front and a bar in the back and started to talk to a man she thought was nice. Morgan may have thought it was a casual conversation, but the man evidently saw a full-grown, somewhat heavy but seemingly flirtatious woman. He invited her to his house, and Morgan, in all innocence, accepted. When he tried to kiss her, she got frightened and headed for the safety of her internal world. Suddenly Toby was back in charge of the body in a situation she hadn't created and didn't like one little bit.

An hour later I got another phone call, this time from Toby, who was still very shaky from the experience. I explained what had happened. She was furious at me. I was supposed to stop this sort of thing, wasn't I? Wasn't that what she was paying me for? I told her that we would talk about it tomorrow during her session, but that was not good enough. She wanted to talk about it now. I said I could not. She started to scream at me. I told her again that I would talk to her about it tomorrow. She did not want me to hang up the phone. She wanted me to keep talking to her and calm her down. I stayed on for a while, but it wasn't helping. Finally, I told her I had to go and hung up. She called back a few seconds later in a rage. I again told her we would talk about it tomorrow. I also said that if she could not control her anxiety, I would have difficulty continuing to treat her as an outpatient and would perhaps need to have her hospitalized. I hoped she would get the message.

An hour later I got a phone call from Anna. She told me that Toby had started to swallow some of the Atavan Maurice had prescribed for her, in a suicide attempt. At the last minute, though, Anna had taken charge of the body and flushed the pills down the toilet. I told Anna to stay in control until she came into my office on the following day. She said she would.

Anna was still in charge when the time for the appointment arrived. We talked for a while about what had happened, and it seemed to me I had stumbled onto a useful fail-safe mechanism. If Toby tried to kill herself again, Anna promised she would step in and stop her. I couldn't constantly hold her hand, and I didn't think it wise to hospitalize her at this point, assuming that in fact I could have had her committed. So Anna's vigilance was as good a solution as I was likely to find.

Next, I decided to deal with Morgan, whom I accessed hypnotically. After a brief chat, it was clear to me that she just wanted to have some fun and had no comprehension about the dangers of New York City. Indeed, she still thought that she was in the decidedly more friendly Midwest. I briefly explained the facts of the big city as best I could and got her to agree to stay inside most of the time in exchange for compensatory time out at Anna's discretion. Morgan liked to watch the Mets, especially when Dwight Gooden was pitching, and the plan called for her to be allowed to watch three games a week. I didn't know if she watched them through Toby's eyes or her own.

Looking back on it, Morgan's behavior was the exception. There seemed to be some sort of implicit social contract under which Toby's individual personalities had given up some of their freedom for the general good of the group. Even as children, they would all answer to the name of Toby so as not to confuse anyone—and to preserve their secret. Now, at my urging, they would have meetings inside and present appeals for time out. As the eldest, Anna would try to mediate any conflicts. I hoped that this would prevent a repetition of the incident.

Before the session ended, I realized that we all had another problem—there were now four patients but only three appointments a week were scheduled for them. They all wanted more time with me, but they could not afford an additional hour, even at my bargain rates. I decided to let them figure out a solution. It might encourage them to take more responsibility for their treatment and, I hoped, speed their cure. Reluctant at first, they eventually held an internal meeting and discussed several proposals. The winning plan would then be presented to Toby, who could not attend, since her dissociative mechanism prevented her from hearing the others.

Again, their system operated democratically despite the tension and hostility among them. Life had treated them so miserably, I guess, that they were very concerned with fairness. They had all decided to give Toby one session a week, since she was one who paid me, and that the rest would alternate on the remaining two days. If one of them had an urgent problem, the others would give up their hour until the crisis was over. They arranged a schedule and presented it to Toby who, after some initial anger at having to share her time with me, approved it. Then, for the first time, she said six words that made me feel as if I was starting to make some progress in at least getting her to accept her multiplicity: "I guess it really is true."

Knowing who was likely to show up for an appointment on a given day made things much easier for me. But I was still barely able to keep up with the turns in the case. Beth was especially difficult. She was, after all, a child, and I was hardly a child psychiatrist. I had never treated a child. I had never even taken any courses in analytic school on how to work with one. To make matters worse, my young patient was frightened all the time, having graphic dreams common to children—nightmares of people chasing her, catching her, hurting her—and causing a lot of trouble for the others on the inside.

Beth would throw tantrums in my office. She demanded her chocolate cookies, wanted me to play with her, but, most of all, wanted to sit on my lap, which she said was the only thing that would make her feel better. Anna counseled me to give in. Hadn't the kindly Dr. Carter, the psychiatrist who lived next door, let little Toby sit on his lap?

I had been trained never to touch a patient, except to shake hands upon meeting for the first time or upon the termination of treatment. Obviously, letting a mature woman sit on my lap was out of the question. But it was also unreasonable for me to expect a five-year-old to behave like a proper adult analytic patient and not like a five-year-old.

Fortunately, I had hypnosis. I also had some children's books left over from when my son was small. And I had Max, a stuffed monkey two feet tall, complete with toes. Max had been given to me a few years earlier by a physical therapist who would work on my fifth lumbar vertebra and listen to me complain about being lonely. The primate had gotten her through some bad times, she had said, and might do the same for me. I had laughed and placed him on top of my bookcase, where he had lived ever since. Beth and Max hit it off from the start. He became like Linus's blanket, what my colleagues term a transitional object. Beth would sit with the monkey in her arms, session after session, while I read her therapeutic stories designed to guide her through childhood difficulties and speed maturity. I borrowed from Aesop, the Bible, Zen, and, of course, Erickson.

Sometimes Beth would tell me her dreams, and then I would try to come up with a story that would help her resolve the issue that had triggered it. I wasn't always successful, but the process seemed to help her build trust in me. I needed that trust. Without it, I would not be able to guide her through her abreactions, much less be able to prepare her to accept her integration, which in her world was tantamount to death. But that, I knew, was a long way off.

Summer was approaching, and soon it would be August, the psychotherapist's traditional month off. At the time of my last vacation, Toby had been in therapy only a few months. Her defenses had still been functioning, and multiplicity was not yet such a consciously disruptive issue. Since then, therapy had been doing what it was supposed to do, which was to wear those defenses down like water on stone, so that the underlying problems could be exposed, explored, and examined. Judging by her reaction during my midwinter trip to Phoenix, I had reason to be worried about leaving for a month.

I talked the problem over with Toby, Anna, and Morgan. They all seemed to think they could deal with my absence. But what about Beth? She had come to depend on me and my stories. Fortunately, I convinced Anna to come out every night and read Beth a story for me. I loaned them Max, and, after promising to send them postcards regularly to let them know I was still alive, I was off sailing to Martha's Vineyard in my thirty-five-foot ketch.

Along the way, I did a lot of thinking about Toby. Despite all I had gone through, I still wasn't completely sure whether she was a multiple or a manipulator. There were numerous inconsistencies that confused me, and there wasn't enough therapeutic time to check them all out. Besides, investigating them made her feel as if I didn't believe her and caused additional problems.

But by giving in, was I reinforcing her problems, whatever they were? How would a more experienced analyst handle her? There had already been one suicide attempt. Some patients kill themselves, they told me in analytic school. It's their problem, not yours. But were they really that tough? Clearly, it is a risky way to think.

I wished to myself that I was more like some of my teachers. They always seemed so sure of themselves. If, while proceeding down one well-defined path or another, their treatment did not seem to work, they simply chalked it up to the patient's resistance. And if the resistance did not get better, then these brilliant clinicians would chide their patients for failing to work through the problem.

Working through. It is a phrase I still do not understand, even when I see patients actually do it. Sometimes I think it means talking about something long enough until boredom forces a person to let it go. Would Toby ever work things through? Was I on the right track with her? As I thought back on it, I realized I had already committed myself. I had returned the first phone call while I was away with my therapy group that first weekend. Once I had started to take calls outside of the sessions, once I had started responding to her, once I had started to use hypnosis, I was being active, directing therapy and thus telling her that I could help take her pain away. I could not return to a classical analytic position. I could not suddenly withdraw and become passive. I had no choice but to proceed down the path I had chosen, hoping that along the way I could get her to take more responsibility for her treatment and her life.

Of course, that didn't mean I couldn't get a second opinion. A colleague, Pat Weltman, and I had been experimenting with joint group therapy for about a year. The purpose was to give our patients the experience of both a male and female therapist. What if Toby were to enter the group? It would give her other people to talk to and give me a break, and when I went away for vacations, one of us would be in town.

Pat said she would let Toby sit in if she agreed not to switch during the sessions. But even if she had switched, I suspect the other members of the group would probably have been too involved with their own problems to notice.

Toby bonded to her new companions and also became very attached to Pat, going so far as to schedule some individual sessions with her, during which she complained about me. Then, suddenly, Pat became ill while on vacation and entered a California hospital for a protracted stay. Once again, Toby's worst fears were realized—she had been abandoned. She berated me for sending her to someone who left her. It was my fault that she was now in pain because Pat was unable to work. I lost my patience and warned Toby to calm down. To be fair, I was under more than a little stress at the time, since I had to cover Pat's practice during her illness and many of her patients were also quite upset.

Anna came to our next session. "Something is wrong with Toby," she said, taking me to task for being so unfeeling. I asked why she had to be Toby's spokeswoman. Toby was too upset to talk, she said. Curious about what was going on, I suggested that she go into a hypnotic trance. As she started to relax, I felt that familiar chill, the one that started at my toes and ran up my spine, the one that seemed to herald the arrival of a new personality. With a mixture of resignation and anticipation I watched as her posture changed. Her eyes opened and looked around the room in a frightened way. By now I was used to it.

"Who are you?" I asked.

"Julia," she said in a sweet, shy voice, her eyes now cast downward.

I had been angry at this particular patient for more months than I cared to think about; my patience was running thin and my countertransference growing strong. And yet it all melted when I got to know Julia. I felt warm and loving toward her. She was seductive in a nonsexual way. Somewhere in the back of my cerebellum a voice warned me to be careful, reminding me that personalities can be created for other purposes than to share the pain.

So now there were five. But who was Julia? Was she new, or had she been there all along? Why did she show herself now? After a brief hypnotic investigation, I learned that Julia was about ten years old, or a little younger than Morgan. Assuming that she had not stopped growing, like Beth, she would have been born in the late sixties, which seemed appropriate, since she could have been the prototype of the 1960s flower child. Her job, in fact, had been to tend the family garden, a chore the others hated. Another of her functions, apparently, was to soften people up when Anna's logic, Toby's rage, Beth's playfulness, and Morgan's assertiveness did not obtain the desired results.

I wasn't sure whether or not Julia had come out in reaction to Pat's illness, a loss that might have reminded Toby of the death of Dr. Carter, or whether it was just a fresh attempt to manipulate me. But I did know that, either way, she was not about to go away. That meant we now had four extra personalities vying for the two weekly therapeutic slots that were available. It took about a month of wrangling before the problem was eventually solved. As before, they shared the time, except if someone was in difficulty. Toby still had title to one session a week, but she was paying for all three—and increasingly resented it.

Scheduling seemed the least of our problems. Although I was fond of Julia, I came to feel that she was the last straw and I the camel. I was increasingly worried about the way I was reacting. I was getting too self-critical and beginning to feel anger toward my patient. Was I losing my analytic neutrality? Was the case getting out of hand? Maybe I wasn't stable enough for such a demanding patient(s). Still, I could not tell Toby to find another therapist because she would think it was her fault. The problem was that there was no one in my circle who could advise me. I again sought Erickson's help, but my second trip to Phoenix proved futile. Erickson had aged, and, although still a great therapist and storyteller, he had no energy to talk to me privately after the group.

Then I discovered a book called *Minds in Many Pieces*, by Ralph Allison, a California psychiatrist. He said he had treated many multiples, many of whom seemed much sicker than Toby. Allison believed that all multiples had what he called an inner self helper, an all-knowing entity with a complete history of the person but no power to change things. Part conscience and part guru, the inner helper might, Allison felt, be mystical, a prospect I didn't take altogether seriously. What gave me hope, though, was that these inner helpers had enabled Allison to solve many of his difficult cases.

Hoping Allison's discovery would work for me, I asked Anna if she knew of any others who might be inside. Yes, she said, there were the ones "cloaked in darkness," over the hill. I told her to go and get them. She said it was a long journey and would take time. She asked Julia and Morgan to take care of

Beth. They begrudgingly agreed, and off Anna went on her quest.

Two weeks later, I was reading a story out of *Winnie the Pooh* to Beth. At the point where Eeyore fell into the river and was floating under the bridge, Anna suddenly reappeared. Apologizing for interrupting, she said she had important news for me—the "Dark Ones" were coming. She looked terrified and exhausted, and I decided not to follow up on this right away.

A few uneventful sessions went by. Then, while I was talking to Julia about—what else—her garden, she became startled. As her eyes turned glassy, I felt that chill again. No, I thought, not another one.

A deep voice came from the depths of Julia's diaphragm. It did not sound like Julia or Morgan or Anna or Beth or Toby.

"Good evening. You sent for us?"

I felt the hair on the back of my neck stand up. The chill intensified. It was like I was talking to a ghost.

The body was Toby's, of course, but the voice, the posture, the very being of the person in front of me had been transformed into something I would call supernatural, if I believed in such a thing.

"Who are you?" I asked, amazed that I was maintaining my calm.

"We are the Dark Ones."

We? I started to question them carefully. They were not a part of Toby, they claimed. Rather, they said they were sent by the Archangel Michael to help her. They claimed that there were three of them, interchangeable but different, and that they spoke as one. They often paused, as if they were consulting one another. They kept themselves "cloaked" from the other personalities, they said, for fear they would scare them. They were, to use their own description, "awesome." And now they were putting themselves at my service.

What in the world was I supposed to do with them? I decided to simply accept what was happening as real, as I had with the arrival of each new alter personality, and hope things would get clearer soon.

The Dark Ones and I talked for a while. I asked some questions, and they gave me cagey answers. Well, what could I expect? They were spiritual, and I was of the flesh. I would never understand. They had other things to do, no doubt far more important than talking to me. They instructed me to let them help me with this case, so they could go home as soon as possible.

I asked if there were any more personalities that I had not yet met.

"Yes," they replied unemotionally.

"How many?"

"Five."

"Where are they? And why don't any of the others know about them?"

"They are in a separate place, walled off," the Dark Ones said.

The Dark Ones claimed they had been responsible for the creation of all of Toby's personalities. They had created the machinery to make the alters many years ago, they said, because Toby was in so much pain. But things had gotten out of hand, and too many personalities had been created. Disturbed about this, they had destroyed the machinery and walled off half the personalities.

"Who were these additional personalities?" I asked.

"Mirror images of the other five," the Dark Ones explained. "When Dr. Carter died, the pain of losing the only person who was kind to them was so great it could not be contained by any of the original five. So they split again, creating Thea, Laura, Ka, Meegan, and Becky, the twins of Anna, Julia, Toby, Morgan, and Beth, respectively."

I met them all in subsequent sessions. The Dark Ones were right. They were just like their twins, only less fully developed, almost caricatures of the originals.

There were now ten patients, three spirits, and one very

confused therapist. We all needed help. Was I the victim of a
giant hoax? If this was manipulation, Toby was far sicker than I
thought. On the other hand, here I was conversing not only
with ten personalities but three supernatural entities. I wondered whether I would end up believing in the spiritual world,
like Allison. Maybe, as Mesmer's more far-out followers believed, the mind *is* open to invasion by spirits.

I had had a religious upbringing, mostly because of my
grandparents. My grandmother's answer to all problems was
to pray to God, although for particularly hard problems she
would travel to Brooklyn and have a consultation with the
zaddik, a Jewish mystic. To her dying day, she claimed it was
the zaddik who had kept her son out of the Army during World
War II and not the fact that he was a pharmacist, an exempt
profession. Although I became an agnostic in college, I had
studied comparative religion. And since then I had studied
with Hasidic mystics, spent time at Esalen, and lived for a
week in a Zen monastery in Vermont. It had all been fascinating, but in the end none of it was for me. I was too much of a
scientist. But now my faith in empiricism had been so shaken
that I feared I might end up as a Jewish exorcist.

Consultation

I had two reasons to be apprehensive as Toby and I drove north on the Connecticut Turnpike. It is unusual for a therapist to meet patients outside the therapeutic setting because it gives them a false idea of the limits of the relationship. But even more, I was unsure about the psychiatrist we were going to see.

When I earlier had mentioned to a colleague that I was considering consulting Judianne Densen-Gerber, he strongly advised me to reconsider.

Stories had been circulating that Densen-Gerber had been using her patients for her own needs. They cleaned her house, drove her car, tended her garden—even combed and set her hair. She had created a cultlike atmosphere at Odyssey House, the drug treatment center she had helped found and now controlled, and she had convinced more than a few addicts from wealthy families to enter private therapy with her. In November 1979, six months before my visit, *New York* magazine had called her "The Mysterious Mistress of Odyssey House," suggesting among other things that she had received $70,000 in fringe benefits in addition to her $107,000-a-year salary from an institution that had officially only hired her as a consultant. The article referred to numerous unusual expenses uncovered in an audit and the fact that Densen-Gerber personally controlled an Odyssey House bank account. No charges were ever filed, but she eventually left the organization.

And yet there was another side. A *Cosmopolitan* article had raved about the Densen-Gerber approach. "Few clinics can boast an atmosphere so humane—so caring—as the refuge Dr. Densen-Gerber has created here at Odyssey House," it said.

It was Toby who found Densen-Gerber. Flipping television channels one evening, she stumbled across a "20/20" segment on multiples. Although she was too upset to watch much of it, she phoned the station afterwards and was given the name and number of Bennett Braun, a psychiatrist at Rush Presbyterian Hospital in Chicago, who was interviewed on the program. She called him the next day and explained that she was a multiple. She told him that although she was already in treatment, she wanted to talk to someone in New York who knew more about multiplicity than her therapist. Braun suggested Densen-Gerber. A substantial number of addicts, it turns out, have been abused as children and turn to drugs to chemically dissociate from the pain. Many sprout multiple personalities as well, for the same reason. Densen-Gerber had treated so many addict-multiples that in Braun's estimation she qualified as an expert.

A few days later I called the "Mysterious Mistress" and had a wonderfully reassuring talk. For the first time since my startling introduction to Beth, I felt there was someone who not only believed me but also understood what my patient and I were going through. We swapped stories for an hour. Densen-Gerber even told me she experienced the same chill in her body that I felt whenever Toby revealed a new personality.

She then suggested that she would like to meet Toby and conduct a workup. The only time I could bring her was over the weekend, but she said it was all right to visit her at her Connecticut country home. I was hoping the trip would confirm the diagnosis once and for all and finally put my doubts to rest. If Toby *did* turn out to be a multiple, I figured I would pick up some pointers on how to proceed and perhaps get networked with other therapists treating the disorder.

Talking with Densen-Gerber made it easier for me to digest all the bad press she had received. Cults were big news in those days, and I knew anything that resembled one would be sure to intrigue a reporter. And residential drug treatment programs do have cultlike aspects. They are typically highly regimented operations, as tough as any boot camp. The techniques needed to socialize addicts are extreme—rituals of public humiliation and punishment for infractions of minor rules; dismissal for breaking the cardinal rules against drug use, sex, and lying; a system where privileges are granted only after the most rigorous determination that they have been thoroughly earned; the requirement that enrollees inform on each other or they, too, will get the boot; heavy-duty confrontations in therapeutic encounter sessions; and house meetings at all hours of the day and night.

On the other hand, I had read two books she had written— *We Mainline Dreams: The Odyssey House Story* and *Walk in My Shoes*—and had been impressed. Densen-Gerber, who came from a very wealthy family, started as a lawyer, later adding a medical degree. She married Dr. Michael Baden, a noted pathologist who was once New York City Medical Examiner, and after the death of a newborn mongoloid child—the couple eventually had four healthy children—she decided to become a psychiatrist.

In 1966, while completing her psychiatric residency, Densen-Gerber tangled with the higher-ups at New York's Metropolitan Hospital, who were refusing to let some addicts under treatment there go cold turkey rather than take cyclazocine, a heroin substitute. Densen-Gerber argued that it made about as much sense to cure addiction to one drug using another as it did to wean an alcoholic off scotch with vodka. She insisted cyclazocine wasn't working: Only eight of seventeen thousand patients had been cured over six years, she said. The bureaucracy contended that addiction was untreatable by the psychiatric methods she advocated, and besides, Metropolitan Hospital had money for a drug maintenance program, not a drug-free treatment program. "It appeared that the hospital was funded to test drugs, not cure patients," Densen-Gerber concluded.

When Densen-Gerber went ahead with her own methods and detoxified a small group of the patients, she was banned from the ward. A few weeks later the hospital discharged the patients. They came to her with the grand sum of $382 they had collected and asked her to continue to work with them. They stayed in Daytop Village, a treatment center in the city, for a while, then camped out on the floor of Densen-Gerber's apartment before their odyssey ended in an abandoned building on East 109th Street, which they rented with contributions from local businesses and others.

At the time of our meeting, Odyssey House International was thriving. It received federal, state, and private grants and had branches throughout the United States, centers in Australia and New Zealand, and plans for expansion in Europe and Asia.

Densen-Gerber had also started the first center in the United States for addicted mothers and children, who were then being turned away by city drug agencies. She had other crusades as well. She was constantly bringing child abuse to the attention of the authorities, who did not seem to want to hear about it, especially from her. Indeed, Densen-Gerber's radical feminism and unrelenting idealism had a way of making people angry. But I was willing to look past that. She just might help me find a way to treat Toby.

Densen-Gerber's directions took us to a beautiful country house behind a high stone wall on several acres in the fashionable Green Farm section of Westport. There was a swimming pool in back and a sauna and Jacuzzi in the basement.

A neat young man in a starched white button-down shirt,

tie, and jeans ushered us into a living room filled with pop art, including chairs that looked like people who were sitting, with anthropomorphized legs that ended in stockings and socks and shoes. To sit in one of them was to sit on someone's lap. All around was a scattering of Odyssey House memorabilia— plaques, paintings, and cartoons.

There were many young people, especially women, and they were busy coming, going, talking, smoking, eating. It reminded me of the mother's country home in *The World According to Garp*. After a wait of about fifteen minutes we were ushered into the doctor's office. Judianne was white-haired and overweight. She appeared to be about my age, which was forty-five. Sprawled on a antique campaign chair, she was a queen holding court, knitting away and apologizing for keeping us waiting and for having a cold. She had an undeniably strong presence. I am rich, powerful, smart, creative, and successful, her body language shouted, and I can prove all of the above. I demand acknowledgment and respect.

No wonder she had gotten herself in trouble.

There were two other women with her. Alice was a tall, thin Scandinavian type with long blond hair, small eyes, and prominent cheekbones. She appeared to be in her mid-thirties and spoke softly, with a cultured midwestern accent. She struck me as friendly but shy.

The second woman's name was Jane. She looked to be just on the far side of forty and was of medium height and slightly overweight, with dark, close-cropped hair and wire-rimmed glasses. Her sneakers, jeans, and man-tailored tweed jacket contributed to an air of asexuality.

As we were offered a choice of coffee, tea, or soda, I wondered about this scene. It certainly wasn't one that would have been included in a textbook on analysis. I reminded myself that Dr. Densen-Gerber was a psychiatrist, and a psychiatrist does not necessarily have to be an analyst (nor an analyst a psychiatrist). Not having been analytically trained, she obviously played by different rules. Many physicians think nothing of being friendly with patients or keeping them waiting.*

Densen-Gerber explained that the two women were also suffering from multiple personality disorder and that she had just finished a session with Alice. Both would now stay in the room to act as "bridges," a concept adapted from her work with drug addicts, who usually do not trust professionals—or anyone, really, who has not been an addict. Densen-Gerber's theory, which I have since accepted, is that multiples, like addicts, speak a language all their own. Especially at the beginning of therapy, another multiple who is further advanced in treatment can function as an interpreter between the patient and the professional.

Bridge or no bridge, Toby was terrified, cowering on the sofa and clutching the bag containing Max. Taking the monkey along was the only way Beth would agree to go. Morgan, on the other hand, had made the trip only after I hinted that she might get to talk to another person her age. I guess we looked quite ludicrous, a six-foot-four therapist and his five-foot patient grasping a paper bag from which the head of a stuffed primate protruded.

Densen-Gerber started to interview Toby, trying her best to be friendly, but Toby continued to shake with terror, clutching the bag and hesitatingly answering the questions, giving as little information as possible. There was no way she would let Densen-Gerber hypnotize her. It was out of the question. Toby just didn't trust her enough. She said she was afraid that if she went into a trance, Densen-Gerber would stab her with one of the knitting needles. Nothing I said helped, either. She just cowered like a hand-shy puppy, edging farther and farther

---

* Analytic training, which occurs after a candidate earns a Ph.D, is open to social workers, psychologists, and medical doctors, all of whom have a different orientation. Social workers are communicative and supportive, psychologists more academically oriented, and psychiatrists, the only ones allowed to prescribe drugs, follow a medical model. In a hospital, the M.D. is at the head of the pecking order, followed by the psychologist and then the social worker.

away from the dreaded doctor whenever she thought no one was looking.

Recognizing a case of unrelenting resistance when she saw one, Densen-Gerber changed tactics and asked Alice to tell us her story.

Alice looked around the room a little tentatively, then began. She was married, had two children, and now lived in Connecticut. She said that she had started to use barbiturates years ago to drown out the voices in her head. It wasn't long, she said, before she had grown dependent on them. When she found herself starting to snort heroin because the barbiturates were no longer effective, she realized it was time to seek professional help. She consulted Densen-Gerber, whom she had heard of because there had been several Odyssey House units in the Midwest, where she was living.

Alice had no inkling then that she might be a multiple. But Densen-Gerber was able to make the diagnosis based on circumstantial evidence. Alice had a childhood amnesia, with no memories before the age of fifteen. And she was also losing time—there were hours and even days she could not account for, and sometimes she would be somewhere and not remember how she had gotten there.

The voices were another telltale sign. They seemed to be coming from inside her head rather than outside, as would be the case if she were psychotic, a more serious problem. She also had persistent headaches, a symptom experienced by many multiples that is caused, I think, by the pressure of the various personalities struggling to gain control of a single body.

Alice also had a school record so uneven it was easy to see how someone could conclude that other people were sometimes in class instead of her. And sometimes people would call her by different names, or she would meet people who knew her, but she would not know them.

Densen-Gerber was right, of course. Not long after she had started treatment, Alice's multiplicity was confirmed by a hypnotic interview during which five personalities emerged.

Alice talked to Toby for a while, trying to calm her. She said that she, too, had been frightened during the early stages of therapy. But although she had not then completely accepted the diagnosis, she said she was relieved when Judi had told her that she was not "crazy" and that she could be cured if she continued in treatment.

Densen-Gerber pointed out that a therapist's first task after making the diagnosis is to convince the patient to fully accept it, which usually isn't easy. Multiple personality disorder is actually an elaborate defense that shields a patient from unpleasant and intolerable childhood experiences—obviously, nothing is more unpleasant to acknowledge than having a father whom you wanted to trust and thought loved you destroy everything by raping you—especially if your mother helped him. Victims try to deny the problem, even to the extent that they often love and protect their abusers. To accept the truth forces them to feel pain not even felt at the time, pain that was dissociated away, pain they do not want to feel but must feel in order to get better, pain that is stored away, festering, burning up energy that could better be used in a thousand ways. It has to come out if a patient is to progress. It has to be felt and to be discharged. To do that, patients have to talk about it. Getting them to accept the diagnosis puts the first chip in the denial mechanism. It starts to allow memories to surface, and it starts to change the relationship with the therapist from one of resistance to one of cooperation.

This acceptance often comes only by means of a severe shock. Take Jane, for instance. A regular churchgoer who thought she lived an asexual life, Jane had great difficulty believing her multiplicity until she woke up one day in a strange hotel room in a strange city. She did not know how she had gotten there or even where she was. Multiple personality disorder provided her with the only explanation.

A waitress in New Jersey, Jane was unmarried, lived alone, and said she hated men. That was hardly surprising given that she had been sexually abused by her father from the age of three until his death, when she was thirteen. Her mother knew about the incest and told her to do what Daddy said. Sometimes when she refused, she said, her mother would tie her to the bed with her legs spread apart. Jane told the story angrily. She had been in treatment for about four years, she said, and felt she was making progress. Still, she wished her father were still alive so she could have the pleasure of killing him.

Densen-Gerber asked Jane to allow herself to be hypnotized and demonstrate her "people" to us. Jane reclined on the couch and was told that a warm wave of relaxation was overtaking her from head to feet. As the induction droned monotonously on, she drifted into a trance.

Densen-Gerber asked to speak to Joe, an eleven-year-old who was obsessed by automobiles. He said he wanted to be an auto mechanic or race car driver when he grew up. When asked why he looked like a girl, he replied unabashedly that he was in "her" body, but when he was inside he was a man with all the right equipment, you could bet on that. Despite his age, he claimed to do the driving when Jane went anywhere. He was unhappy because he wanted her to buy a sports car with a stick shift, or better yet a motorcycle, but she wouldn't.

We then met Mae, who was also a waitress, but in a different restaurant than the one Jane worked in. Mae also worked a different shift than Jane. Somehow or other this woman managed to hold down two jobs.

The fourth personality was named Eva. She was a maid who would clean the house every Thursday. She didn't say what she did the rest of the time.

Listening to Alice's story and watching Jane's alter egos helped reduce Toby's anxiety. Finally, she allowed herself to be hypnotized, but by me, not Densen-Gerber. I started the induction by instructing her to focus on a spot on the wall. Then I began counting from twenty to zero, telling Toby that at some point before I finished her eyes would become tired and close and she would drift into a trance. When I reached zero, her eyes were shut, her breathing had slowed, and her facial muscles had softened. I noticed from the pulse in her neck that her heart rate had eased. She was ready.

"Can I talk to Anna?"

Her body became rigid, her eyes opened and she crossed her legs and placed her fingers together in Anna's inimitable style. Anna looked around the room, fully in control of herself, as usual. She focused on Densen-Gerber, ready to put her to the test. How long had Alice and Jane been in treatment? she asked. Was it going well? What were the problems? Did they like their therapist? Would they recommend her?

Anna interrupted her inquisition, suggesting that Densen-Gerber put away the knitting needles because they would scare the others. When I questioned Anna about her fear of the needles, she told us that Toby's mother used to knit and occasionally would take one of them and stab at her. She showed us a scar on her left hand where she said a needle had been plunged in.

Anna finally stopped asking questions and became silent. I knew she was satisfied, or at least as satisfied as she could be.

"Can we talk to Beth now?" I asked.

"It's okay with me, if it's okay with Beth. I'll ask her."

She closed her eyes for a moment, then opened them. "Beth will come out if she can have a cookie," Anna said.

Densen-Gerber rang for a servant to fetch them and some milk. In a flash Anna was gone and Beth had arrived, saying she hoped they would be chocolate. I told her that they were on the way, but she still seemed fidgety and nervous. Like Toby, she immediately started to inch away from Densen-Gerber. I took Max out of the bag and Beth let out a squeal, hugged him, and seemed to calm down. "Who are all these people?"

I introduced her to Jane, Alice, and Densen-Gerber. She caught a glimpse of the needles and said, "Are you going to stab me with one of those?"

We tried to reassure her, but it was tough going. After a few minutes, she dropped the subject. "Are there any little girls here?"

Unfortunately, neither of the other two patients had any personalities who were Beth's age. At that moment, thankfully, the cookies arrived. "Oh good, chocolate, my favorite. Can I have one, please?" she said in her most polite voice. She quickly devoured it with one hand while holding Max close to her face with the other.

Then Judi made the mistake of offering her a glass of milk. Beth's back stiffened. Her face took on a look of terror and then went blank. A split second later, Morgan said, "Geesch, you people are stupid. Don't you know we hate milk?"

I would think about her reaction to the milk later. For now, I concentrated on her choice of pronoun, "we," which, I would learn, is characteristic of multiples.

Morgan looked around the room, then down at her left hand, the one holding Max, and discreetly dropped the monkey. She tried to cover her embarrassment by saying, "What took you so long to let me come out?"

Not waiting for an answer, her eyes fell on the knitting needles. She glared at the world-famous psychiatrist, who was also twice her size. "If you make one move toward me with one of those needles, I'll tear your throat out."

I quickly reassured her that no one was going to hurt anyone. Satisfied, Morgan turned to more important business. She was very interested in Joe, the boy who resided in Jane. It had been a long time since she had talked to someone her own age.

Jane obligingly switched into the eleven-year-old, and the two adult females had an adolescent conversation about cars and baseball cards. It reminded me of my childhood, only I couldn't quite believe it was really happening. Perhaps this is the only way to work with this strange disorder, to believe it and not take it altogether seriously at the same time.

We watched, fascinated, for about half an hour. Then I brought Toby out of the trance, and she and the other two women left the room to have a more adult conversation. Densen-Gerber and I then had a case conference.

Judi got right to the heart of it. There was no doubt in her mind that Toby was a multiple personality. She said that I could expect to find male, female, homosexual, and heterosexual alters. I was told to watch out for a personality that was probably homicidal, created for the purpose of killing the abuser. That one could be dangerous to me. Densen-Gerber said that she never worked with this personality without a backup. She also said that there should be an internal self-helper, which I already knew about, and a switch, a personality who was in control of the mechanism that determined who was out of the body.

I told her that I had isolated the personalities, but although I had found the "Dark Ones," who were the closest I could come to internal self-helpers, there was no sign of a switch or a male. From my observation, the system seemed to operate democratically. Densen-Gerber could not believe this. There had to be a switch and a male someplace, she insisted. The patient was holding out on me.

She also berated me for being too soft on Toby. She felt Toby was manipulating me, taking advantage of my sympathetic nature, and not working hard enough in therapy. I tried to argue that unless I bent over backwards, Toby would not stay in therapy, but Densen-Gerber wasn't convinced.

Changing tack, Densen-Gerber told me there was a small group of researchers and clinicians who were working on multiple personality disorder, trying to win acceptance for the diagnosis from a still suspicious profession and trying to develop a systematic method for treatment. Among them was Bennett Braun from Chicago, the reason I was in Densen-Gerber's home in the first place. He had written papers demonstrating that hypnosis is the method of choice to work with and that it does not cause the disorder, as some previous researchers had fearfully suggested. There was Dr. Richard Kluft of Philadelphia, who was gathering demographic data on patients and their various personalities, compiling a census of multiplicity. Dr. Frank Putnam of the National Institutes of Health in Bethesda, Maryland, was researching brain waves and physiological responses of patients and their alters. Dr. David Caul in Ohio had treated Billy Milligan, the first to avoid a death sentence due to multiplicity.

These physicians were circulating papers and developing an oral literature that would later be published. In so doing they were forming the nucleus of an organization that would be known as the International Society for the Prevention and Cure of Multiple Personality. In 1984 it held its first international conference, attracting more than four hundred participants from the United States and other countries. Judi gave me copies of some of their papers. At last I was hooked into the network of professionals who, unlike Arnold, wouldn't think that the problem would simply go away.

Their research was clearly more advanced than I had been led to believe from the various articles Toby had tracked down for me. Briefly, Densen-Gerber filled me in on the emerging field with broad brush strokes. Research was showing that nine out of ten multiples were female, perhaps because many more women than men are abused as children, or perhaps because there are sex-related differences in the brain that predispose women to dissociative reactions. There are also many more women than men in treatment, though some argue that most men with multiple personality disorder are not correctly diagnosed and many probably end up in prison. This obviously reflects differences in the ways men and women handle feelings such as anger, aggression, and hostility. Women internalize these feelings, while men act them out, becoming criminals instead of patients.

Ninety-seven percent of all known cases of multiplicity are people who have been severely abused as children, usually but not always by a family member. Other family members sometimes deny the abuse is going on and sometimes are even facilitators. The abuse is usually sexual but can also be physical or psychological. It often reaches the proportions of torture. Billy Milligan was repeatedly buried in the ground up to his head by his father. Sybil had implements such as ice picks and curling irons thrust into her vagina. In any event, the abuse is usually frequent, giving the child no opportunity to recover, and it characteristically continues over a long period of time.

There was still not a good answer for why some abused children develop multiple personalities and others do not. Some think it could be genetic. Others believe it has to do with the age at which the abuse takes place. Densen-Gerber told me she believed that the number of personalities a patient develops might be connected to the amount of abuse, although she knew of no research that had yet confirmed this. There have been reports of multiples begetting multiples, but no one knows whether it is learned behavior or genetic.

Multiples are thought to be unusually creative, especially in the arts, and appear to have higher-than-average intelligence levels. But multiplicity cuts across racial, religious, and economic lines. Victims come from the right and wrong sides of the tracks, from religious as well as atheistic families. They are educated and uneducated. They can be parents, lovers, and spouses. They can be heterosexual, asexual, homosexual— or any combination of the above.

One study found that nine out of ten multiples had been misdiagnosed at least once. Another found that the average multiple had been in treatment seven years before the correct diagnosis was made. Some are severely incapacitated and need hospitalization. But not all are. The three multiples in the room with Densen-Gerber and myself, after all, all held responsible positions.

Circling back to Toby, Densen-Gerber clearly believed she was very ill, one of the most difficult cases she had seen. This was the same message the psychiatrist I had sent Toby to, Maurice, had given me earlier and one of the reasons I had been so attentive to Toby. But now I realized that my efforts to prevent further decompensation might be undercutting any motivation I could instill in her to face up to her dilemma and try to change.

Densen-Gerber called Toby back into the office. She told her she was a multiple and that she could be helped and would get better. Then, to my analytic surprise, she berated Toby as sternly as any angry parent. She accused her of demanding too much of my attention and time. "You have eaten enough," she said. "It is now time to shit."

I was shocked. I had never talked to any patient that way. I would never even consider it. I had been taught to be neutral and understanding.

Toby and I thanked Densen-Gerber and left, each engrossed in our own thoughts. Toby was relieved to know what she had and that there was actually a course of treatment that promised success. But it was overshadowed by her rage at this woman with the knitting needles who had criticized her behavior and told her that she would never get well if she continued to expect me to be as attentive as I had been. "There are no men," she muttered. "We do operate democratically. What does she know?"

Toby was frightened as well as fragmented. If I weren't attentive, she would surely stop coming and get worse. But if Densen-Gerber was correct, I would have to change my approach if Toby was to make progress and get better.

As I thought it through, I realized that Densen-Gerber had a different angle on the case than I did. She had spent most of her professional life developing Odyssey House and dealing with hard-core drug addicts. These were people the *Diagnostic and Statistical Manual of Mental Disorders* calls "chronically antisocial individuals who are always in trouble, profiting neither from experience nor punishment, and maintaining no real loyalties to any person, group, or code. They are frequently callous and hedonistic, showing marked emotional immaturity, with a lack of sense of responsibility, lack of judgment, and an ability to rationalize their behavior so that it appears warranted, reasonable and justified." In other words, they have no conscience, do not care about right and wrong, and are masters at manipulation. To treat them, you first have to give them a conscience. And if you allow them to manipulate you, they lose respect for you. So Densen-Gerber and her colleagues took a hard line at Odyssey House, and it certainly seemed to work. Would such toughness be effective with a paying patient in private practice who can walk out the door? I had my doubts.

Still, it gave me an idea. I could use Densen-Gerber's approach against Toby. I could put her in a double bind by emphasizing to her that Densen-Gerber thought I was too lenient and that she would not get better unless I drew the line. If Toby wanted me to continue to be so attentive, she would have to prove this lady with the knitting needles wrong. To do that, she would have to get better—and I would be able to defeat Hydra.

I was in an upbeat mood the whole way home. It was good for Toby to chat with other people suffering from multiplicity, especially people further advanced in therapy than she was. It made her feel less crazy and gave her hope that she could be cured.

As for me, I learned much in Westport. My diagnosis had been confirmed and I had met someone who could back me up if I needed it. More important, with the "mean" lady and her knitting needles as a threat, I had the beginnings of a treatment plan.

Saint or sinner, Densen-Gerber had helped us, and I liked her.

6

Two for One

One crisp September morning, four months after my trip to Connecticut, I got a phone call from a Jean Lothian, who handled public relations for Dr. Densen-Gerber. Would I be interested in treating a multiple who had recently been uncovered in the Odyssey House center on East Eighteenth Street in Manhattan? The fee would be low, but the case would be interesting.

It sounded intriguing, and I had some open time. I accepted.

Ms. Lothian suggested that I come to the center the following week to meet the patient and discuss the details of the case with Dr. Densen-Gerber. When the day arrived, I walked east from my Tenth Street apartment to Third Avenue, then turned north past the junkies, winos, and prostitutes and the porn theaters and the Salvation Army shelter. As I crossed Fourteenth Street the neighborhood started to improve. By Gramercy Park, it had become fashionable. Cities have multiple personalities, too.

Odyssey House occupied a four-story brownstone that had seen better days. I walked in and encountered a young neatly dressed Hispanic man who politely asked me what I wanted. I told him, signed the guest book, and was led upstairs to wait for Dr. Densen-Gerber.

I had never been inside a residential drug treatment center before. I guess the model in my mind was some squeaky clean country place with rolling lawns, a swimming pool, and nurses in starched white cotton. Not so different, now that I think about it, from Densen-Gerber's country home. Odyssey House, on the other hand, was dilapidated, crowded, and noisy, but at least it was clean. There were all sorts of people roaming around. Some wore sandwich boards that said things like "I have been too noisy, I am not allowed to talk today." One woman had a telephone hanging from her neck with a sign explaining that she had made a call without permission. Another was carrying a very large baby bottle. Still another had donkey ears and a tail with a sign that read, "If I act like an Ass, I should look like an Ass." An extreme way to teach people, I thought. Then again, to reach the hard-of-hearing you have to shout.

I was ushered into what looked like a boardroom on the second floor and told to make myself comfortable. The doctor was running a little late. As my guide left, I poured a cup of coffee from an urn at the back of the room and took a look around what had once been a magnificent chamber. The ceiling boasted a plaster floral design and still had a huge chandelier in the center. The walls were paneled in walnut and hung with sconces, photographs, awards, and diplomas. At one end of the room was a large mahogany table surrounded by twenty armchairs covered in worn red velvet. At the other end was an old sofa upholstered in silver-colored cloth and three club chairs. The grouping faced a fireplace that looked like it hadn't seen a spark in twenty years.

Up the stairs flowed Judianne Densen-Gerber, with an entourage that included a man to get the door, a woman on either side, and another woman bringing up the rear.

She apologized for her lateness and introduced everyone so quickly and offhandedly that, except for Jean Lothian, I was not able to remember their names or jobs. After an all-too-quick round of pleasantries, she got right to business.

"I have two patients I would like to refer to you. Howard"
—she looked at her assistant, a tall, thin man of about thirty-
five—"tell Dr. Mayer about Lauren." Howard took one of the
folders he was carrying and proceeded to read Lauren's case
history.

Lauren was thirty years old and of Italian descent. Born
and raised in New Jersey, she was one of eight children from a
devout Catholic family. She was currently married, with a
four-and-a-half-year-old daughter.

Lauren's husband, Roger, constantly beat her, fracturing
her jaw on one occasion, her nose on another, and two ribs on a
third. She had been hospitalized more than twenty times in all.
Roger was also in the habit of bringing men home and forcing
Lauren to have sex with them, after which he would beat her
some more, calling her a whore all the while. Sometimes he
would bring women home, have sex with them himself while
Lauren was forced to watch, then force Lauren to have sex
with them while he watched. He also abused their daughter
and wanted Lauren to join him when he did. Her refusal led to
more beatings.

Lauren had been sent to Odyssey House at the insistence of
the Bureau of Child Welfare, which had investigated com-
plaints from neighbors of violence and child abuse in her
household.

Both Lauren and her husband took drugs, having met in a
methadone program. Roger had shot heroin intravenously for
years and also took amphetamines and drank heavily. After an
interview with the Odyssey House counselors, he had refused
treatment and was last seen leaving the city for points west.
Lauren was the heavier drug user. She had started snorting
and skin-popping heroin when she was nine and continued
sporadically until the age of fifteen, when she switched to
opium, which she augmented with occasional shots of heroin
and nips of narcotic-based cough syrup. She also dabbled with
LSD. But her favorite drug was Tuinal, which puts me to sleep
but sends drug users like Lauren sailing. She took up to forty

capsules of the barbiturate a day, sometimes souping it up with alcohol or marijuana. Her repeated use of LSD and marijuana, which are hallucinogens, was unusual for a multiple, but the other drugs fit the pattern. They were central nervous system depressants, probably used to mute voices in her head and allow her to chemically dissociate from her problems, past or present. I was amazed that her body could build up a tolerance to all these pharmaceuticals and wondered if each personality had its own favorite. Different alters within the same multiple can have different reactions to the same drugs, and some can even be allergic to one substance while another is not. One of the reasons multiples are difficult to treat with drugs is because a prescription cannot always be counted on to affect all the personalities the same way. Perhaps in Lauren's case those forty Tuinals were really split among five people.

Over the years Lauren had overdosed a half-dozen times and wound up in hospitals having her stomach pumped and being detoxed. Some of these occasions apparently were bona fide suicide attempts. The first had come when Lauren was a teenager. She was having an "S and M" affair with an older girl who liked to play mother and spank Lauren for being bad. Eventually, it would evolve into lesbian sex. After a while, the playmate broke off the relationship, sending Lauren into a fit of anger and depression during which she swallowed dozens of her mother's sleeping pills. She was discovered in time, and she was rushed to the hospital.

During her marriage, her self-destructiveness had taken the form of "accidental" drug overdoses designed to manipulate her husband into treating her normally, or at least better. In fits of rage she would sometimes swallow whole bottles of whatever pills happened to be at hand, and her husband, Roger, would have to rush her to the hospital, promising that he would never do whatever he had done again. Hospital records showed that she was usually put into thirty-day detoxification programs and released, after which time she promptly went back on drugs. She certainly didn't make it easy for anyone trying to help her. She managed to go to a different hospital for each attempt and was diagnosed differently each time. After the attempts she was often referred to therapists, but she would stop treatment after a few months, invariably claiming that the psychiatrist did not understand her.

I later found out that neurological examinations had determined that Lauren—or at least the host personality, I suspected—was an epileptic. I requested but was never able to see the report, which left me wondering, like Dr. Charcot a century earlier, whether some patients with this malady could be misdiagnosed multiples.

After arriving at Odyssey House, Lauren was detoxed yet again, put on an antiepileptic drug called Dilantin, and started in the program. Six months later, after making relatively good progress, she confided to the resident psychiatrist that there were other personalities living in her body. She said she had made them up and given them names when she was a frightened, lonely child.

Lonely? With seven siblings and two parents? That was as good an indication of what her household was like as any, I thought. Lots of people but no real interaction, much less love. It made me think of Toby's three sisters, all whom were beaten but none of whom talked about it to each other or anyone else.

During the next few months Lauren's multiplicity became more acute, with more shifting from alter to alter. She obviously felt safe in Odyssey House, safe enough to be herself. The plan now, I was told, was for Lauren to continue at Odyssey House under a neurologist's care for epilepsy while I took her into therapy for multiplicity, with both treatments monitored by Densen-Gerber. "She is a wonderful multiple," Judi said before I had a chance to respond. "You'll love her. Now tell him about Susan."

Howard pulled out another folder. Susan was a twenty-eight-year-old from Odgen. One of ten children, including two sets of twins, all girls, she was from an upper-middle-class Mormon family. She has been sent to Odyssey House Utah by a judge after an arrest and conviction for drug possession and prostitution. Then she had been transferred to New York to get her away from her environment. Now, three years later, she had reached level four, the stage at which the staff often recommends that patients receive therapy from a private, outside analyst before they graduate from the program and reenter society.

In Susan's case, therapy was necessary. She said she had no memories from before the age of twelve. There was no evidence that Susan was a multiple, but Densen-Gerber's experience told her that she was, just as it had told her Jane and Alice were. Later, under hypnotic investigation, it turned out that Susan had indeed been abused from age seven to nine by her father, who felt that it was all right since she had not yet been baptized and therefore wasn't really a person. He had also abused her sisters, invoking the same rationale.

"Let's meet the patient," Judi said.

An aide picked up the phone and asked for Susan to be sent in. She entered a few minutes later. She was a tall, blond, blue-eyed woman who looked to be about thirty pounds overweight despite a loose-fitting top.

Susan said she still didn't fully understand what had happened to her. She had been brought up in a respectable, religious family but had somehow fallen in with the wrong crowd in high school. She had started to use drugs and quickly graduated to the big leagues of illicit pharmaceuticals, heroin. Then, spiraling downward, she had begun to sleep with the men who would keep her supplied with the stuff. After she was busted, she had been thrown in jail and had had to detox cold turkey.

Susan was anxious to enter private therapy to find out what had caused her slide, which she now felt was bizarre, given her background. I asked her to come to my office the following Wednesday, and she said she would.

Even though I looked hard, I saw no signs of multiplicity in

Susan. All multiples may be sexually abused as children, but clearly not all sexually abused children become multiples.

Now it was time for Lauren. It was clear as she came into the room that she was as flamboyant as Susan was reserved. It would have been hard for her not to be, with her silky blond hair that flowed down to her waist, brown eyes, and the pale complexion typical of a blond. She walked like Bette Davis, leading with her hips, confident, tough, and sexy. She greeted everybody and sat down, crossing her legs and rearranging her dress.

"Hello, Scarlett," Densen-Gerber said. "It's nice to see you, but we were expecting Lauren."

The voice of Scarlett replied and said that Lauren had had a panic attack just outside the door and that she, Scarlett, had taken charge of the body. After chatting for a bit, Scarlett and I were formally introduced.

Densen-Gerber reminded her that they had talked about her multiplicity and her need for psychotherapy. I was billed as an expert—which made me wonder. Still, Lauren looked me over and appeared reasonably satisfied.

Densen-Gerber asked her to tell us about herself and the others inside, so I could decide whether or not I could help her. She agreed.

Scarlett was thirty, the same age as Lauren, and was her assertive, sexual personality. She usually came out when Lauren faced a situation that required cunning or sexuality. She had worked as a cocktail waitress, supplementing the tips by giving twenty-dollar "B.J.s," as she called oral sex. When asked to describe herself, Scarlett said, "I am tall, I am sexy, I am smart, I am shrewd, I am pretty, I have long red hair—and whatever Scarlett wants, Scarlett gets." (Well, she didn't say she was modest.) When I pointed out that her hair was blond, Scarlett said yes, the body's hair is blond, but when she is inside her hair is red. And when she is outside, she went on, she usually wears a wig.

Her stay in Odyssey House had been upsetting, since she

didn't think she should be there. Scarlett insisted that, unlike Lauren, she was not an addict nor had she ever been one and did not even suffer when Lauren was detoxed. Scarlett did drink, but only Southern Comfort.

Densen-Gerber asked her whether she had gotten her name from the character in *Gone with the Wind*. She replied that Lauren, who had named her, had seen the movie.

Scarlett contended that she was usually in charge of the body and knew everything that happened to Lauren. She had the memory, although the feelings were spread among the rest of the personalities. Scarlett, not Lauren, knew all the others inside and decided who came out and who stayed in. She was a combination of switch, internal self-helper, and host personality. But she said she was getting tired of having all this responsibility and wished Lauren, whom she didn't respect, would get stronger and take on more of the administrative burden of multiplicity. After all, wouldn't that make Lauren healthier? Could I help them achieve that goal?

Probably, I told her, but I would need to meet all of them and know much more of their history before I could make a judgment. Scarlett agreed. She started by telling me about her family. The mother was religious, strict, stupid, and not very caring. She had eight children and was constantly complaining about how hard life was. She was angry about the fact that her husband had made her leave Italy and come to the United States. Lauren appeared to be her father's favorite. Scarlett said that "the woman"—that was how she always referred to Lauren's mother, who she evidently did not accept—would beat Lauren for very small offenses, forcing her father to step in and stop her.

Lauren's father, according to Scarlett, was a laborer who also did "odd jobs" for the mob. I found it hard to believe, but Scarlett insisted that he would often come home with blood on his clothing and make Lauren either wash or bury it. He once handed her a bloody knife to clean, saying that he had borrowed money to gamble and had had to kill someone to pay off the debt. Another time, he said he had "cut someone into small pieces" who had threatened to steal Lauren and sell her to satisfy a debt. It was right after that incident that Papa "disappeared." He had gone swimming in a cement bathing suit, I suspected.

Scarlett felt that he, like Lauren, had had a number of people living inside of him. In fact, he sometimes answered to different names—Joey, Cosmo, Roberto, Guido, and Sean.

"Sean? That's an Irish name," I said.

Scarlett shrugged. It was Sean, she said, who anally raped Lauren when she was five, telling her he would kill her if she told anyone. He continued to sodomize her until she was fifteen, which was when he disappeared. He would tell her that it was all right, that she needn't confess it to the family priest. They weren't breaking any rules since he was preserving her virginity and anyway, anal sex really wasn't sex.

Not content only with incest, her father inhibited Lauren's efforts at a normal social life by chasing her would-be boyfriends out of the house. It was all right, however, for her to go out with *his* friends. (This was surely what she was recreating when she consented to have sex with men her husband brought home for her.) Her father also had sex with all of her sisters. On many occasions, Lauren suggested that he take a sister instead of her. Later, in therapy, it was clear that she bore a tremendous amount of guilt over this. Scarlett, on the other hand, recounted all these travails with a noticeable lack of feelings. It was clinical, almost as if she were reading a report about someone else.

Howard, Densen-Gerber's aide, cut in at this point, saying that two of her sisters had been interviewed. They were both married, living in New Jersey, and heavy drug users. Their children also had severe behavior problems. The sisters did not admit to being sexually abused as children, probably because they did not trust the interviewer but more probably because they simply did not remember or, like nearly all incest victims, had been threatened by their abuser and were still too terrified to tell anyone.

Neither could recall very much about her childhood, although they did confirm that their father seemed to go by different names. They, too, said they had different people inside of them, but they felt they were stable and were not interested in psychotherapy.

Densen-Gerber thanked Scarlett and asked her if we could now meet the others.

She agreed and walked out of the room. A few moments later the door opened and she walked in again. Well, it was she but it wasn't. She had the same blond hair and body, of course, but she carried herself entirely differently and had different mannerisms, too. She bounced into the room with the walk and body language of a teenager. She was chewing gum furiously and cracking it loudly. She had gone from sexy to sixteen.

Her name was now Loverly, and she said she was a "dumb blond" with a wink that meant she wasn't. She knew that the Cockney "loverly" was from a song from *My Fair Lady* in which Eliza Doolittle is contemplating what life would be like married to her teacher, Henry Higgins. A father figure, I thought to myself.

After hearing her story, Densen-Gerber asked if we could talk to Peg. With a wave of her left hand she bopped out the door, and about fifteen seconds later in strutted a woman named Peg. Again, it was the same person, but it wasn't. The voice was deeper and the walk more assertive. There was anger in her demeanor. "That fucker always chews gum," she said, depositing it in an ashtray. "I hate it."

She reached into her bag and pulled out a pack of Salems. "Fuck," she said, throwing them on the table and rummaging in her bag. She pulled out Newports and Marlboros before finding her brand, which was Kools. Sighing, she took one out and lit it, exhaling the smoke through her mouth and nose. If I ever get confused as to who is who, I thought to myself, I can always recognize them by their cigarettes or gum.

Peg started right in with a tirade against Loverly. She was very angry because Loverly used to come out and seduce an older man, a distant cousin named Sal. As soon as he would try to put his hand between her legs or on her breast Loverly would get frightened. Peg would have to take over, verbally or physically fending off Sal or anyone else.

Scarlett would play the same game sometimes. She once went out on a subway, flirted with a man sitting next to her, and when he started to respond she went away and Peg appeared and had to take care of the man. Then Peg left and Lauren was suddenly in charge of the body, with an angry man sitting next to her, not knowing what was going on.

Next, Sadie paraded into the boardroom with her chest out, her shoulders back, and her head high, cursing at the cigarette in her hand and stubbing it out in the first available ashtray.

She spotted the Salems on the table and lit one. Sadie was from the South and had the drawl to prove it. Before entering treatment, she said, she had earned money by taking "packages" to and from Europe. She claimed not to know what was in them but got paid well for her troubles.

I was not prepared for what came next. Sadie did the door routine and then Jefferson entered, walking like a stereotypical gay male. He was cursing the mentholated cigarette he found in between the first two fingers of his right hand, his left hand being partially raised and cocked at the wrist. He smoked Marlboros, it turned out.

Jefferson was twenty-eight and did everyone's hair—they owned five wigs, one for each personality—and took over the body whenever there was something mechanical to be done. He also cooked. He did not like Lauren's husband, calling him "that disgusting man," although that did not stop him from enjoying sex with Roger. Jefferson also enjoyed it when Scarlett and Loverly picked up men, which gave him variety. Apparently it was Jefferson who performed oral and anal intercourse. What a system—Scarlett or Loverly picked them up,

Scarlett arranged the finances, Jefferson or Scarlett had sex with them, and Peg got rid of them.

Jefferson left to get his "sister" Honey but reentered a few minutes later, saying Honey did not want to come.

"This is important," Densen-Gerber said. "Tell her to come or the body will lose its privileges." (Odyssey House functions on a behavior modification principle: If you are good, you get rewarded and move up the "levels"; if you aren't you get punished. You might have to wear a sign, or you might lose the right to smoke or to go to parties. Serious violators can be dropped down a level or two, and those who break a "cardinal" rule are discharged. This was an obvious problem for multiples because the personality who transgressed would not exclusively be the one to pay for it.)

Jefferson shrugged his shoulders, walked through the door, and closed it. For what was probably only a minute but seemed a very long time, I wondered whether Densen-Gerber's threat would work. Then the door opened and in came Honey.

"What do you want?" she said crossly. It was the same body, but now it seemed more erect and masculine. She strutted over to the chair and sat down. She didn't smoke.

She told us that she had short brown hair, and was, as she said, "into women." In fact, she was appalled that Lauren, Peg, and Loverly were attracted to men, after what men had done to them. The best time she ever had was when Lauren had gone to Plato's Retreat, a sex club in New York, and Honey had made love to another woman for the first time. She hated Lauren's husband and did not understand why Lauren stayed with him, but she didn't mind it when he would bring back another woman and force Lauren to make love to her, a task she eagerly came out for when Lauren freaked out in horror.

I was having trouble keeping all of them straight, and I still hadn't met Lauren. She proved to be an anticlimatic host personality. She walked in slowly and cautiously, deemphasizing her ample chest by lowering her head, rounding her shoulders and hunching her back. She found the same chair the others had used and sat down, primly pulling her skirt about her knees. She was, as Scarlett described her, a shy, backward, almost uneducated, unsophisticated housewife.

She rummaged in her bag and found a pack of Spring cigarettes. Yes, it was a problem, she said, as she put the other packs back in her purse. "And I have to have many different wardrobes."

As we talked, it became apparent that her self-image matched her body language. She felt not only that she was ugly and stupid but also that the only thing she could do was make babies and take care of her house. She could remember creating Scarlett, Loverly, Jefferson, Sadie, Honey, and Peg when she was lonely and hurt as a child. But she could not remember any of the early sexual or physical abuse to which she had been subjected. Then again, she said, she hated sex and didn't like to talk about it. It was bad, dirty, sinful.

What was fascinating about this case was that they all knew about each other. Unlike Toby, they had co-consciousness. When Lauren was inside she could talk to Peg or Jefferson or Scarlett or Loverly or Sadie or Honey. She also was aware of what was happening on the outside, as were the others. Lauren was so aware of the often outrageous experiences of her alters that she felt terribly guilty and would go to church quite often to confess and do penance. She did not understand how her "people" could do such terrible things—she was prudish and sex, especially prostitution and homosexuality, were anathema to her. That was one of the reasons for her drug addiction. She used heroin and barbiturates, she said, so she would not be so conscious of what they were doing.

After a brief silence, Lauren went over to Judi and kissed and hugged her. She thanked Dr. Densen-Gerber for taking her and her child into the facility and explaining all about multiple personality. Then she looked at me through teary eyes.

"Can you help us?" she said. Then she left to await the answer.

"The case of Susan should be easy and straightforward. She has a childhood amnesia," Densen-Gerber said. "You are a good hypnotherapist. I would suggest that you investigate hypnotically what is going on in those missing years. Then we will have a case conference and decide where to go with it. My suspicion is that she was abused as a child.

"With Lauren, it is more complicated. But after seeing you with Toby, I am sure you will know how to handle it.

"Lauren has no money, but Susan does. That is the deal." Treat one for free, the other pays. Two for one.

I liked being connected with Dr. Densen-Gerber and Odyssey House because these patients were quite different from my normal vanilla neurotics, and my professional life was bound to be far more interesting. And then there was Lauren. Somehow, I felt I understood her and already had a handle on the case, even though it seemed atypical from most multiples in the quickness and ease with which she switched from one personality to another. My mind had been processing what I had seen. Lauren had been abused as a child by a father who also appeared to be a multiple personality. His "Italian" personalities were the good daddies, while his "Irish" personality, Sean, was probably the pedophile, thus allowing him to resolve any psychological or moral conflict. In his own thinking, he did nothing wrong—it was Sean.

Her mother, meanwhile, resented Lauren because her husband was paying more attention to her than to his wife. This removed a source of love, if indeed she had ever been one. To take out her anger, the mother had simply not protected Lauren from the continuing nightmare of abuse.

As for Lauren, she had little self-respect and was utterly lacking in the ability to assert herself. She was frightened and timid as a child, trying to be a good girl. The only nurturance she got was from her abuser, so she solved her problem by forming other personalities. It might have been easier for her to do this than it had been for Toby because she had a handy example of multiplicity in her father. In so doing, Lauren put all the problems into neat little compartments. Lauren may only have tested average on the Odyssey House IQ test, but she was creative. The personalities, once invented, helped her deal with situations she could not otherwise handle. Because she was insecure and nonassertive and had a bad self-image, Scarlett, Loverly, Honey, Jefferson, Peg, and Sadie were available to manipulate the environment depending on what was needed.

Scarlett was strong, assertive, rational, in charge, the person Lauren would like to be. Scarlett was not afraid to use her charms or temper to get what she wanted. Scarlett also represented her anger toward men through her prostitution.

Lauren's disillusionment with her father was expressed in the choice of the name Loverly, which, if it did come from *My Fair Lady*, would clearly point to a young girl's wish for a daddy who would teach her and whom she could eventually marry.

Through Honey, the lesbian, Lauren's hatred of her father was transferred to all males. Identifying with her father's maleness, even though she had a female body, could also represent a desire to be loved by her mother.

Jefferson was the homosexual, nonthreatening male she needed to take care of things that needed a "man." The name could be a reference to Thomas, but I was inclined to suspect that it referred to Jefferson Davis, the leader of the Confederacy, Scarlett's homeland. Through Jefferson, Lauren got the last laugh on men, because in her mind heterosexual men were being forced to have homosexual relations with him. In Odyssey House, she would often change into Jefferson and come on to the male residents.

Lauren was the type of person who felt guilty for leaving her fingerprints on the doorknob when she entered or breathing more than her share of the air in the room. Unconsciously, she was probably feeling the guilt of breaking the incest tabu even though it wasn't her idea. In some way, she may have felt the beatings from her husband were deserved as proper punishment for her "crimes."

Peg, the opposite of Lauren, was tough as nails, providing the anger that unassertive Lauren was frightened of but needed, the anger born of the physical pain of the rape and the emotional pain of the paternal betrayal. Peg protected Lauren.

Sadie was also a reaction to Lauren. She was a sociopath, an antisocial personality who feels no guilt. She got even with society through crime.

Lauren had already undergone a lot of therapy at Odyssey House and co-consciousness of her alters. That was a big advantage. The memories of the abuse were now available as well. What was needed, I thought, was for someone to break down the "feeling" barrier. She would have to be taught to feel what the others were feeling, what she should be feeling in response to past and present situations that she now fended off. Then and only then could Lauren take over the functions of the others. Then and only then would all the parts form a whole.

The problem, as almost always, was resistance, which was evidenced by Honey's refusal to meet me. I did have one thing going for me, though. Odyssey House was threatening to take away her child and send her to foster care if Lauren didn't continue to progress. That could be a powerful incentive.

I looked at Densen-Gerber for a moment.

"Judi," I heard myself say, "you just bought yourself a therapist."

7

SUSAN

My professional life was certainly getting busier. After the meeting at Odyssey House, the organization frequently called on me to apply hypnotic Band-Aids to its residents. The Odyssey House hierarchy believed that most of its charges needed psychotherapy from someone not connected with the treatment center, an outsider to whom residents could say things they might not be able to reveal to a drug counselor. Therapy from someone not directly connected with the center would also serve as a bridge between the cloistered life inside Odyssey House and the reality beyond its door.

I found many of these Odyssey House cases fascinating. Listening to residents' histories was like going to the movies. I could mentally wander through an underworld of drug users, drug sellers, and deviants of all stripes. It was quite a contrast to my comparatively tame, middle-class practice.

It was Odyssey House that sent me Edward, a fifteen-year-old ex-addict who had the distinction of being the only white person to travel with an especially vicious Chinese youth gang specializing in extortion and drug importing. Arrested and sent to the treatment center on probation, he was referred to me, amazingly enough, for bed wetting. Upon investigation, I believed he was unconsciously using this problem to gain attention, albeit the negative variety. Because the bed wetting occurred while he slept, Edward felt helpless to control it. I started by training him to go into a hypnotic trance, and when he mastered that skill I took him on an imaginary motorcycle ride in which he "felt" sensations such as his hand on the throttle, the bike between his legs. As Edward, an avid biker, made his way along an idyllic country road, I pointed out that he didn't have to think much about what he was doing—he automatically stayed on the right side of the road, he automatically slowed down when he approached an intersection, he automatically sped up when he went up a hill, he automatically leaned into curves and applied just the right amount of pressure to the brakes so that his bike did not stop short and pitch him over the handlebars. He could do all this, keep his balance, and still think about other things. My plan was that he would make the link between all the unconscious muscular control he exerted while riding the bike and the unconscious control of his urinary sphincter muscle. This connection was established in the first sesssion and reinforced in subsequent ones. The next step was to transfer his thirst for attention that had generated the symptom. This turned out to be easier than I thought. Edward had a good voice and liked to sing. I suggested, while he was in a trance, that he join the Odyssey House choir, a group that was getting a lot of publicity at the time. He soon became one of the lead singers.

While all this was happening, his bed wetting began to taper off. Eventually, it stopped.

Another Odyssey House referral, Dorothy, an ex-prostitute and drug user, had a similarly mundane affliction: She stuttered. I know, it seems like the least of her problems. But Dorothy was getting ready to graduate from the center and reenter society, a process that was hindered by the terrible time she was having at job interviews. Again, there was a simple solution: I hypnotized her and transferred the symptom to her fingers. When on an interview, she was instructed to place her left hand into her pocket and let her index finger do the stuttering instead of her mouth.

Susan, the woman I had met at the Eighteenth Street center, was more challenging than either Edward or Dorothy.
Brought up in an upper-middle-class home, with upper-middle-class privileges and values, she had descended into addiction and depravity. Why? The amnesia she was now suffering
from was a major clue. Susan remembered virtually nothing
about her childhood before the age of twelve. I was to give her
general therapy as an adjunct to her treatment at Odyssey
House. Our goal was to find out what had happened to her
during the years her memory was blanking out.

I decided that I would work slowly, using standard therapeutic techniques. I would try to get Susan talking, striving not
to make judgments about what I heard. Eventually, she would
come to trust me. Eventually, we would confront the resistance that was keeping her memories locked away, unresolved. Susan had about a year and a half before she was
scheduled to graduate from Odyssey House, so we had some
time to work.

I started my first sessions with Susan by asking her to tell
me the story of her life, with the standard analytic instructions
that she report whatever came into her mind with as little
conscious censoring as possible. Even though at this point in
my career I was enamored of Milton Erickson's brand of hypnosis, I decided to save that tool for later. For now, I would rely
on the traditional Freudian approach of free association, hoping it would enable my patient to summon up the years that
had disappeared.

When we started, practically the only thing Susan recalled
from her childhood was a fragment of a memory of her mother
kicking her. She did not understand her mother's behavior.
The amnesia seemed to end at about the time Susan entered
junior high. What she told me about those years could have
been made into a grade B movie called *Reform School Girls,*
featuring sex, drugs, and rock 'n' roll.

Susan said she had her first sexual experience at the age of
thirteen and was one of those girls my generation would have

said had a "reputation." She said she would have sex with the boys because it was the only way she could get them to pay attention to her. In high school, this desire for attention resulted in numerous broken hearts and uncountable fights with her parents. She also had two abortions.

Susan's father, a successful and respected environmental engineer and church deacon, was naturally disturbed over his daughter's behavior and tried hard to control her. The more he tried to clamp down, the more Susan resisted and rebelled. In the end, she would sneak out at night to meet her friends, who were mostly troublemakers—something else that hardly sat well with her father. When she would bring her friends and lovers home to dinner, her father would usually throw them out, making the relationship with his daughter even worse. Sometimes he would chase her friends down the block, and once or twice he even took a baseball bat to their cars. When he was really in a rage he would storm back into the house and beat his daughter.

Where had Susan's mother been during all this? According to Susan, she was a sickly woman who spent a great deal of time in bed. With nine other children and a tyrant of a husband, she was clearly overwhelmed. Little wonder she became addicted to Valium.

Susan's rebellion included drug use—first marijuana, then cocaine, and finally heroin, which she started out snorting and later injected. When her parents learned of her drug use, they threw her out and Susan had to earn money for her fixes through drug dealing and prostitution. Many heroin addicts function fairly well in the early stages of addiction, and Susan managed to pull herself together and even started college. But she didn't do very well, flunking out after two years. She then became obsessed with her weight, which did not appear to be a problem, went on a stringent diet, and lost her appetite. She became so weak her father had to take her home. Susan recovered, detoxed, and got a job in a local exercise club. She soon fell back into her old ways, and her father kicked her out a second time.

She moved in with her lover-dealer—I suspect it is very easy to love one's dealer—and not long after that came a middle-of-the-night knock on the door. The voice on the other side claimed to be that of the building's superintendent, who was looking for a leaky pipe. When Susan opened the door three undercover police officers waving guns and badges burst in, threw the pair facedown on the floor, cuffed them, searched the apartment, found drugs, needles, and other paraphernalia, and arrested Susan and her beau.

Through this point in her history, which was related over many sessions, I had tried only to be a sympathetic listener, asking questions merely to keep her story coming. Then one day she came into my office terribly upset. She had a dream the night before that she couldn't get out of her head. It was the first dream she had reported since we had started therapy, so I was eager to listen and analyze it.

"I was in my room, sleeping," she told me. "I looked up, and there was a shadow in the doorway. I was terrified. I called to my sister, who shared the room with me, but she wasn't there. Where was she? I don't know. I just lay in bed. I was frozen. I couldn't move. Then everything went black and I couldn't see. Then I was in the water. It tasted salty and it was easy to float in. I was on my back. The water was very warm. Then I felt myself sinking slowly under the water, like in quicksand. I tried to scream, to call out for help, but I couldn't. I opened my mouth and tried to scream as loud as I could, but nothing would come out. It was terrifying. There were people standing around me, in the water, watching. I tried to call to them for help. But nothing would come out of my mouth. I looked at them, but they just watched as I sank lower and lower."

She paused.

"I woke up in a pool of sweat, terrified. I stayed up all night.

I was afraid to go to sleep. I didn't want to turn out the light for fear that I would have the dream again."

She turned and looked directly at me. "Help me. I don't know what to do."

As she related the dream she had become more and more upset. Now there was a wild look in her eyes, and her body was shaking. She was now lying back on the couch, curled up in the fetal position, sweating. This is what therapy is supposed to be about, I thought. You wait and wait and wait until you get a break, until your patient gives you a signal that she is finally willing to face a problem. I didn't need much analytic training to realize that this was such a moment. It was time for me to bring out the heavy therapeutic artillery. We could have gotten to the meaning of the dream through free association, but I decided that it would save time to work hypnotically. I had a sense that, given her body language and her fear, hypnosis would be more efficient. Besides, I was anxious to try out my newest technique.

"I think I can help you with this if you will allow yourself to be hypnotized, so we can uncover the meaning of the dream. Are you willing to do that, Susan?"

An affirmative answer would commit her conscious mind to the process.

"Yes," she said. "Anything. I'll do anything to end this awful feeling."

"You don't have to face the terror and fear right now, Susan. Just close your eyes and try to take yourself in your mind's eye to a pleasant place, a place where you feel safe, a place where no one can bother you, a secret place that only you know about. While you are going there you will hear my voice, you will always stay in contact with my voice, it will go with you wherever you go."

"Now Susan, picture yourself walking down a country road. You might feel the gravel under your feet. You might feel the wind on your face. You might hear birds overhead, or the rustling of leaves in the trees. You might see some flowers beside the road. Stop and look at them. Touch them. Smell them. It is an enjoyable walk, a pleasant walk. See yourself coming to a clearing, a grassy knoll. Let yourself lie down on the grass. Feel the warmth of the sun on your body. The sun is life-giving, it is nourishing, it makes things grow. Let your body soak up the nourishment. Let your body rest. Let the tension drift out of you. Let yourself sink further down into this nice, pleasant state of relaxation. That's right, stay with it."

Susan's face softened, her body stopped trembling, and she looked peaceful. I was pretty sure she was in a trance. I had assumed that by giving her a suggestion to go "inside" to this safe and special spot—to dissociate—she would be more than willing to leave the terror of the dream outside, and she was. After all, she had already shown a tendency to dissociate rather than face pain. That was the reason for her amnesia.

The next step was to test the trance.

"Susan, tell me what is happening to you."

"I am lying on my back on the grass. The sun is warming my body." Her voice was sluggish.

"Did you have a pleasant walk to that place?"

"Yes, there were bluebirds and the mountain laurels, the prettiest I have ever seen. I picked one up and am holding it in my hand. It smells so nice."

Good enough, I thought. She was having visual, tactile, and olfactory hallucinations—she was feeling and smelling objects that were not present in my office, retrieving memories of these sensations from the appropriate compartments in her brain and experiencing them as if they were happening at that moment. Such is the power of hypnosis.

"Think back to your dream of last night. Tell it to me again."

For what seemed like a long time, Susan did not speak. I wondered what was wrong. Patients are supposed to follow instructions when under hypnosis. I thought she might be frightened and in need of some additional support. I decided to try again, but first I sought another commitment, this time from her unconscious mind.

"Susan, you have been troubled by something all your life. It has made you do things that perhaps you would not otherwise have done. Now it is time to find out why. Are you willing to do that, are you willing to face your fear, to find out about it and try to eliminate it?"

Still she was quiet. Then she finally spoke.

"Yes."

"Okay, Susan, that's fine. Now let me start you off. You dreamed that you were in your bed and there was a shadow in the doorway."

Almost immediately, Susan started to tremble and cry. "I don't want to talk about it." she said crossly. "I don't want to remember. I won't."

What was I going to do now? Obviously the events were extremely painful for Susan to remember. Her conscious mind was willing to give it a try, but her unconscious mind, even though it had agreed, would not cooperate. I decided to try another technique to make it easier for her. Sometimes the mere knowledge of an event troubles people; sometimes it is the reliving of the feelings associated with the event, the pain of the experience.

"Susan, you don't have to feel the pain of this memory at this time. Let's take a little journey, okay?"

I was giving her permission to dissociate the feelings from the cognition. I was also sowing the seeds for the next phase of therapy.

"Okay."

"See yourself getting up from that nice, grassy spot. You can go back there later and rest, if you want. Now go out to the road and follow it into the city."

I waited for her to nod.

"In the city, see yourself walking down the main street to a theater. All right, now inside the theater are a group of actors rehearsing a play."

Another nod.

"This is a special day, Susan. They are letting some of the public in to watch them rehearse. Go in, find a comfortable seat, and sit down."

"Oh, this is fun. I always wanted to be an actress and be in the theater. I am finding a seat and sitting down."

"The director is giving instructions to the cast," I went on. "He is saying that a young girl is lying in bed in her room. It is the middle of the night. It is dark. The door opens and someone walks slowly in."

"Yes, I can see it. There is a little blond girl lying in bed."

"How old does she look?"

"Five or six."

"Is there anyone else in the room?"

"Yes, there is another girl sleeping in the other bed. She looks about nine or ten."

"What happens next?" I prompted her, sensing that Susan was no longer reporting freely, that she was beginning to grow apprehensive.

"The man walks in. I can't see his face, it is in the shadows. He walks over to her bed. He strokes her forehead and hair very gently, then"—she paused briefly—"no, it's awful, he takes the covers off and pulls down her p.j.s. She looks very frightened. I don't want to look at this any more. I don't like this play. I want to go home."

"Okay, Susan, you don't have to look at that scene anymore. You can leave the theater, if you want. But then you will never know what happens in the story. Aren't you curious to take one last look before you leave? Take one last peek, Susie."

I deliberately used the name she had been called as a child, trying to trigger the childhood memories and at the same time cast myself in the role of the helping adult, so she would feel safe in releasing them. If used judiciously, a name like this can be a very powerful tool.

At that moment, Susan let out a scream. It surprised me. Before I could fully recover, she screamed again.

"It's Daddy! I'm in the bed! It's me!"

"What's Daddy doing?" I asked, realizing as I talked what was about to happen.

"He is pulling the covers off me. He is taking off my jommies and he is putting his head between my legs."

She spoke slowly and deliberately, with a tone of astonishment. It seemed to me that her voice had become more childlike.

"Tell me what is happening now," I coaxed, as gently as possible.

"Daddy is licking me in my privates. It feels so strange. He is making it all wet. He takes his finger and rubs me, then licks his finger and puts it in me. He is not supposed to do that, it's wrong. Don't do that, Daddy, it's wrong. Don't do that. Don't do that."

Her voice got quieter, as if something was muffling it. Susan began to sob.

"Tell me what is happening, Susie."

"Daddy is on top of me. I can't see. I feel crushed. Oh, it hurts, it hurts."

"Where does it hurt, Susie?"

"Down here, down here." She was now whimpering on the couch, tears streaming down her checks. Her legs were crossed and her hands were holding her vaginal area.

"What's happening now, Susie?"

"I hurt. I am all wet and sticky. There is blood on the bed. My older sister Carol is coming over and looking at me. She goes out of the room and is coming back with a washcloth and a basin, and she is cleaning me up. She puts me in her bed and tells me not to cry, everything is going to be all right. Then she comes into bed with me and holds me. But it hurts, it hurts. It really hurts."

I decided to let her feel the pain for a while, in an attempt to get it all out of her. The memories were encrusted in her unconscious and were probably the source of much of her trouble functioning in life. Now that they were being freed, I wanted to make sure that they all came out, that nothing was left. I was not sure that we would have such an opportunity again.

Then I told her that Carol was putting on some soothing ointment, hoping this hypnotic suggestion would gradually lessen the pain until it finally went away. I told her to go to sleep, to sleep deeply and let her body heal the hurt. Even though I would let her rest for just five minutes, I told her, it would seem like hours. After that she would wake up and take the memories with her, if she felt she could handle them.

When Susan came out of the trance, she looked dazed. She sat up, glanced around the room, then seemed to withdraw deep into her thoughts. After a few minutes she looked straight at me.

"My father raped me? I can't believe it. Why would he do such a thing? I was so young. Did I make it all up? It couldn't have happened. My father wouldn't rape me. He always protected me. I must have made it up."

I told her that I didn't know, but that it would certainly explain a lot about her childhood and what followed. Perhaps she would have additional memories that would prove or disprove her suspicions, I added, sowing seeds for future work.

She still appeared shaky, so I told her to rest in my waiting room for a while before she walked the ten blocks or so back to Odyssey House. I asked Susan to come again tomorrow, even though we had no appointment scheduled, so we could talk more about what had happened.

When she arrived the next day, Susan was enraged. "It really happened," she said. "I have been remembering lots of things. He would come in every few nights, from when I was about five until I was eight. I would talk to my sister Carol about it. She told me that he had done it to her, too, and that after a while it became her job to get me ready for him and to clean me up afterward. When I turned eight, he stopped and started doing it to my younger sister Ann, and I had to take over Carol's job.

"I didn't believe it at first, but I called Carol last night and asked her. At first she didn't want to talk about it, but I pushed her. She said that for years she hadn't remembered anything about it either. But when she recently entered Alcoholics Anonymous and began psychotherapy, the memories came flooding back. So she confirmed it. She said he did it to all of us. That bastard!"

Susan had a stunned, pained look on her face as the full realization of her father's betrayal of childhood trust hit her. It was beyond rape. It was soul murder.

After a long pause she looked me in the eyes and asked, "How could my father do that to me?"

During the next few sessions memories came back to Susan, as they had to her sister. Gradually, the missing years came into focus like a Polaroid snapshot. It seemed that Susan's father had abused all his daughters. Susan's mother probably knew all about it but did nothing, probably because of her own psychological problems. (Studies show that mothers in incestuous families usually know what is going on but either consciously or unconsciously deny it in order to keep the family together. In many cases, they, too, were sexually abused children who, with a seemingly mystical sense, chose a mate who would replay the scene.)

Now that her childhood memories had been restored, Susan wanted to kill her father. It was my job to try to help her work out her rage in a way that would not end with her in prison. Vengeance has its satisfaction, but Captain Ahab did die with the whale.

Susan's case reminded me of another patient, Lisa, a thin, attractive twenty-one-year-old. She had been raped by one of her mother's live-in lovers when she was five and then forced to have intercourse with him regularly for several years. When she got older, Lisa refused to give in to him and he left her alone. No doubt he preferred younger children.

It seemed that Lisa's mother, a southern belle type, fancied herself a great artist even though she never sold a painting. She would serve her daughters up to her lovers in exchange for financial support. One of them was later jailed for child abuse.

Lisa joined a tough crowd in high school but was still able to finish and get a job as a secretary. She experimented with drugs but did not become an addict. While Susan had childhood amnesia, Lisa could remember some of the details of the abuse, but not the feelings. It was an odd experience to listen to her. She would tell me about what had happened to her as if she were talking about another person. She had split off the feelings from the memory and thus could talk about the abuse without experiencing the pain.

I had firsthand knowledge of the phenomenon. Years before, when I had started analytic school, a close friend had suffered a psychotic breakdown and later killed herself. I used to go to the hospital to visit her, and although her condition greatly pained me I knew I had to put my feelings aside or my visits would be of little use to her. So on the long subway ride to the hospital I would distance myself from what I was about to experience. "Robert is now on the train going to visit Betty," I would tell myself in an internal dialogue. "Robert is now getting off the train to visit Betty." Thus I was able to depersonalize myself, enabling myself to visit Betty without feeling any sorrow. Only when I was back home, alone, did I allow the pain to take hold.

My therapeutic plan for Lisa was simple. I allowed some time for her to get to know and trust me, after which she consented to let me hypnotize her. In that state I told her that we live intellectually *and* emotionally, and that to protect herself she had split off the pain of the abuse from her remembrance of it. "I am asking you to go inside and bring back the feelings, so that they can join the memory and be complete."

She understood, and her body relaxed. Her face was turned

slightly away from me. I put her into a trance and asked her to find the emotions that accompanied those early, dreadful experiences.

When she came out of the trance, Lisa looked terrified. Her body was frozen except for her eyes, which darted rapidly back and forth. Her legs were crossed tightly, and she had put her hand between her thighs in an effort, she said, to ease the pain she felt in that spot. As the emotions took hold, her body started to tremble, then shake. I could see her alternate among terror, pain, sorrow, and rage but forced back my natural impulse to make it all better. This was a process she needed to go through. When it was over, she would be left with a full awareness that she had been victimized as a child. At least then she would know what she had to deal with.

There was a side effect, however. Like Susan, reliving the memory made Lisa almost uncontrollably angry. In both cases, working through the rage became the therapeutic problem.

Susan became a junkie, and Lisa almost did. Both had failed to get an education that would have prepared them for the world. Both had a poor self-image, which led them to associate with people who were abusive to them, repeating their childhood experiences. Both suffered from depression. Above all, both had been betrayed by the most important people in their lives—their fathers or father figures, who abused them, and their mothers, who failed to protect them.

This violation of parental trust can occur even in the absence of physical abuse, as I learned from another patient. Joan had given up dancing to obtain a Ph.D. in literature from Columbia University. Now, at thirty-five years of age, she was a veteran of two brief and disastrous marriages and had a personal life that was in shambles. For that, the entire male population of New York City was not spared from blame. But first and foremost Joan hated her father, who had taken her to Europe when she was sixteen years old and upon arriving in Paris had rented a single room for the two of them. During the night he had crawled into her bed and fondled her. She said she had not encouraged him, nor had she resisted him. During the rest of the trip, she had been her father's escort for business luncheons and social affairs.

Later that year, her father walked out on her mother and went to live with a woman with whom he had been having an affair for years. However, when he came to see Joan he would act more like he was on a date than on a visit with one of his children. He would take her to dinner and then sometimes to the theater.

Was it incest? Joan had full memory of the incidents, and hypnotic investigation turned up nothing other than fondling. Although it was not as traumatic as physical penetration, it was nonetheless a violation. Fathers are not supposed to use their daughters as sexual objects or surrogate wives.

Although these cases constituted neither a large nor a random sampling, they did begin to give me some ideas about why children who are abused react the way they do, and why some become multiples and some do not. Joan, for example, felt betrayed and victimized. She did not, however, dissociate the experience, perhaps because she did not suffer a physical trauma but most likely because the event occured after puberty.

It is generally acknowledged—at least among those of my colleagues who recognize that a person can have multiple personalities—that two factors are associated with the disorder: a natural capacity to dissociate and an exposure to severe trauma, especially during childhood. I suspect other factors are involved. After all, Toby, Lauren, Susan, and Lisa fit both categories, but only Toby and Lauren were multiples.

Toby and Lauren grew up in households they described as lonely and isolated. Although Toby shared a room with an elder sister, she did not have any recollection of being friendly with her, either as a child or as an adult. Her mother actively worked to keep her children separate from one another. I suppose she was operating on the divide-and-conquer theory; keeping her children from talking about the abuse with one another constituted another form of abuse, since talking about it might have helped them. It seemed much the same for Lauren, who told me that even though she had grown up with seven siblings she constantly felt lonely.

In contrast, Lisa and Susan—and no doubt some of my other abused but nonmultiple patients—had siblings with whom they were close. Indeed, both had sisters who took care of them after episodes of abuse. They had someone to talk to about what was happening, someone who could tell them they weren't crazy, someone who could soothe them.

Toby and Lauren had no one. Isolated from the rest of their families, they had to rely on their own resources—which, as children, were not great. What options did they have? Well, they could kill themselves, they could go crazy, or they could use their imaginations, creating other personalities to help them. For reasons still not known, they chose the latter.

8

LAUREN

When I was a young man under-going the rigors of eight years of analytic school, I used to amuse myself by daydreaming of how cushy life would be when I finally became an analyst. I had two models—Sigmund Freud, of course, and my first training ana-lyst, Hendrik Ruitenbeek.

Freud had a wonderfully rich life. He lived and worked in Vienna, which at the turn of the century was the artistic and intellectual capital of the world. Freud thought of himself as an archeologist of the mind. He would sit in the chair behind the couch in his overstuffed Victorian consultation room, his two pug dogs at his feet, his cigar in his mouth and his collection of ancient artifacts all around him, and listen to his patients. Every so often, like a coherent Delphic oracle, he would pull their verbal productions together with a brilliant analysis based on his knowledge not just of patients or pathology but also of history, music, art, archeology, and religion. Resistance would crumble, and the case would spring forward. His patients came on time and paid their bills. In the evening, the master would dine, spend a few hours with his family, and then retire to his study, where he would think and write until bed.

Dr. Ruitenbeek, a Dutch-born analyst trained at the best European universities and the London Psychoanalytic Insti-tute, was of the same old world mold. He even spoke with a

European accent, which automatically made him seem authoritative to a young student such as myself. He, too, lived graciously, in a ten-room apartment that took up half a floor in a beautifully maintained baroque building on Manhattan's lower Fifth Avenue. Every room I was permitted to see was filled floor to ceiling with books, including the thirty-six volumes Ruitenbeek had written. (Ruitenbeek published thirteen more volumes than Freud, but, unlike Freud's, many of Ruitenbeek's books were collections of articles.) I remember being impressed that he had the complete works of Freud in German as well as English. Hendrik didn't trust translators. (It turns out he was right. In retranslating Freud's letters from German to English, Jeffrey Masson found many errors.) While Freud collected antiquities, Ruitenbeek acquired French art and furniture, circa 1800. A butler opened the door and ushered patients into a waiting room. When it was time to see the doctor, they would be escorted into the consultation room, where Ruitenbeek, always impeccably dressed and groomed, would bow slightly and motion toward a sofa that looked very similar to one Freud owned.

Most analytic schools require their students to be in classical analysis while they are in school. There are three reasons for this: One, the only way to understand and practice psychoanalysis is to experience it; two, it ensures that new analysts are healthy and in touch with their countertransferences, which are feelings a therapist has that are based on his past, not the patient's; and three, it generates business for the senior members of the institute. There was one big problem with this system, however—the training analyst was also on the board that determined whether or not his patient, the neophyte analyst, would graduate. So a young, insecure, anxious analyst-to-be had a dilemma. Should he initially appear a little sick, then become sicker and finally gradually get better, all for the benefit of his training analyst? If so, how much pathology should he display?

As my training analyst, Ruitenbeek was a gentleman. Four

times a week for four years he and I waltzed through the corners of my mind as if to a melody by Strauss. Someday, I used to think, I too would be doing this type of work in my own ivory tower of psychoanalysis, far from the noise, the dirt, the poverty, the reality of New York.

However, my sessions with Ruitenbeek didn't prepare me for Toby, and they certainly didn't prepare me for Lauren. On the day of her first appointment, I answered my office bell and found three men—a Puerto Rican and two blacks, neatly dressed but wearing earrings and tattoos—standing at my door, escorting my blond-haired patient. She was too new to Odyssey House, her chaperones explained, to be trusted to travel the short distance between the center and my office alone. They were prepared to wait while Lauren and I met. I live where I work, and the hallway I use as a waiting room did not have enough seats, so I asked them to come back in an hour to retrieve their charge.

I wondered if my neighbors in my somewhat snooty apartment building would object to my new clientele as I ushered Lauren into my consultation room and offered her a seat. Before I could settle down, Lauren became Scarlett. No problem, I thought. Toby had taught me to handle sudden switches. But as I started to talk to Scarlett, she suddenly became Loverly. And as I started to question Loverly, Lauren returned.

The session continued on like this, with her constantly switching from one personality to another, sometimes in mid-sentence. It was like watching people dance under a flashing strobe light at a disco. I lost all track of the conversation, which I imagine was just what she wanted. It was an effective form of resistance that, looking back on it, I probably should have anticipated. This was the first time Lauren had been in a private psychotherapist's office. She was undoubtedly frightened, a state in which her considerable defenses would be mobilized to the hilt. Lauren had not sought out private therapy; it was

Odyssey House's idea. Nor had she chosen me; Odyssey House had. I was someone not yet to be trusted, and therefore she was not about to give me any information. I got the feeling Lauren would have been much happier seeing me once a month, instead of the twice a week we had scheduled.

The question was, what should I do about all this? Confront the resistance? Join it? Do nothing and hope it would go away? I decided to try gentle confrontation and watch her reaction. It was the most honest approach.

"I'm sorry, I can't follow you," I told her. "You're switching much too fast for me to follow and talking too low for me to hear you."

Immediately, Scarlett came out and remained in charge for the rest of the session. She may have started out by testing me, but I sensed that despite Lauren's attitude she—Scarlett, that is—wanted to work. Scarlett told me she was fed up with the way Lauren had conducted her life and accused her of being too wishy-washy and depressed. Scarlett also gave me some of her personal history, including the childhood horrors and traumas I was now becoming quite used to. I noted, however, that she again presented everything in a cold and clinical way, as if it had all happened to someone else.

After the session ended, I congratulated myself. This was going to be much easier than with Toby, I thought. After a little initial resistance, I would access the main personality, flesh out the history, and obtain a treatment contract—an agreement with my patient about the structure of the sessions, the fee (which in this case was nothing), and the goals we were trying to reach. I knew there would be additional resistance—there always is—but I was confident I could resolve whatever she threw at me. I was looking forward to our next session.

As it turned out, I had a longer wait than I expected. Lauren did not show up for her next appointment. After about half an hour waiting, I phoned her. She told me that she had forgotten all about it. I gave her my best "That's interesting," the one where I raise my voice slightly at the end to imply a question, trying to force her to think about the reason for her forgetfulness. Then I reminded her of the date of our next appointment.

After hanging up, I rethought what had so far transpired between us. My first attempt to resolve Lauren's resistance had temporarily worked, and I had obtained her cooperation and a little bit of her background. However, that had led to a stronger and more destructive resistance, as manifested by her failure to show up for her next appointment. I didn't quite know what to make of this. Again, I could confront it or do nothing, letting whatever was happening happen a little longer. That is one of the nice things about my profession— there are times you don't have to do anything. (And, of course, much of the time you don't have to say anything, either.)

When Lauren arrived for the third session, I remained silent, waiting to see what she would talk about. Avoiding the issue of the missed appointment, she went on and on about her life at Odyssey House. She had been put in charge of the kitchen and was feeling overwhelmed at the prospect of cooking for so many residents. How much pasta does one put in the pot for eighty-five people, anyway? After a while, I had heard enough.

"It strikes me as curious that you have not mentioned the fact that you forgot all about the last session. What do you make of that?"

At first she looked at me quizzically. Then she started to berate herself for being so stupid as to forget the appointment. People had always told her she was flaky, she said lamely. She apologized several times, reaching for a cigarette as she did so.

I told her that it wasn't stupidity that had caused her to miss the session. I suggested that I must have touched on something so threatening to her in our first meeting that she had sought to avoid further contact with me.

I glanced at Lauren and realized from the way she was holding the Marlboro between her thumb and forefinger that Jefferson was now sitting in front of me. Moreover, he seemed completely uninterested in the discussion Lauren and I had been having. He was more concerned with his own problems at Odyssey House. He had to help Lauren with the cooking and was upset because the food was starchy and the condiments limited. He also found many of the young men at the treatment center very attractive and was having a hard time obeying the rule that residents refrain from sex. He rambled on about how he was going to miss the annual drag queen ball that was coming up in his hometown, Newark, even though he had spent weeks making a wonderful outfit. I didn't allow myself to even consider how a gay male alter personality in a female body could gain admittance to a party for men who dress as women. I was confused enough as it was. I listened to Jefferson for a few more minutes and asked him if I could speak to Scarlett.

"What's going on?" I asked when she emerged. "You and I had a nice talk last week. You seemed to be feeling better when you left. Then all of you missed the next session, and when I tried to talk to Lauren about it she disappeared."

"You criticized her," Scarlett replied. "See how sensitive she is? I'm fed up with taking care of her. She was frightened and sent Jefferson out to deal with you, man to man."

Jefferson hadn't dealt with me—or perhaps couldn't—but I let that go for the time being. I wanted to stay focused on the main issue, her resistance. It seemed obvious to me that a strategy employing directness was not going to work in this case. Lauren, the host personality, was so sensitive that she interpreted any question about her behavior as an attack that made her defensive, and presto, she was gone, Sometimes I could get answers from Scarlett, but if a topic bothered her she, too, would switch to another personality. It was a conversation stopper, far more effective than trying to change the subject.

For the next few weeks, I pulled back and simply listened to Lauren, letting her proceed at her own pace and trying not to say anything that would make her feel guilty for being so resistant—because she would then get sidetracked beating herself up for being stupid rather than working through the resistance, which was the main issue. Resistance is tricky that way. Mainly, Lauren talked about her husband and how he mistreated her and their daughter. He was the kind of man who said he wanted to have a daughter so he could be the first man to have her sexually. Now he had moved to another state and was refusing to pay child support. When I asked why she had remained with such a man for so long, she told me that she had never been popular, that she was uncomfortable in most social situations and was convinced that no one else would want her. Besides, with a small child she didn't have any place to go or any way to earn a living.

She also talked about her childhood, which had been sad, lonely, and frightening. Her mother was always picking on her for one thing or another, and she would wait patiently for her father to come home because he would protect her. She remembered making up the alter personalities and naming them after characters she read about or saw on television. I was amazed at her casual attitude, since the names seemed so meaningful, but decided not to pursue the point at this time, since she would undoubtedly interpret it as an attack and switch personalities to avoid the blow. At the moment, I was more interested in building a relationship with her, gaining her trust and learning how she functioned.

Unlike Toby, Lauren had full consciousness of her internal personalities. She knew all of them very well, and she knew what they were doing at any given time. They would comfort her, keep her company, and help her when she found herself in a tight spot. Knowing she could not handle her assignment in the Odyssey House kitchen, for example, she had asked Jefferson if he would do it. If she found herself in a position where sex, which truly frightened her, was inevitable, she would call for one of her alters to come out.

I was gradually filling in the blanks in Lauren's life, although I was still far from understanding her multiplicity. She would not yet let me hypnotize her, though, because she was frightened of losing control. She needed more time to become familiar with me and the way I work. Still, we were making progress, albeit slowly. Her life outside the office was progressing positively as well. She was steadily working her way through the Odyssey House program. The feedback I was receiving from the staff there was good.

I wasn't surprised the morning Lauren appeared at my door about six months after we started our sessions without her escorts. She told me she had reached level three and was now allowed to travel alone. One more step to level four, at which point residents prepare to leave the Odyssey House cocoon.

I congratulated Lauren on her achievement. Then I noted that although the room was quite warm she had not bothered to remove her coat, which was an ankle-length, long-haired, dirty white, fake furry thing that made her look like an orphaned sheep. My analytic mind reasoned that keeping her coat on was one more form of resistance, another layer between the two of us. What had caused it? Things were going well, weren't they? Maybe too well. Perhaps Lauren felt she had gotten too close to me, had become scared, and was trying to pull back.

Lauren told me she had just obtained the coat in a "procurement," which is what Odyssey House calls it when clothes are donated by people or businesses. As a privilege, residents are allowed a quota of garments from the collection. Then Lauren got out of her chair, stood up, turned around to let me see the coat, then faced me and opened it, demonstrating that she was a natural blond.

I had heard about patients trying to seduce their analysts, and vice versa. It was a sensitive subject to me, since one of my professors in analytic school had lost a well-publicized case—along, of course, with his job. He had been accused of having sex with a patient.* It had been drummed into all our heads that the first commandment of the analytic profession was "Thou shalt not sleep with thy patients." (But if you happened to break it, we were told, the second commandment was "Do not abandon the patient.")

The classic explanation is that the patient forms an erotic transference to the analyst, who in the female patient's unconscious represents the father. But I had my doubts. In years of conducting therapy I had come across only two patients who admitted to sexual feelings for me based on the Oedipus complex, and only one who wanted to act it out. She was a young woman who in her first session told me that she could not pay for therapy and offered her body as barter. After a discussion failed to change her mind, I referred her elsewhere and never saw her again.

Of course, seduction can happen the other way around. There is a psychoanalytic joke repeated in Janet Malcolm's book, *Psychoanalysis, the Impossible Profession,* which goes: "A new woman patient comes to a male analyst's office, and he says, 'Take off your clothes and get on the couch.' The woman gets undressed and lies down on the couch, and the analyst gets on top of her. Then he says, 'You can get dressed now and sit in that chair.' She does so, and the analyst says, 'Okay. We've taken care of my problem. What's yours?' "

"Lauren or Scarlett or whoever you are at this moment, close your coat," I commanded.

She gave me a sly, sexy smile—was it Scarlett or Jefferson?

---

* The patient wrote a book about it, and the doctor later ran workshops on how to deal with extreme stress. The scandal rocked the institute and made sense out of an incident for which I had mistakenly blamed a patient. When I was a student, I had sent a very attractive female patient to him for medication, since he was the medical director of the institute. She told me that he had had her remove her clothes and gave her an injection in her bottom. But I never really believed her, since most medications come in pill form. I assumed that she had made it up to discredit him, me, or the process of therapy. He had such stature that it would have been unthinkable for me to phone him to ask if he had actually done it. I guess I was like Freud, who couldn't believe that so many of his patients had been abused by their parents. The patient eventually terminated therapy without having made much progress.

—and seductively drew her coat around her as slowly as possible, leaving her right breast exposed to the last possible moment.

"I think you should go back to Odyssey House and clothe yourself. I will see you Tuesday, assuming that you are dressed properly."

Giving her no chance to reply, I stood up, walked past her, opened the door, and ushered her out of the office.

When I had a chance to think about what had happened, I could only thank the gods of therapy. Lauren had tested me, but training had defeated lust. The men in her life had been nice to her in order to have sex with her. I was nice to her, ergo I must want to have sex with her. She wanted to see what kind of man I was, so she had devised her own Rorschach of flesh. I had passed this test, but I knew there would be others.

Lauren was properly attired when next we met. I brought up the events of the previous session, and she blamed everything on Scarlett, whom she claimed had overpowered her. I asked to speak to Scarlett, and, to my surprise, she not only accepted responsibility for the incident but also said she did not know why I had been so upset about it—or, for that matter, why I had rejected her. Scarlett said she liked me and wanted to show it, which translated into going to bed with me. Sex was the only thing she had to give. After all, she wasn't paying for the session.

Although she seemed sorry that she had upset me, she also told me she was hurt that I didn't want her. I told her I was flattered she found me attractive, but that I was her therapist and it was my job to analyze what she said. We were here to talk, not to act. She did not seem to understand.

"You don't like me?" she asked. "You don't find me attractive?"

"A father doesn't go to bed with his daughter because he

loves her," I said, looking her directly in her eyes and emphasizing the "because."

She took a few deep breaths and started to cry. I remained silent, giving her a chance to experience her sadness. Scarlett wasn't very emotional. She was cool, hard, and logical, the essence of pragmatism. This was the first time, to my knowledge, that she had allowed herself to express sadness. There was an interesting dynamic to Lauren. She had created different personalities as a way of handling the traumas, and all of the personalities seemed to split off feelings from their cognitive states as an extra level of protection. It was as though she were split both vertically and horizontally.

When she finished sobbing, I asked her what was going on. She said she was feeling sad not just about me but also about her father. She had always remembered the awful things he had done to her but had never allowed herself to have feelings about them. I watched her reach into her bag and pull out a pack of Kools—she evidently hoped a cigarette would help her settle down—and waited for the right moment to resume our discussion. "That bastard," she muttered. It was Peg. The cigarette was the clue. Peg smoked the Kools.

Scarlett had become sad and then angry when she thought about her incestuous father. She could tolerate the sadness, but the anger was too much. The system overloaded, and she switched to Peg, who was able to express pure rage without any feelings of love, loss, or sadness. Feelings are the key to this case, I suddenly realized.

Given my experience with Lauren thus far, I expected more resistance would follow such a difficult session—and I was right. For a couple of weeks after that, Loverly showed up at my office. She said Lauren and Scarlett didn't want to come. Our sessions would focus on such mundane matters as her punishment for skipping a few Odyssey House meetings and laughing when she was not supposed to. I used these hours to get to know Loverly better. I would access Lauren and Scarlett hypnotically every so often and point out to them that they were avoiding me because they were frightened of the realm of feelings. They didn't argue, but they also didn't make any effort to change the situation, so I let things ride. I know that changes occur only when a patient is ready, so I decided to trust the process.

At this point, my seemingly stalled case got an unexpected and fortuitous push. For reasons that I was not made aware of, officials at Odyssey House decided that Lauren was an unfit mother and tried to convince her to put her daughter up for adoption.

There was little chance of that. Like a lioness, Lauren swooped up the child and left the center, moving in with some friends on Avenue C in the East Village, a neighborhood in-fested with drugs and those who market them. Odyssey House contacted the Bureau of Child Welfare, which tracked Lauren down and threatened to take the girl away unless she returned to the facility.

It was a real mess. In the back of my mind, I half suspected that Lauren had somehow created the situation in order to justify her departure from Odyssey House—perhaps because she found therapy and the feelings it had summoned up too threatening. Then again, maybe the timing was a coincidence. I had no idea how good or bad a mother she actually was. Maybe someone in Odyssey House simply couldn't accept the idea of someone with multiple personality disorder trying to raise a child. Sometimes mental health workers like to play God.

Lauren set about building her new life as only a multiple can. Scarlett got a job working for an "escort" service. Peg handled her difficult clients. Jefferson, meanwhile, kept the Bureau of Child Welfare at bay, going to meetings, talking to them, promising them cooperation, and basically tying up their bureaucracy. He also purchased Scarlett's clothes, did her hair, and kept house. Loverly took care of the daughter. The others—Peg, Sadie, and Honey—seemed to be in hiding, or at least quiescent.

Lauren maintained sporadic contact with me throughout this period. She would attend a few sessions, then miss a few, complaining that she had no one to leave her daughter with or some other such excuse. She also complained about my fee: Under the arrangement I had made with Densen-Gerber, Lauren initially got therapy free, but I had been charging her $20 a session since she left Odyssey House. It is very difficult to confront or resolve a resistance based on finances, although if someone thinks therapy is valuable he or she can generally find a way to pay for it.

Lauren spent a large part of her couch time during this period trying to find out whether I approved of her new life. Even though she wasn't the prostitute, she had enough co-consciousness to know that Scarlett was. This made Lauren feel guilty. She had me in an interesting dilemma. If I suggested that it was degrading, she would no doubt complain that she was not trained for anything but housewifery or prostitution. She could not earn enough to support her family on the minimum wage. As a prostitute, on the other hand, she could make the most money for the least work—$400 in one night. It was an interesting moral issue. I have always been opposed to victimless crimes such as prostitution or gambling. Moreover, what was someone like Lauren to do in a city where a studio apartment in a decent neighborhood can cost $1,000 per month? It made sense, financially at least, that she market the only asset she had—her body. However, as her therapist I had to be careful. If I accepted and perhaps, in so doing, encouraged what she did, I became her pimp. My problem was how much to charge: If my fee was high, it would encourage prostitution; if it was too low, it would have no meaning.

Two months later the Bureau of Child Welfare caught up with Lauren and under court order placed her daughter in a foster home, allowing her to visit her once a week. Losing her daughter was a real blow to Lauren. Her life became more chaotic. She started using drugs again, mostly marijuana and cocaine. Scarlett continued her prostitution, arguing that even more money was needed now to hire lawyers to get the child back.

Things got worse. On her third visit, her child told Lauren that her foster father had fondled her.

Peg and Jefferson wanted to kill the man. Scarlett wanted to take the child and flee. But Lauren was too frightened to do anything, and her internal system was stalemated. She came into the next session blaming everyone from God on down for her misfortunes. I could hardly blame her. I tried to explore her options, one of which was to call in the Bureau of Child Welfare again and ask it to assign the child to another set of foster parents.

Lauren thought about it for a moment. "But how can I guarantee that it won't happen again?"

I answered that whenever I wanted to do a job right, I found that I had to do it myself. I thought I was giving her a message that if she didn't want these things to keep happening to her, she had to take charge of her life. Lauren, however, took it as a directive to take immediate action. She left my office, went to the foster home, talked the foster parents into letting her take the girl out for a few hours, and headed straight for Odyssey House, which she formally reentered. Upon hearing the child's allegations, the organization demanded a full investigation. Meanwhile, the child was to remain at Odyssey House to be with her mother.

Lauren began working harder in therapy. She attended sessions regularly. She allowed herself to be hypnotized and started to face her childhood memories. At Odyssey House, she quickly rose from border—those who leave the center and reenter it have to start back at square one, no matter how far they had progressed—back up to level three.

Society had put her in a bind. Not being a protective mother had subjected her daughter to abuse by her husband.

Failure to be a good mother at Odyssey House had caused her to lose custody of her child and likely led to more abuse. She had no choice. She had to pull her life together. Lauren at least had to try to change.

9

The Dark
Ones

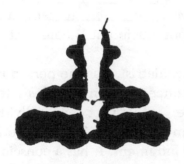

Buddhists believe that the only thing worse than not getting what you want is getting it. That was the position I found myself in with Toby. When I had set out to access her internal self-helper, and succeeded, what I found was not one helper but a trinity. They claimed they were not mere alter personalities but angels from the spiritual world.

It confused me. In fact, it confused me more than my first encounter with Toby's multiplicity. By now I was thoroughly used to dealing with multiple personalities within one person. The phenomenon even made sense to me. I could recognize how I sometimes operate as different people during the course of a day. At one point I am a son, at another a father, at another a therapist, at another a teacher, at another a writer.

Toby had an amnesiac barrier that made it impossible for her to remember what she did in her different states. This concept of forgetting was also familiar to me. I dream every night but do not always remember the content. Nor am I aware that I am dreaming while I am sleeping. I have also noticed that when I have to get up at an unusual time, say to catch an early plane, I wake up before the alarm goes off. How can I tell time while I sleep? Is some other part of me monitoring the clock, some other part I am not aware of?

In the same way that we all have a touch of multiplicity, we all have internal self-helpers. Like a conscience, they are a part of us that is usually more objective and rational, and when they take the other side in our internal debates they are usually the more logical. My self-helper is clear, logical, knows what is going on, and has access to my memories. It makes me wonder sometimes why I don't always listen to him (or it?).

At the turn of the century, Pierre Janet reported that he had found self-helpers within two multiples he was working with, Lucie and Leonie. Each of these self-helpers knew the patient's entire history. They were even able to remain in touch with reality when Janet put Lucie and Leonie into a trance.

Ralph Allison, a California psychiatrist, was the person responsible for popularizing the concept seven decades later. The internal self-helper, he wrote, "is that part of an individual's consciousness that is free from emotion. It is not neurotic. It is pure thought and uses good judgment. It has a conscious awareness of God and a strong sense of right and wrong. It does not necessarily respond to cultural demands."

Allison noted that the self-helper could be a resource for the therapist, since it knew so much about the patient's past. Indeed, the first self-helper he came across, in a case he wrote about in the *American Journal of Clinical Hypnosis* in 1974, emerged spontaneously during treatment and assumed, of all things, the role of therapist.

Densen-Gerber once told me about a similar experience in which she had received a phone call from a woman who had introduced herself as a psychiatrist and requested a consultation about one of Judi's patients. When the psychiatrist showed up for her appointment, it turned out to be the patient—or to be more exact, another personality of the patient. Although not formally trained, the personality was well versed in psychiatry and took on the role of cotherapist. Thanks to their periodic consultations, Densen-Gerber said, the case had a successful conclusion.

Self-helpers, however, have no power to effect change by

themselves. John Watkins, a professor of psychology at the University of Montana, notes that what the internal self-helper "has in knowledge, it may lack in power for whatever reason— or else the problem would have already been solved."

To approach self-helpers from another angle, think of the mind as an orchestra, with many parts—or personalities—that are different but nonetheless must work together in order to work properly. In this analogy, mental health would be harmony and mental illness dissonance. The self-helper is the conductor, whose job is to make sure the ensemble functions as a unit. The conductor knows each instrument's part, but he does not actually play an instrument. He is effective only if the individual musicians follow his lead.

I was looking for Toby's conductor in the hope it would unstick the case. I was not prepared, however, for a self-helper that was a trinity of angels. I am certainly no expert on the spiritual world and have avoided thinking about spirituality, the afterlife, the existence of God, and other such matters. Quite frankly, the subject confuses me. I prefer to operate under the theory that there has to be some scientific explanation for such phenomena, even though it might not be immediately apparent, and that any additional energy I spend thinking about them is a waste of time. However, at this stage of my career, Toby made me question what I had taken to be objective reality. I felt compelled to try to understand what I was dealing with.

The simplest way was to ask this trinity who or what they were, which I did. However, they—I will refer to them in the plural even though only one of them talked to me at a time, usually after extensive conversations with the other two—rebuffed all my attempts to question or analyze them.

"Where do you come from?" I asked.

"That is a concept that you would find hard to believe," they curtly replied, in that flat, emotionless, self-assured voice that told me they were in control.

"Try me."

"We come from beyond."

"Beyond?" I answered in my best analytic tone, with a slightly raised voice that requested more information, and that any normal person would feel compelled to answer.

"That is correct," they answered, not taking the bait and forcing me to keep asking for more information.

"I don't understand what you mean."

"That is what we told you. It is a concept that you would not understand."

"Who are you?" I continued, ignoring their attack designed to make me defensive. The duel continued.

"You would not understand that, either. Let us say that we have been sent to help her."

"Who sent you?"

"We were sent by the Archangel Michael. We suspect that you know who he is."

"You mean to tell me that you are some sort of angel or spirit that lives in the spirit world."

"That is correct."

"Are you assigned specifically to her, or do you float from one person to the next?"

" 'Float' is trite and shows a lack of understanding of the spiritual world. We are assigned to her, but we wish to caution you, we are not part of her, so do not think about integrating us."

I felt that they had read my mind. I had been talking about integration with Toby from time to time and was just thinking about what I would do about the Dark Ones when it came their time to merge. "I don't understand," I said.

"Haven't you ever heard of guardian angels? You have one also."

"I'm not aware of it."

"That is because your spiritual awareness is that of a flea."

"What happens when Toby dies?"

"We are assigned elsewhere."

Our conversation went on like this for a while. I was chided for my lack of spirituality. They argued that in dilemmas of this nature one has to make a leap into faith. They held Buber and Kirkegaard up as models for me. Hadn't I ever prayed to God for help? they wondered, implying that I knew of a God but that I thought of him as a Santa Claus. What did I think happened to the soul after the body dies? They treated me with patronizing disdain.

But if they were indeed from the spiritual world, I countered, why didn't they simply make Toby better? Even though I had read the literature, I couldn't get it through my head that, given their supposed spiritual origins, they did not have access to power. Why would they require a mere mortal like myself, with a flea's spiritual awareness? They answered that they had only the power of argument, and Toby's internal personalities were too frightened of them for direct communication. Thus my role became that of an intermediary. I was the one Toby had chosen, the one she had formed an attachment to, and even though I had my limitations, the Dark Ones were now stuck with me. It would be too traumatic for Toby to change therapists now, however much they would have preferred it. The Dark Ones told me they had been around since Toby was a child. They were there when she was being abused but had no way to stop it. In response to the abuse, however, they had created the machinery Toby had used to create other personalities to help absorb her pain. The problem, the Dark Ones said, was that the machinery had gotten out of control. Instead of learning to deal with stress, Toby had repeatedly created new personalities. What had been a useful adaptation device for a child had become a pathological tool for an adult. The Dark Ones were afraid she would continue to create new personalities rather than deal with new and difficult situations. This was why, they said, they needed my technical "expertise." I guess they considered me their psychological mechanic.

After about fifteen minutes, the Dark Ones abruptly stopped talking. Toby's eyes rolled up to the top of her head for a moment, then came back. "My colleagues are concerned," she said in the Dark Ones' voice, "because the questions you are asking are essentially those of a spiritual doubter. There is no way to explain to you, given the framework in which you think, what and who we are. Therefore, this conversation is serving you and not her. You will simply have to accept that what is, is, and that is that."

"There is another matter. These sessions"—the voice paused for a moment as if looking for a word—"cost her money, and we know that she does not have much of it. Therefore we are wasting time. We are quite unfamiliar with this body and cannot spend too much time in it."

This seemed so curious that I could not resist pressing them about what they meant.

"It is hard to explain," they said. "We are not used to being in a body. It exposes us to all sorts of sensations that we are not accustomed to."

"What's so wrong with that?" I asked.

"It is tempting, and that is not good."

"Why not?"

"There is sex. There is food. And better angels than us have fallen."

I decided to leave it at that, for the time being. I told them that we would proceed with the work and with a curt "good evening" they were gone.

I was spooked. In my line of work I have heard people say many incredible things. I have wandered through the world of incest, and pedophilia, where grown people have sex with children, and met people who wanted nothing more out of life than to be punished or abused. But this was something else again.

Could this Dark Ones business be some new form of resistance, or even an attempt by Toby to gain power over me? Any therapeutic relationship—including ours—is structured so that the patient feels he has no power, or so he thinks. As the analyst, I set the fee and the time and decide when to end a session. Patients do have the ultimate power of firing me, of course, but they usually feel so badly about themselves—and so respectful of the therapist—that they rarely do. Even when they do dismiss an analyst, they usually feel they are the ones who have failed.

Just because I did not believe in angels or ghosts did not mean there weren't any. When I was much younger, I would have vehemently disputed anyone who claimed I had an unconscious that controlled much of my behavior. I was convinced of my absolute free will. After I lay down on my analyst's couch, the machinery of my unconscious was demonstrated to me. I now have quite a different philosophy. If my unconscious is like a fourth dimension, was it really so farfetched that there may be a fifth dimension, a spiritual one? The eminent Swiss psychiatrist and onetime favorite of Freud, Carl Gustav Jung, believed in the conscious, the unconscious, and a collective unconscious, within which all things are connected. The great American psychologist William James also believed empirical science was limited and advocated the study of spiritualism. Even in our own materialist age, churches, synagogues, mosques, and temples are all well attended.

Once again I sought out Densen-Gerber for advice. As I told her about the grilling I had gotten from the Dark Ones, she nodded wearily. "I have the same problem," she said. Judi told me about a patient who had claimed to have a reincarnated fifteenth-century Welsh poet living in her body. This personality could even speak a strange tongue that a linguistic expert confirmed was a fifteenth-century Welsh dialect—although the patient had never been to Wales or studied any of its dialects, past or present. Judi had no explanation for it.

She also told me about another patient who had claimed to have a demon living in her body. After isolating it hypnotically and talking to it, she confessed that she was thinking about asking a minister to help her "bury" it in hallowed church ground.

The thought of a psychotherapeutic exorcism, however incredible it seemed to me, was already part of the psychiatrist Ralph Allison's modus operandi. He claimed to have once exorcised a spirit from a patient in two and a half minutes. In his view, some patients suffering from multiplicity could be possessed by evil spirits.

"In many of these cases, it was difficult to dismiss these unusual and bizarre occurrences as mere delusion," he wrote. "In the absence of any 'logical' explanation, I have come to believe in the possibility of spirit possession."

"I went to the Bible and began reading about possession," he wrote. "The New Testament discusses Christ's casting out of demons and I chose to follow this concept. It seemed fairly simple as I interpreted it."

"It is important to remember that religion and mental health are not as contradictory as they may seem," he wrote. "In earlier times, the church cared for the mentally ill. The fact that doctors have taken over this function doesn't mean that bringing religion to a treatment program is wrong. Essentially, I was bringing mental health full circle, combining the best of medicine and religion. Since my family has produced a long line of ministers"—Allison was also a descendant of the elder William Brewster, a minister who came over on the *Mayflower* —"it seemed quite natural for me to mix a religious act with my psychiatry since this seemed to be in the best interests of my patient."

My own view is that Allison might have been better suited for the family business than his chosen profession. Still, he is not an easy man to dismiss, even though he did come from California. Allison is a fellow of the American Psychiatric Association and past chairman of the psychiatry department of Dominican Santa Cruz Hospital in California. The field owes him a tremendous debt because he did a great deal to bring multiple personality disorder to the attention of his colleagues by convincing the American Psychiatric Association to hold a teaching seminar on the subject at its national meeting in 1979.

Allison was not even the most extreme proponent of spiritualism. Some believed multiple personality was the result of multiple possession, a theory that was tidy if not credible. "My view is that these cases are probably uncontrolled mediums who are multiply possessed," wrote another Californian, the psychologist Edith Fiore, in a recent book. "The 'personalities' are actually other people—spirits. The reason these patients are generally unresponsive to therapy—at least with lasting cures—is that the main cause, possession, is not treated. When it is, the 'personalities' disappear." Like Allison, Fiore cures people by exorcising the demons and claims great success.

This type of treatment is practiced widely in South America and the Caribbean, though usually not by psychologists or psychiatrists. But it may be making inroads, for in the fall of 1987 the American Society for Psychical Research held a conference in Manhattan on multiple personality and mediums—people who claim to use their body as a conduit for spirits.

Pierre Janet wrestled with the same subject more than eighty years ago. He was treating a thirty-three-year-old man who, in a state of agitation, would strike himself, curse, and sometimes speak in a strange voice. These states would afflict him intermittently for months at a time. The patient, who came from a highly religious family, believed he was the victim of "devilish possession."

However, Janet regarded such symptoms not as a result of things spiritual but as manifestations of hidden material erupting from the subconscious, without the conscious participation of the patient. This would become the theoretical basis for those of us who subscribe to the psychological view of man: that the mind can control the body, that ideas have power.

Using hypnosis, Janet learned that his patient had been unfaithful to his wife. He had tried to forget the incident by pushing it out of his mind, but could not. It was like a balloon—

squeeze one end, and it pops out at the other. In Janet's view, the man was suffering not from the grip of demons but from a guilt-provoked delusion that had its roots in his marital indiscretion. He was possessed all right, but not by the Devil—by an idea, an *"idée fixe."*

"Man, all too proud, figures that he is the master of his movements, his words, his ideas and himself," Janet wrote of the case. "It is perhaps of ourselves that we have the least command. There are crowds of things which operate within ourselves without our will."

Such ideas are like prehistoric monsters frozen in the ice of the unconscious. When the ice thaws, the monsters will emerge into the patient's consciousness.

Janet cured his patient by putting him in a trance and then suggesting that his wife would forgive him. This caused the symptoms to disappear. Although the delusion persisted in the man's dreams a while longer, Janet eventually was able to expel it completely. Like the Catholic priests who administer confession, he knew that the way to disarm a fixed idea is to get it out in the open. Once pathological secrets lose their secrecy, they cease to be pathological.

Jung was even more mystical than Janet. But after studying a young medium who was supposedly able to embody the spirit of her dead grandfather, he came to a similar conclusion. What appeared to be a mystical personality, he theorized, was actually the split-off contents of her unconscious. Or, as I understand it, the various nightmares, images, and thoughts were gathered together and expelled from her mind to form a demonic entity.

Like Janet and Jung, I was convinced that chasing after spirits would take me down a false trail. There are various aspects of our behavior that we all would like to feel are the result of possession—or at least some force outside of ourselves that we cannot control. Not being able to give up cigarettes, for example, or getting lost on the way to an appointment we don't want to keep. Blaming a demon is like suing a distillery for making one an alcoholic. Since Janet, the scientific community has generally concluded that any demons that may be lurking around are our own unconscious invention.

I once had a patient who would often hear a voice berating and cursing him in Yiddish. This voice would not leave him alone, and it drove him into my office—which I'm sure was not the voice's intention, since I ended up "exorcising" it. The patient had been born and raised in the United States, spoke perfect English, and understood but did not speak Yiddish. He was convinced that he was possessed by a *dybbuk,* a Jewish demon, which, he added, would yell at him but which he could not respond to, since he could not speak Yiddish. Upon investigation I found that it was not a demon but an internal psychological representation of his mother—in effect, a tape of her voice, words, ideas that had become part of his personality. Once he understood and accepted that concept, he knew how to handle it. He simply stopped listening. A person cannot play tennis alone. Another demon was demystified.

In Toby's particular case, the Dark Ones were right. My job was not to engage in metaphysical quests. Toby had hired me to help her resolve childhood traumas and unify her personality. If she were a Haitian peasant, a Californian canyon dweller, or some other mystically inclined sort, I might have called in someone to exorcise her. But she wasn't. It really didn't matter whether her three internal self-helpers insisted they were angels or Martians. They were simply the tools I would need to treat the case.

10

TOBY

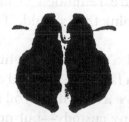

I was sitting in front of a fire, combating rather than joining winter by reading an advertisement on chartering a sailboat in the Virgin Islands, when the phone rang.

"Dr. Mayer, my name is Special Officer Hanson. I am in charge of security for a midtown department store. I have a woman here who has been arrested for shoplifting. She says she is your patient and that you can explain the situation to me."

I didn't have to ask him her name. Actually, I had been expecting something like this for a few weeks. With the Dark Ones' emergence, Toby had been doing much better. The double bind Densen-Gerber had inadvertently put Toby in when she had chided her for being too demanding of me—and me for being too ready to fulfill those demands—was working. Toby, furious with Densen-Gerber, who had become the bad mother figure, would do anything to prove her wrong—even if it meant getting better.

Over the past few months, she had stopped being so demanding and the midnight phone calls had ceased. She no longer spent our sessions complaining and no longer expected that I could simply supply a magic solution that would make her well. She was actually trying to understand how she had gotten the way she was and trying to figure out what she would have to do to change. She had stopped seeing me as a child sees

a parent—someone who can make everything better—and begun to view me as someone who could help *her* begin the job of
getting better.

Although this change in her was encouraging, I didn't fully
trust it. It has been my experience that people in therapy take
at least one step backward for every two steps forward. And
there was another reason to be apprehensive: Christmas was
approaching. Psychiatric practices, like many other enter-
prises, have busy and slow seasons. The holidays are usually
busy for therapists because people are reminded of all the
things they don't have but somehow think they should. 'Tis the
season for depression.

When I got to the store, I found a confused, frightened
patient. Officer Hanson was polite to a fault. He listened to my
explanation, seemed impressed to have a real, live Sybil in his
office and agreed to release Toby in my custody—but not before taking the time to give her a lecture. I have never understood why people think that if they tell someone sternly to stop
doing something that is obviously psychologically motivated,
the person will stop, just like that. It works about as well as
Prohibition did.

I had my cab drop Toby off at her home and reminded her
that we had an appointment the following morning. Then I
went home to wonder who had actually shoplifted and why.

The next morning Toby arrived at my office half an hour
early. She was anxious to straighten things out, although she
claimed she had no knowledge of what had happened. She had
gone uptown to do her Christmas shopping and remembered
walking around the store's main floor. The next thing she
knew, she was apprehended just outside the building by Officer Hanson. He reached into her purse and took out a ring—
costume jewelry, not very valuable—that she—or one of her
alter personalities—apparently had stolen. So we had a mystery.

I put Toby into a trance and asked to speak to Anna, who
told me that Becky, Beth's twin, was the guilty party. In fact,

she said, Becky had shoplifted many times before. She would come out while Toby was shopping, pick up objects seemingly at random, and put them in Toby's purse or pocket before going back inside. Upon further investigation of these shoplifting incidents, I could discern no pattern in the items stolen—they included a pen, a pin, a jewel box, a ring, a miniature doll—except that they were all small enough to fit into a pocket or purse. Fortunately for her, Becky had not been caught until now.

When I asked Anna why she hadn't told me about all this, she angrily replied that she was not her sister's keeper. Furthermore, she was starting to resent my reliance on her to explain what was going on whenever a problem cropped up. Even though she was the eldest, she told me somewhat testily, she did not want to take care of all the others. She wanted to stay inside, where it was safe, and do what she liked best, which was to think.

When I asked her what would happen if one of the alters were arrested and convicted, Anna replied that while Becky, Beth, Toby, or whoever would actually go to jail, she would just stay inside. It wasn't her problem, and it wasn't going to bother her.

I didn't agree with Anna. The shoplifting had to be attended to before more harm was done. But I needed her desperately. She was the only internal personality who acted like a rational adult—most of the time, anyway. (Thea, Anna's twin, was also an adult, but although I didn't know her very well she didn't seem to be as complete a person as Anna.) Toby, when she went inside, inhabited a separate spot in the internal world, so she wasn't useful to me, and Ka, her twin, was generally uncooperative. Moreover, since she had come from the "other" group, the members of the original group did not trust her enough to let her take care of them. The rest of Toby's alters were children.

I set out to win Anna over. First, I empathized with her. It was hard to be the eldest, I said. Then I made her feel special by acknowledging that I probably had been relying on her too much. I even used one of the most potent weapons that I had learned from that great psychologist, my mother—guilt. I told her that although I wasn't Christian I had always liked that religion because I thought Christians took responsibility for one another.

I could see from her expression that the strategy was working. Anna was quiet for a few moments. Finally, she said she would think it over.

I suggested that she go back inside. I would, for now, go directly to the source of the problem and ask Becky why she had stolen the jewelry. Of all Toby's personalities, Becky was the most difficult to talk with. For one thing, she was quite young—the same age as her twin, Beth. But a far bigger problem was that she was also very strange. If I had to diagnose her, I would say that she was schizophrenic—even though I am not sure how a person who definitely is not schizophrenic, like Toby, can have a personality who is.

I brought Becky out without much trouble.

"How are you today?"

"Are you going to kill me?" she asked, sliding away from me on the couch in terror. It was typical Becky.

"No, of course not. I'm here to help you. Would you like to hold Max?"

We had gone through this scenario a few times before. Sometimes holding Max calmed her. Sometimes it didn't, and she would scurry off, trying to hide in a corner of the room. I would "join" this behavior by helping her construct a barricade of chairs and pillows, attempting to make her feel safe enough so I could talk to her. Sometimes even this didn't help, and Morgan or one of the others would spontaneously appear as Becky fled inward. I could only speculate on how brutalized Becky must have been to have caused her to act like this.

I gave Becky the monkey, which she held with one hand while putting her other thumb in her mouth. I noticed for the first time that she was left-handed. Beth was right-handed. They were mirror-image twins.

"I heard you went shopping," I said, trying to edge into the matter at hand. There was no reply, just the slurp as she sucked her thumb and looked wildly around the room.

"Who's outside?" she said, momentarily startled by the noise of the radiator.

"Nobody. It's only the heat going up these old pipes. Should I open the door so we can take a look?"

That frightened her even more. She shook her head violently and cowered farther back on the couch.

"I have to have it," she said, almost wailing.

The abruptness of it startled me and threw me off course— but then again, Becky always did. I could never get used to the twists and turns of her responses. She always seemed to be coming at me from left field.

"What do you want?" We had had this discussion before, without any results. I knew what was coming.

"It," she said. "It." Then, louder: "I need it."

"Well, you certainly can have it," I said, trying to humor her, "but I have to know what it is so I can help you get it."

"It. It," she said, as if I were stupid and didn't understand what was completely obvious, at least to her. "I need it."

Changing the subject slightly, I asked her if she had found it when she was in the store the day before.

"I thought that was it, but it wasn't. I have to have it."

"If that wasn't it," I said, "why did you take it?"

"Because I have to have it."

She was getting more frantic. Obviously, this discussion was not helping. I still didn't understand what she was talking about. But whenever I tried to change the subject during one of these sessions with Becky, she would just ignore me and keep demanding "it."

I had no choice but to end the encounter. I told her I would try to help her find "it," but first I would have to know what "it" was. Becky lay back on the couch, closed her eyes and dropped Max as she went back inside. There was a body on my couch, but who was it? It seemed sort of like a garage without a car, or better yet, a car without an engine. I had once asked Toby what happened in these situations. She explained that she and her alters lived in a garden that had a gate. When one of them wanted to come out they simply went through it. One of my other patients, on the other hand, drew me a picture of a structure that looked like a light bulb. All the people lived in rooms inside of the bulb. There was a corridor leading to the spot where a normal bulb screws in. When one of them wanted to come out, he or she went down the corridor to that spot and then came out.

I wondered what to do next. Then I thought of the Dark Ones. According to Allison and others, self-helpers were made for situations such as this.

"Good morning," came the perfunctory reply as the Dark Ones sat up on the couch and gazed at me coolly through Toby's eyes.

"We have a problem," I said, trying to get straight to the point. "It appears that Toby was arrested for shoplifting, and Anna says that Becky did it. I talked to Becky about it, but all she said was that she was looking for something called 'it.' Do you know anything about this? Can you help me?"

"First of all, there are no problems, only situations. And it is you and Toby who have the situation, not us," they said.

"Have it your way. I meant Toby has a situation and I am trying to figure it out. Can you help us?"

"We will try. What would you like us to do?"

"Can you tell me what 'it' is?"

"Excuse us," they said. My patient's head—it wasn't really Toby anymore—tilted back slightly, the eyes rolled up toward her forehead, and she went into a trancelike state for a few minutes. She was already in a trance, of course, but there can be trances within trances. I have also found that when I hypnotize the host and then bring out an alter, the second personality must be hypnotized all over again if I am to gain access to its unconscious or its memory bank.

After what was probably only a minute, Toby's body slackened, her eyes met mine, and the Dark Ones spoke again.

"Years ago, when she was a child, she would go next door and visit with Dr. Carter. She was very fond of him, and grew very attached. She would sit on his lap while he would read her stories. Sometimes they would have tea together. At some point, Dr. Carter became sick and died. Before he got too ill to see her he tried to explain that he would be going away. He gave her a ring with a large clear stone mounted in it. It looked like a diamond but was probably only quartz or crystal. He told her that she should keep it to remind her of him.

"She went home and worried about where to put it. She was afraid to wear it because her mother would notice it, wonder where she got it, and possibly take it away or forbid her to visit with Dr. Carter again. Her mother didn't like him. Toby shared a room with her sister and had no privacy. Both her sister and mother were constantly going through her things. So she went up to the attic and hid the ring in an old jewelry box. After Dr. Carter died, she would periodically go and look at the ring, thinking about the fun she had had with Dr. Carter. Then one day it was gone. Nobody in the family seemed to know what had happened to it. And that is what she is looking for at the various stores, her ring."

"Do you or any of the others know where this ring is or what happened to it?" I asked.

"Excuse us for a moment." Again her eyes went up, there was a pause, then recontact. "No. We checked with all ten. There is no knowledge of what happened to it in any of their memories. Either the mother or sister must have taken it. Is there anything else you require from us today?"

"No. Thank you."

The body lay back on the couch. As I saw it relax I knew the Dark Ones were gone.

I asked to speak to Anna, who immediately came out, sat cross-legged on the couch and put her hands together in her familiar pose.

"I'm really angry at you," she said crossly, picking up exactly where we left off, what seemed like hours ago. "You put me in conflict. I don't want the responsibility of taking care of them, but I know that you are right and if I don't do it then nobody will. Besides, if I don't, I won't be a good Christian. Why did I have to be born first? It's just not fair."

"I think we're making progress with your problem," I said. "But I'm concerned about Becky's shoplifting. I want it to stop. Do you have any suggestions?"

"I could bump her inside, out of the way, but that would mean I would always have to be on the alert and watching her. I don't know if I want that responsibility. Look, I didn't shoplift, so why do I have to be the responsible one? I didn't do anything."

"I understand that," I said, trying to commiserate. "Can't anyone help you?"

"I can't trust the young ones. Julia is too timid, she hates to look outside. And I don't know her twin, Laura, that well. That leaves Morgan and Megan, and they're a little irresponsible. They just want to have fun."

"I know it's hard to be the oldest and in the position of responsibility. But that also gives you the power."

"Well, I guess it's our problem and not yours," she said after a moment. "I'll have to take care of it."

The session was about over. I asked Anna if she would go in and summon Toby, in line with my rule that whoever walks into my office also walks out. She reclined, said good-bye and closed her eyes. In a second Toby was back in charge of the body, albeit in a trance. I let her relax for a few moments and then woke her. As usual when the Dark Ones had been present, she had a taste in her mouth that reminded her of copper pennies. (I once investigated this with the Dark Ones, who said it was a chemical reaction to having a foreign substance enter and leave the body.)

"Feels like someone was walking through my brain—or maybe ruffling through it with fingers. What happened?"

I explained that the Dark Ones were able to access information from her memory and that we were trying to solve the mystery of her shoplifting.

"That's it," she exclaimed, shaking her head slowly in disbelief. "It feels like there are files in my head and someone has gone through them. It makes me feel creepy."

She got up and walked out, slowly shaking her head.

For my part, I felt quite pleased. Aside from the minor victory of getting Toby (through Anna) to take some responsibility for her safety—a start on the problem of multiplicity, which is partially a disorder of responsibility—I had used my new tool, the self-helpers, and they had worked wonderfully. Through them, I had immediate access to Toby's memories, something which could save years of couch time, since I did not have to separately hypnotize each personality.

I even had an idea how to deal with the shoplifting. But that would have to wait, because I had some catching up to do with the others. I hadn't talked to them for a while, and the natives were getting restless. So I went through a couple of weeks reading stories to Beth, discussing plants with Julia, helping Morgan plan what ball games to watch on television, and commiserating with Anna because of the burden she bore by being the eldest. I was also getting to know the other twins, Laura, Thea, Ka, and Megan. They were timid and not as comfortable with me as the original personalities. Indeed, they would have been happy to skip their hour on my couch, which was the reason why I would not let them.

When Becky's turn finally came around again, I put my antishoplifting plan into effect. After putting Toby into a trance, Becky came out and, as I had come to expect, immediately asked me if I had found "it" yet.

"Not yet, Becky. But I think I have a way that we can both look for it and possibly find it."

"How can we do that? I have been looking for it and I can't find it. I have to have it."

"Let's try something which might work. It's magic, so you have to close your eyes. Make believe that you are watching a television show with a bunny rabbit on it, okay?"

She nodded yes, put her thumb in her mouth, closed her eyes and started to smile.

"Now, watch the bunny. He is jumping around. He finds a carrot and he sits down and eats it. It's a good carrot. Now he's finished and he is so, so tired. Watch him rub his belly and yawn. Watch him lie down, get comfortable, and go to sleep. Now move next to the bunny, cuddle up with him, and go to sleep." Which she did. Children are easy to hypnotize. It's only after they get to be jaded adults that it becomes difficult.

"You're safe in your bed, Becky. There's nobody but you and Sally"—a cousin she trusted—"at home. Now, get out of the bed and go upstairs to the attic. Find the nice jewelry box that you have hidden and take it out. Open it up and see the pretty ring that Dr. Carter gave you. Take it out, look at it. That's right."

I saw her smile, a sign that she was following the instructions.

"Hold the ring in your hand, Becky. Feel it with your fingers. Put it on your finger. Hold your hand out and look at it again. Look at it carefully. Make sure it's the right one. Nod your head when you're sure."

She nodded.

"Now, take the ring and put it in your left pocket."

She put her hand in the pocket of her jeans.

"Now, whenever you need to, you can close your eyes for a moment, take a deep breath, put your hand in your pocket, clench your fist around your thumb and you will feel the ring in the palm of your hand. You will know that the ring will be with you, always. You will have the memories of the ring and the feeling that it is with you, always."

I let her stay in the trance for a few minutes, so she could have the experience of possessing this "genuine imitation" object that was so important to her. It represented the unresolved grief over the death of a man who was one of the few loving people in her childhood. It probably also represented the unresolved grief over her entire traumatic childhood. How does someone come to terms with the fact that people who are supposed to love and care for you, don't? The real ring was gone, stolen perhaps, but the hypnotic ring would now take its place, though I knew it would not be enough. All the personalities would have to learn to mourn Dr. Carter in order to resolve a loss of such magnitude. One of the reasons people become multiples—or dissociate, for that matter—is a reluctance to experience unpleasant feelings. I had to make them take this medicine, however bad it tasted. I had to convince them it would be good for them. Perhaps more important, I felt, his death had been a screen that covered up an even deeper loss, the abandonment by their mother. I was supposed to be the replacement for Dr. Carter and this mythical mother. But Toby and the others had to learn that they could not solve their problems by finding someone to love and nurture them. Prince Charming was not going to come.

When Toby came out of the trance, she appeared calmer than usual. I discussed what had happened earlier with Becky. She listened to me and seemed to understand, but I noticed that she didn't seem to be feeling anything. There should have been some sadness triggered by thoughts of Dr. Carter, the tea parties, and most of all the ring. Toby had memories, but no feeling. The pain they had all felt when Dr. Carter died had been passed from the original personalities to their twins, which was why they had been created. It was now time for all those first personalities to experience the grief, especially Toby. The pain had to go out the way it had come in.

"I have some homework for you," I told Toby. "You obviously are upset over Dr. Carter's death but have never mourned him. Did you go to his funeral?"

"No. We tried to visit his house one morning just after he died, but his wife came to the door and angrily told us to go home. She said Dr. Carter had gone away. We were hurt."

"Did you cry?"

"We never cry. To cry would be to let her"—that was the way Toby always referred to her mother, just as "her"—"know she was winning. She would hit us, and we would look her straight in the eye and that would get her madder. But we wouldn't cry."

"Don't you think that if you lose somebody you love and feel close to that you should feel some grief and go through a mourning process? If we don't get the emotions out of us, they bottle up and clog our systems. That is what tears are for, to flush out the system, like rain cleans the air. Did you ever notice how clean the city smells after a storm?

"Look at the Jewish religion, which you were brought up in. When a loved one dies, there is a public funeral and burial, during which it is acceptable for mourners to cry and wail. Then there is a seven-day period of heavy mourning, where friends and relatives come to the house to help grieve. Then there are thirty days for less intense mourning, during which you go to work but do not take part in other pleasurable activities. Then there are nine months of light mourning, after which the tombstone is set and the matter put to rest. During this time one goes to temple daily and recites the Kaddish, the prayer for the dead. So you are made aware of your grief every day for ten months. Now, Dr. Carter was the most important person in your life, but you never even mourned him."

I could see what I was saying made some sense to her. But quickly her resistance flared. I did not really expect her to easily forego the dissociative mechanisms that were designed to protect her from the very feelings I was now trying to make her face.

"I have no one to help me mourn. And besides, what about Anna? She's Catholic."

"Go to a temple," I replied, joining the resistance. "During every service they say a prayer for the dead and the mourners get up. You can get up with them and feel like you're a member of a community and other people are sharing your grief. And every so often, on a schedule you and Anna agree on, go to a church and light a candle for Dr. Carter."

I waited for her reaction. I had put her in a bind. She had to let herself feel the grief over Dr. Carter's death rather than delegating it to her alter personalities. To do that, she had to start breaking down the dissociative barriers she had carefully erected years ago. If she refused, she knew by virtue of the years she had already invested in therapy that she would lose credibility with me. I would think she was the kind of person who wanted someone else—namely me—to solve her problems. She was becoming too proud for that.

As she sat there thinking about all this, a few tears rolled down her cheek, and I suspected she felt some sadness.

As Erickson might have said, the cow had started to go into the barn.

11

The Twins

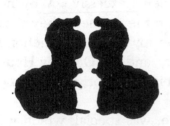

"Dr. Mayer, my name is Jennifer," a clipped, Australian-sounding voice said over the telephone one frigid December morning. "I am an aide to Dr. Densen-Gerber. She instructed me to invite you to a probe a week from today."

I was getting to like these calls. They always promised a welcome change from my normal routine. Tunnel vision is an occupational hazard for psychotherapists, who typically work too long with the same patients, sometimes at the expense of meeting enough others. You can begin to believe the narrow segment of the population you work with is representative of something more than a narrow segment of the population. Even the great therapists aren't immune. After the Nazis captured Austria, Freud, a Jew, was so enmeshed in his writings and his patients' inner worlds that he had no concept that he was in danger from the outer world. Friends had to take him out of the country to England.

During my work as a consultant for Odyssey House, I had heard about probes, which I understood to be a sort of psychiatric rite of passage, but I had never attended one. Every new Odyssey House resident spends two or three days with a more experienced resident, who teaches him or her the ropes. After about a month in "pretreatment" doing what people in pretreatment do—cleaning all day and taking great pains to be nice to everyone they meet while they get oriented to the program and used to their surroundings—they are put into groups to begin therapy. At some point along this path they can request a sponsor, someone who recommends to the higher-ups that they are ready to formally enter the community. It is then time for the probe, during which the candidate appears before a panel chosen from all levels of the facility, including at least one staff person, which will determine whether or not he or she will be accepted into Odyssey House. To the uninitiated, this probably seems excessive. Why not begin treating all new residents from the moment they show up? Because it's not that simple. Therapy for drug addiction is at best a difficult and lengthy process, and the Odyssey House counselors have to be sure a resident is truly motivated and not just there to get in out of the cold.

This probe, Jennifer assured me, was special, which was why my presence was being requested. It seemed that in the course of the normal psychiatric workup given to new residents, an Odyssey House psychiatrist, Paul Hansch, had uncovered two new cases of multiple personality—in identical female twins. Not in any of the professional literature that I have read—before or since—have I heard of such a case.

The probe was to be held at a division of Odyssey House specializing in treating addicted mothers and their children. Located on Ward's Island, a patch of land in the East River, the Mabon, as the facility had long been called (although no one knew quite why) was a tribute to Densen-Gerber. Before the Mabon, there was no place in New York or anywhere else that I know of where an addicted mother could go for treatment with her children.

As I drove north along the Franklin D. Roosevelt Drive and approached the Triboro Bridge, I thought about the people I was about to meet. Identical twins, each with a number of separate internal personalities. Would each have the same number of personalities? Would these alters be twins of the other, twins of twins? If so, would they be identical or fraternal? Imagine it. Mirror-image multiples. The possibility was mind boggling.

One out of every 150 births results in identical or monozygotic twins, the product of a single fertilized egg that splits in two after fertilization. Fraternal or dizygotic twins, the result of the separate fertilization of two eggs, occur more often, about one out of every 100 births, producing siblings that are genetically different.

Twins have always interested me. It is more than the inherent cuteness of two little Munchkins dressed alike. By their very existence, twins deflate the myth of human uniqueness. Imagine what it must be like to be a twin and have the opportunity to see how you look and act in various situations.

Medical journals have recounted some remarkable sets of twins. Take Chang and Eng, who were born in Siam in 1811, joined by a thick band of tissue at the breast. (P. T. Barnum made them and their birthplace famous.) Chang died first, and poor Eng had to endure another hour of life tethered to the corpse before he followed suit—some say from sheer fright.

The Chaplin sisters, Freda and Greta, were two identical but separate twins who lived in Yorkshire, England, and seemed to have the same mind. They dressed alike, walked in step, and could complete each other's sentences. If they were given two pairs of different-colored gloves, both would take one glove of each color, so they would remain exactly alike in all respects. They even knitted from the same ball of yarn and arranged flowers together. But the Chaplin sisters went too far when they fell in love with the same man, who happened to be married. They pestered him intolerably for fifteen years, to the point of throwing themselves in front of his car. Finally, in 1980, he filed a lawsuit to be relieved of their attention.

Then there is the case of June and Jennifer Gibbons. Born of Barbadian parents and living in west Wales, Great Britain, they stopped talking to the rest of the world at an early age and developed a secret language enabling them to communicate only with each other.

A dozen years or so ago the New York City tabloids were filled with stories about the Marcus brothers, who chose the same branch of the same profession, gynecology, and even served as cochairmen of their hospital department. Their emaciated bodies were found lying amid an accumulation of garbage in a trashed apartment on Manhattan's Upper East Side. They had died of drug-related causes within a few days of each other.

Strange as some of these siblings are, there is an even more mysterious phenomenon—the vanished twin. In one European study, 71 percent of nearly seven thousand expectant mothers given ultrasound examinations prior to the tenth week of pregnancy started with two fetuses but gave birth to a single child. What happened to the other twin? It is possible that many of the fetuses were imperfect and either absorbed by the placenta or aborted, the two ways in which the body deals with such problems. However, doctors have reported finding fetal hair and bones within tumors removed from their patients, perhaps indicating that some of a vanishing twin may have "survived." The most startling example of this is a fetus *in fetu*—a fetus that is found enclosed in the body of a normal person, who was apparently a sibling. In Portland, Oregon, in the late 1940s, for example, a half-developed fetus was removed from the abdomen of a thirteen-month-old girl.

Could a fetus "absorbed" by its mother or a sibling actually be a nascent alter personality? Is this the reason some people become multiples? Patricia McDonnell, a British housewife, seemed to think so. Doctors found two kinds of blood flowing through her veins, type A and type O. After three years of tests, she related, the doctors told her that "my mother should have had twins, but that I absorbed the embryo of my twin into my body, where it has been producing its own blood." The physicians told her the type A fluid, which accounted for 7 percent of the blood in her body, was hers, while all the rest belonged to her twin—a male, according to the chromosomes in the white cells. So Mrs. McDonnell was her brother's keeper. Indeed, in her case, the dead may have lived on psychologically. "I have two personalities," she once said. "Sometimes I am a cheerful extrovert. The next day I will be an introvert. I have no control over it. It just happens."

I was nearing the tollbooth on the Triboro Bridge by now, and from experience I knew I had to concentrate on my driving, especially since it had begun to rain and visibility was declining fast. The bridge connects Manhattan with the Bronx and Queens, and the turnoff to Ward's Island and the Mabon is hard to find. Miss it, and I would be in big trouble, lost in an unfamiliar world of one-way streets in what Manhattanites call the "outer boroughs."

Fortunately, I found my turn and headed down the ramp onto Ward's Island. It was like going back fifty years. There was very little traffic, and the road took me past bleak gray institutional buildings that looked as if they could be prisons.

A little way down the road was a three-story, red brick building that I took to be the Mabon. I parked my car, walked through the front door, and immediately knew why residents often called the place "Mad Barn." The din was overwhelming. Adults and children crowded the corridors, walking, talking, smoking, and playing. An aide led me up a flight of stairs and down a long hall to the room where the probe was to be held. There were a couple of couches, a few easy chairs, and about thirty folding chairs fanning out into a rough circle around two three-legged stools. I was glad I didn't have to sit on one of them.

I was a little late, and most of the seats were already taken. A comfortable-looking club chair was vacant, but I guessed it was reserved for Dr. Densen-Gerber. I took one of the folding chairs next to Arlene Levine, the clinical supervisor of Odyssey House, whom I had met a few times before, and struck up a conversation. Arlene was surprised by the size of the crowd. A normal probe has only five or six participants, she said. Usually there were representatives from all four levels of the Odyssey House program as well as a staff member or two from that particular branch. But gathered at Mabon that day were visitors Arlene recognized from Odyssey units around the country, along with a few people she had never seen before, including the man on my right. I turned to introduce myself and learned he was an Israeli who was neither a psychoanalyst nor in the drug treatment field. In heavily accented English he said he felt like a fly on the wall. He was a bureaucrat and was in New York to negotiate the establishment of an Odyssey House in Israel, but he knew nothing about drug treatment and didn't quite know why he was here, other than that Densen-Gerber had invited him and he had accepted.

After a few more minutes, which I spent making small talk with Arlene, who, it turned out, was also an identical twin, Densen-Gerber and an entourage of about a half dozen came into the room. She walked quickly to the easy chair I had correctly guessed was saved for her and apologized for being late. Without pausing, she went around the room asking everyone to introduce themselves. When she got to Dr. Hansch, the last person to speak, she congratulated him for his brilliant diagnosis of the double-edged case we had been summoned to learn about.

The twin girls had been born to a middle-class Connecticut family. Twin births can cause problems. They are often a surprise, especially in the era before sonograms; they can cause a financial burden; and, of course, they are a handful to take care of. In this case, their parents already had two boys. An Odyssey House staff member who had gone to the house to interview the mother reported that she was high-strung and held a grudge because her dream of being a ballet dancer had been ended by an early pregnancy. She obviously did not want her children, and probably not even her husband. The twins' primary childhood memories were of screaming, yelling, and hitting. They were forced to keep the house obsessively clean.

Meals were a major horror, with severe punishments for leaving food on their plates or for spilling their milk.

If the mother was described as a witch and a terror, the father was lovingly viewed as a friend and protector. The twins remembered him reading them stories when they were sick and taking them on outings on Saturdays. And it was the father, concerned about their drug use, who had brought them into Odyssey House in the first place.

But, we were to learn later, this good, loving father had sexually abused them—something they had obviously blocked off. He had molested them separately, telling each twin that he was only doing it because she was his favorite. He also gave each instructions not to tell anyone, thus preserving their "special relationship." They didn't, either. Perhaps to lessen his guilt, but more likely to keep them friendly so they would continue to be available to abuse, the father was extremely loving and kind to both of them. Thus he was their sodomizer and their only nurturer. His inconsistent personality, loving one minute and horrendously hateful the next, made him appear to be two different people. If not a multiple himself, he possibly provided the model for his daughters' multiplicity.

To the best of their hypnotic memory, one twin was sodomized by the father at age two and a half, after which she formed the first of her alter personalities. The other twin watched her sister switch from one personality to the another and followed her lead, forming an identical alter personality, which she could use when she, too, was abused. That was the theory, anyway.

The trauma continued, and more personalities were born, first in one sister and then in the other. For example, one twin formed an alter when she was left alone in the house locked in a closet—something her mother often did to save the expense of a babysitter—and the house caught on fire. A neighbor heard her screams and rescued her. This personality was a male, and became the one that would fight her battles. The other sister also formed a warriorlike personality, but after a different episode in which she was thrown into a lake by her father, who wanted to force her to learn to swim.

So these twins had parallel sets of personalities who could converse, befriend, and console each other. It was like two people learning to dance but constantly changing partners. If one switched, the other could switch and match her. Twins normally bond together in a symbiotic knot. How much closer can you get than to have shared the same womb at the same time? Well, in this case we had twins within twins.

There is a downside to all this, of course. As confusing as it is being an ordinary multiple, it is even worse to be part of a set of multiple twins. The drugs they took probably helped keep their alters out of awareness when the dissociative barriers surrounding and protecting the host weakened. These barriers help us all keep from being overloaded. They are why we often do not remember our dreams, even though scientists say we have them every night.

"Let's bring in the patients," Densen-Gerber said.

An aide returned with the twins. They appeared to be about twenty-five years old, with long blond hair. One of them —Mary, I learned later—had crinkled hers slightly with a curling iron. Despite a few extra pounds and shabby jeans and sneakers, they had a seductive sort of look. They glanced around at the crowd but seemed only slightly frightened. Good composure, I thought to myself. Then they looked at one another and sat down on the stools, two fish in a fishbowl.

"Well," Densen-Gerber started, "you know why you are here and what this is about. This is your probe, a most important moment in your odyssey. This is where we decide whether you become a member of our community. I urge you to be honest, to answer the questions as best as you can. You can start by telling us why you want us to treat you."

Marcia glanced at Mary and in an instant they silently agreed that she—Marcia—should be their spokeswoman. "We were born and raised in Connecticut," she started out matter-of-factly. "We went through the public school system there.

Our home life wasn't good—we didn't get along at all with our mother—so after high school we left and moved to New York, where we shared a place. But we found it hard to earn enough money here. We both drank, and I guess gradually we started using dope. Pretty soon we were shooting it. By that time we were also engaging in . . . well, you know, we were prostitutes. And we also danced nude, and did a few movies . . . adult movies. We have both been on dope—heroin—for about five years, and we wanted to get off it. So we came here. And that's about it."

They both looked around furtively to see if the crowd was buying it.

"You're full of shit," a young man on the far side of the room spat out.

The twins, stunned probably not so much by his conclusion as the forcefulness with which it was expressed, spun to face their accuser.

"You don't want to be here," he continued. "Your father dragged both of you in. You're only here because there's no other place for you to go. It's cold outside. As soon as it gets warm, you'll split and we will have wasted months of time and energy on you."

"Okay. You're right about our father bringing us in," Marcia pleaded. "But the other stuff isn't true. We're working hard here. We're trying to get through the program. We don't want to go back to using. There are no old addicts."

"I don't believe you," said another resident, taking up the attack. "You took two months to get a sponsor. It shouldn't have taken you that long. People usually get one right away. And why did it take so long for this probe to happen? You didn't seem the slightest bit interested in it."

"All right, we weren't sure we wanted to stay here. We thought we would hang out for a while and see what we thought and leave if we didn't like it."

I could see why they called it a probe. The questions were confrontational, designed to throw the twins off guard and see how honest and motivated they were. As the grilling went on, it got more and more heated. Mary tried to help Marcia face the inquisition, but their answers clearly were not good enough. They were exposed, in the center of it all, with no place to go and no place to hide. One of them would fend off one questioner, only to have another pop up. I noticed there seemed to be a competition among the interrogators to see who could ask the most pointed question. They were scoring points with their peers and no doubt impressing Densen-Gerber with their insight. It reminded me somewhat of my Ph.D. orals at Rutgers University, where I had been the pawn between two professors who had been feuding over an academic point for years. One would ask me a question, and after I replied the other would attack it. Then I would answer him and the first professor would open fire. After a while I called them on it—and walked out with an apology along with my degree. I didn't think Mary and Marcia were going to come out as well.

I saw that when one twin would answer a question the other would remain completely silent, never indicating any disagreement. They also would turn to face opposite sides of the room, in effect guarding each other's flank. They were obviously communicating with each other through some non-verbal means indistinguishable to the rest of us—a glance, a finger motion, a raised eyebrow, a grimace. It was as if they could read each other's thoughts.

It didn't take extensive psychological training to know they were hiding something. After a while Densen-Gerber must have had enough, because she abruptly sent Mary out of the room.

"Look, Marcia, you two are obviously going to fail this probe if you keep going on like this. We'll have no choice but to put both of you out on the street." Then Judi's voice, which had been harsh, became velvet. "Come on, Cookie, we're here to help you. You know that. But you're hiding something." She turned on her famous charm, leaning forward and looking Marcia in the eye. "What's the secret? Is it so bad?"

Others joined in, putting gentle pressure on her. "Come on. You can tell us."

With that, Marcia started to cry. "Please, we can't go back on the streets. He'll kill us, he really will."

"Who'll kill you?" Arlene Levine asked. "Who are you protecting?"

"Nothing," she said, stiffening and returning to the defensive. But it was too late. Now that they had an opening, the others started firing queries. Marcia would start to answer one person, only to have another interrupt. It didn't take long for the staccato bursts to throw her off balance.

"Mary does not want you to know about her rape," Marcia said, trembling. "She asked me not to tell anyone, ever."

"That's ridiculous," Levine said. "We're here to help you. But how can we if you aren't honest? Do you want to protect your sister at the expense of your own treatment?"

Marcia thought for a few moments. "We can't leave. There's nowhere to go. If we leave here, he'll get us. He'll find us and get us."

"Who will?" somebody else asked.

"Martin."

"Who?"

There was frustration and fear in Marcia's voice. "Martin is the man that set us up. We used to run this 'S and M' business on Twenty-third Street. He rented a brownstone for us and paid for us to redo it. We hired other people—it was a big business."

She paused for a second, thinking about whether she wanted to continue.

"We built this dungeon, with rings in the walls, racks—the whole thing. We would advertise in *Screw* magazine—'English discipline by single or twin mistresses,' we called it. It was a great gimmick. Where can you get twins dressed in black leather who will spank you, whip you, or whatever?"

Well, I thought, there's probably a market for anything in Manhattan.

"Business was good, and, you know, we loved it. We would get these men, ask them what they wanted, whip them, hit them, and despunk them. It was wonderful. We didn't feel guilty, we were simply giving the client what he wanted. Look, they thanked us, they paid us—some wanted to marry us. And these were nice people, executives and lawyers and all that. We felt like we were doing good work, sort of like a shrink. And you would not believe how much money we were making."

The room had gotten quiet. I heard someone mutter, "Like a shrink?"

"Look," Marcia said, "these were unhappy people, there was something burning inside them. They would come to us and we would give them a good time. That would help them get through the week, until they came back again to us. Anyway, you know how men are, they have to be relieved every so often, or they get mean. We did that for them. That was our job. Maybe by coming to us they didn't go out and rape someone. It's possible, right? Who knows?"

"Let's get back to Martin," said a man sitting on the left of Densen-Gerber, his voice filled with disgust.

"Okay. We were supposed to give Martin a piece of what we got. In the beginning it was nice. We had tons of money. We could do anything we wanted. I spent more on cabs the first year than I had earned in my whole life. But then came all the drugs, and Mary started cheating Martin to pay for them. When he found out, he came in and grabbed my sister and tied her to one of our special tables—"

"Special tables?" someone asked.

"Yes, we bought these examining tables from a medical supply company and fitted them with hooks for the ropes, and mounted them so they could be tilted and rotated in whatever direction we wanted. Anyway, he tied her feet to the stirrups and her hands to the hooks, gagged her, and burned his initials into her breast with a cigarette. Then he started to rape her.

Somehow, at that moment, I walked in with an old customer, saw what was going on and there was a fight. Ed—"

"Ed?"

"Ed was my customer. He pulled Martin off Mary and pushed him onto the floor. I cut Mary loose. The three of us ran out of the building onto the street. Fortunately, Martin had his pants down and couldn't run too fast. It was quite a scene, myself and my naked sister running down Twenty-third Street. I remembered there was a boutique down the street and ran in and bought some clothes. Then we got in a cab to Penn Station. We took Amtrak to Connecticut and stayed with our father for a few days. But since we didn't have much money and couldn't cop drugs we started getting sick. We stole some money from our father, and when we were going to buy the dope he caught us and got pissed. He said he would turn us in himself unless we kicked. He locked us in separate rooms until we were clean—it took about three days—and then brought us to Odyssey House. We didn't want to come here at first, it's true. But now we feel safe here, and we don't want to leave."

She looked around the room, then at the floor, and started to sob. "You know, Mary will kill me for this, she will absolutely kill me. I shouldn't have told you."

"Nonsense," Arlene Levine said. "I'll take care of her. You won't get in trouble. Trust me. Now go outside and send in your sister. And Marcia, tell her we know."

A few moments later Mary sheepishly walked into the room and sat on the stool.

"Okay, I'll tell you what I know. I was tied up on this table and my breast was burning—that bastard put an 'M' in it with a cigarette. He was starting to rape me when Marcia and Ed walked in. They cut me loose and we got away."

When asked about what had happened that had led up to those events, Mary said she did not know. It seemed to me that she was lacking a lot of knowledge about the S and M parlor and her life during the past five years. If she was a multiple, it seemed possible—even probable—that some other personality was the S and M mistress. Arlene Levine must have come to the same conclusion at about the same time I did, because she asked Mary what she thought was going on.

"Damn," she exclaimed. "It must have been Camille or Madeline. Damn."

"Who are they?"

"They live inside me. She used to be a nude dancer before we renovated the brownstone, and I haven't been in contact with her for a while, but she hates me. She is always fucking me up. Madeline is my age, very attractive and strong. She's the one my mother likes best. She sang, danced, wrote poetry, drew—everything my mother liked. Madeline hates men, and I think she is the one that ran that S and M business. My mother also hated men."

"Does anybody else live inside you?"

"Yes, there are others, but I'm not sure how many. There is Jerry, but he's only twelve and doesn't come out much. I sometimes hear the rumbling of others, but I'm not sure."

No one talked. Then Arlene Levine broke the silence. "Can I talk to Madeline?"

Probably relieved to get off her hot seat, Mary's eyes closed, then opened and a refined voice with a slight English accent took over. "I am Mistress Madeline, dominatrix extraordinare."

I had to admit it was a handy way to get even with men.

Madeline said she knew nothing about the rape by Martin or what had led to it. She thought Camille must have been involved, since Camille often let Mary take the rap for things that Camille had started. Moreover, Camille had been getting more and more upset since she was forced to quit dancing when Madeline put the body into the S & M business to make more money. Although some multiples could pursue several occupations at once, she couldn't, for reasons I still don't understand. So Camille was out of a job, sinking deeper and deeper into drugs. And Camille took the money Madeline had earned—Martin's money—to buy heroin.

I didn't have a chance to indulge in private thoughts long because at that moment, Judi asked to talk to Camille. Again the body slackened, and after a second or two a tough voice from the streets said, "What the fuck do yoose want?"

To my right, Arlene answered in the same tone, if not accent. "Why did you let Martin rape Mary? You were the one who took his money."

"I hate that little fucker. She deserves it."

"Why do you hate her? What did she do to you?"

"When we were little, that man would come into the room . . ."

"You mean your father?"

"That perverted piece of shit was not my father. He was her father."

"Who is your father?"

"I don't know . . . I don't have one."

"So, tell us what *that man* would do."

"He would tell her that she was sick. He would stroke her head with his hands, then put his lips on her forehead. He would then tell her he was going to take her temperature. He would turn her over, rub her back for a little while, take her pajamas down, and then fuck her up the ass. At that moment that little shit Mary would go away and leave me to take it. She set me up, and I was sick of it. I try to get her back for it every chance I get. I am no longer going to take it. Let's see how she likes it."

After a while, Mary was sent to join her sister in the hall, and it was time for the decision. There was no discussion at all as to whether or not the twins should be accepted into the program. That appeared to be a given, at least to the treatment staff if not to the prospective patients. Rather, the talk was mostly about how to treat them, assuming the twins would stick it out when things got rough, as they always do for Odyssey House residents. Although no one would give me figures—either they don't keep them or they do not want the world to know how much money is spent to get such meager results—I have observed that about 80 percent of those that enter Odyssey House leave before being cured. That is a terrible failure rate, although of course one could argue that it is better than nothing. My opinion was that the twins should be treated together, at least for a while, so they could support each other. Then they could be separated. But I was always more gentle than the Odyssey House people, who decided to put them in separate centers. That way, they reasoned, if one twin wanted to leave the program, she wouldn't take the other away with her.

The other problem they discussed at length was how to put a multiple through a program such as Odyssey House. In reality, two tracks were needed, one for drug addicts, the other for people with psychiatric disorders who happened to be addicted to drugs. In this case the twins used drugs to cut out the voices in their heads or gloss over the blank spots in their memories that occured when personalities other than the host were in control of the body. During the period when they were dominatrixes, for example, Madeline ran the business and Mary was nowhere around. Occasionally, though, she would come back, find herself in a situation she couldn't explain, and be very confused and want to go away. Drugs helped.

The Odyssey House approach is basically behaviorally oriented, designed in part to teach reponsibility—consequential thinking, as my Odyssey colleagues call it—something usually absent in the hard-core addict. That is why the best drug counselors are former drug users who know all the scams. But with a multiple, one personality can violate a rule, then go away, leaving another personality to pay the price. What does one do about that? How can they be held to the same rules as the others?

Furthermore, two of each twin's personalities were ex-addicts and one or more were not. In Mary's case, both she and Camille were addicted to heroin, but Madeline had never been. And while the first two suffered terrible withdrawal while they detoxed, Madeline did not. So two of the personalities needed the full Odyssey House program and one did not. On the other hand, they all needed multiple personality therapy.

It was decided that the two addicted personalities would go through the program, each on different days, and the nonaddicts would have two days for themselves, since they also needed time off and time for their therapy. A schedule to that effect was devised. No one was happy with this solution. There was even more confusion in the center when one twin's personality became a level four and the other had been busted to level one. Imagine what a problem it was to have identical twins with different rights, privileges, and duties.

While the group was discussing these nettlesome details, I noticed that it was time for me to head back to my office. I had appointments with patients that evening, and I would have to hurry.

I excused myself and left with my thoughts and questions. On the way, I noticed that the Israeli was still there, looking very confused.

12

Perpetrators

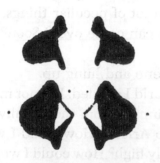

It was 8:45 on a Friday evening in January. The last patient of the day had just left, and it was the end of a busy week. I was glad it was over. I felt burnt out. My patients had been particularly demanding during the past few days, and I had somehow gotten sucked into the middle of a stupid bureaucratic battle at the college—one of those who-was-going-to-get-the-better-office affairs—that had been consuming a lot of my energy. Even if an issue is unimportant, one has to make a stand or people might think you are weak, or so I found myself thinking.

I poured myself a Glenlivet and settled down. I was meditating on what I would do for dinner—my wife, who supervises the printing of fabric at textile mills, was on a business trip to South Carolina—when the phone rang. It was Arlene Levine from Odyssey House.

"Mary is in trouble," she said after an all-too-brief moment of pleasantries. "On Wednesday she suddenly took off from the center and went home. She wanted to confront her father about how and why he abused her as a child. We told her not to go, but she went anyway. You know how she is. As I understand it, the confrontation went very badly and she ended up switching into a personality of hers who is a mute child. Her sister Marcia got her out of the home and called me in a panic. She didn't know what to do.

"I sent a group from here to bring them both back, because I was afraid their father might not let them return. Both twins are here now, but we have a major problem. Mona"—that was the name of the child Mary had switched into, according to Marcia, who of course had a similar personality—"is in control of Mary's body and won't let go. All she does is try to crawl up on Marcia's lap, sucking her thumb and crying. It's the strangest thing you ever saw, a whimpering adult trying to nurse at her twin sister's breast. I've seen a lot of peculiar things, but . . . listen, Bob, do you think you can come over? Soon?"

Damn, I said to myself.

"Give me an hour," I told Arlene and hung up.

This was the last thing in the world I needed. I'm not much of a drinker, and my head was spinning from the Glenlivet I had finished just before I talked to Arlene. How could I walk into a drug treatment center slightly high? How could I work if my head wasn't perfectly clear?

A cold shower brought me back to reality. I decided to walk the mile to Odyssey House, figuring that the exercise would burn off any remaining alcohol in my system and allow me to enter the center with a clear head—and no guilt.

When I arrived at Eighteenth Street I was greeted by Arlene and Paul Hansch, the center's psychiatrist. They led me upstairs, where I found Mary just as Arlene had described her: sitting on Marcia's lap, resting her head on her twin's breast, thumb in her mouth, alternately sucking it and whimpering. Her sister was holding, rocking, and stroking her, looking quite confused.

I walked in, sat down, and waited to see what would happen. Arlene and Paul began making small talk. I couldn't understand why they were wasting time. Then it hit me. They were waiting for me to take charge. That was why they had called me. They couldn't figure out what to do and had summoned me, an "expert" on multiplicity, to help.

I must say, it threw me. I have respected—maybe been

intimidated by is more accurate—medical doctors like Hansch ever since I was a child, when they would tame the chronic asthma attacks I thought would surely kill me. Some part of me still felt doctors were all-knowing. Also, I was on Arlene and Paul's turf and didn't expect to be in charge.

I felt insecure but chose not to give in to it. First, I decided, I would eliminate anything that would inhibit me and my ability to work, such as any feelings I might have about being watched and judged.

So that meant getting rid of Hansch. I told him, in the most assured tones I could muster, that given the delicacy of what I would be trying to do, it would be best to do it in circumstances familiar to the patient. Hansch, who had not had much contact with the twins, got the message. He quickly mumbled something about having plans for the evening and seemed only too glad to be excused.

Feeling more confident without him looking over my shoulder, we retired to the wonderful old boardroom where I had first met my patients Lauren and Susan. I had to lead Mary in by the hand, just like a child, and sit her down on the beat-up couch. As soon as I let go, she started to crawl up onto the lap of her sister, who was sitting beside her.

Marcia filled me in on what had happened in Connecticut. Mary had accused her father of anally raping her. He had handled the confrontation like a typical abuser. They will usually do anything to avoid responsibility—even tear apart the ego of their victim. Mary's father had denied everything and gone on the counterattack, accusing his daughter of being crazy. He was trying to make her feel like Ingrid Bergman in *Gaslight* and, judging by the results, had done an even better job than Charles Boyer. He had then compounded his sin by trying to make both daughters feel guilty, telling them he loved them and reminding them that it was he who had saved their lives by taking them to Odyssey House. How could they be doing this to him?

Mary was so angry and at the same time so guilty that she couldn't cope with her confusion and switched to the helpless, hurt child, Mona. It was a personality I had heard about but never met, since Mona had rarely been out.

Marcia was also in shock, but not as deeply as Mary. She must have had a better sense of the kind of man her father was —and a more realistic expectation of what her sister's confrontation would accomplish. She was able to maintain her composure and call Odyssey House for help.

I would normally have relished the opportunity to work with Mary—or, rather, Mona. It was a rare opportunity to get right to the core of Mary's problem: Here was the hurt child, normally buried inside her but now accessible to me and my colleagues. But working with a young and troubled personality such as Mona might have taken months, and she would have to be cared for all the while. I asked Arlene Levine whether it would be possible, in effect, to hospitalize Mary at Odyssey House while I developed and carried out a treatment plan. But Dr. Levine said the center was not set up for a case like this. Who would take care of this baby in an adult? There was no nursing staff. The only available person was her sister, and it was unrealistic to expect Marcia to give up months of her life to hold and feed her regressed twin. Even if Marcia were willing, the special attention given to Mary would likely disrupt the entire center, and the other residents would soon resent her. They might even suspect that she was faking the whole episode to get out of doing her chores. Who knows, after a week there might be twenty babies crawling around Odyssey House.

What about a nursing home or a hospital? That was out, too. Mary simply could not afford a private facility. And to my knowledge there wasn't a hospital on the East Coast that truly understood multiplicity.* If we sent her to an institution, they

* As of this writing, there are only two places in the United States that have programs specifically for multiples: Rush–Presbyterian–St. Luke's Medical Center in Chicago and Ridgeview Institute in Smyrna, Georgia. Arlene Levine has been negotiating with Gracie Square Hospital in New York City to become the third.

would most likely diagnose her as psychotic, load her up with drugs, and, since hospitals are professionally xenophobic, not let me or Arlene anywhere near her, since we wouldn't be on staff.

Mary still sat whimpering in her sister's lap. I tried to make contact with Mona but could not get her to talk. She didn't even know who I was. The more I tried to soothe her, the more I frightened her. I asked Arlene to try, reasoning that she had been around Mary more than I, but Mona was scared of her as well. The only person she trusted was her sister.

It would be a long process building up enough trust to work with Mona, and we didn't have much time. I had to get her to go back inside—but how? Children are usually easy to hypnotize, but there was no way this child was going to let me put her into a trance.

Then I had an idea. Why not let the only person she trusted, her sister, be the hypnotist?

Marcia was still shaken by what was happening with her sister, so I started by putting her into a trance and asking her to switch to a personality who knew—and was trusted by—Mona. In a moment she went inside and out popped Rose, who had been created by Marcia when she was first abused. Perfect, I thought.

I asked Rose to rock her "baby" sister, telling her that Daddy was bad and that we loved her. I don't know whether Mona understood the words or the body language, but whatever it was, it had a calming effect. Mona's whimpering grew softer.

After another ten minutes of rocking, it was time for phase two.

"Tell Mona to close her eyes," I told Rose. "Tell her to relax, like she was going to sleep. Tell her to let herself go back inside, where it's safe and no one can hurt her. Remind her that she knows how to do it."

Rose followed my instructions, and I held my breath.

Would it work? What would I do if it didn't? I looked at Mona. Her facial muscles seemed more relaxed. Then her thumb dropped out of her mouth, and I knew she had gone back inside.

"Let me talk to Mary," I commanded in the most gentle but authoritative tone I could muster.

Her eyes opened. She looked around and recognized us. "Arlene . . . Dr. Mayer. What are you doing here?"

I could see by her expression that she was starting to remember what had happened. She looked like she was waking up from a short nap and reorienting herself.

"The last thing I remember I was at home, yelling at my father. What happened? What the fuck is going on?"

Yes, Mary was back, to my great relief. As I helped fill in the blanks in her memory, the tension that had been building in the room dissipated. Marcia looked at me like I was some sort of guru. I just felt lucky.

On the way home, I thought about how we had gotten into this mess. It was a classic case of trying to solve one problem and creating another. What makes the trauma of child abuse much worse is that it doesn't go away. Bad enough that a child is raped, but many have to endure living with, eating with, and loving their rapists—even as they continue to rape them. Little wonder incest victims tend to assume the role of victim over and over again during the course of their lives.

A year or so before Mary's disastrous journey to Connecticut, I had sought out an expert in the treatment of physically and sexually abused women and children. Dr. Nancy Halloran had impressive credentials—a medical degree with board certification in pediatrics and psychiatry—was analytically trained, and had written and lectured widely on a subject then given short shrift by the mainstream of our profession. I had been encountering more and more incest victims in my practice during that time, and I was hoping to pick her brain on how best to help them.

Her most successful, if controversial, method was to have the "survivor" confront the perpetrator. By winning such a confrontation—having the abuser admit it is wonderful, of course, but on a more basic level it is important that victims learn that they can confront their attackers and survive—Dr. Halloran believed, a patient would regain the power taken from her by her assailant. She would defeat the one who had defeated her and thus feel like a victor, not a victim. Her sense of self-esteem and self-worth would be renewed.

Dr. Halloran's "don't get mad, get even" approach, however, could be a tricky business. Because abusers could hardly be counted on to be cooperative, Nancy took great pains to increase her patient's odds for success, staging thorough rehearsals that covered every eventuality. And she was not above tricking abusers into showing up for confrontations, which she insisted on staging on the therapist's home turf.

A lot of this did not sit well with the profession. Conventional analytic training holds that you cannot undo the past, as Dr. Halloran seemed to be trying mightily to do. Rather, what is important is how the patient feels about the past—assuming a therapist is sure a patient has an accurate recollection of it. But it had already been my experience that even with extensive psychotherapy, incest victims often feel powerless to change. So I made arrangements to study with Nancy and eventually became coleader of her incest therapy group, meeting several women who had successfully confronted their rapists—mostly their fathers—and had won. Most felt it was the turning point in therapy. Convinced of the value of confrontation and encouraged by Nancy, I decided to use the technique on my own patients.

I was successful on my first try. Carmela, a Cuban American, had been abused by a neighbor when she was a child. Two years after she started seeing me, her abuser was arrested in

Florida on charges of rape and child pornography. As his trial drew near, I convinced Carmela to contact the prosecutor and offer herself as a character witness. Frightened, she reluctantly flew to Miami and confronted the man, albeit through the grillwork of the county jail's visiting room. He admitted everything. Later she testified in court and helped send him to prison for three years.

When she returned to New York I discovered a most amazing change—Carmela seemed stronger and more sure of herself. The proof was in her dreams. Before the confrontation she had had a recurrent nightmare of someone coming into her room. The door would open and a faceless person would approach her bed. She would lie there, paralyzed by fear, as the intruder came closer. She would try to scream, but nothing would come out of her mouth. She would try to get out of bed, but her body would not respond to her commands. She would try to fight him off, but her arms and legs would not move. She felt paralyzed with terror. Finally, as the man came within inches of her bed, Carmela would wake up with a jolt, soaked with sweat. Sometimes she would just lie there, thinking he was still in the room, not knowing what was real and what wasn't. But after her Miami confrontation, the dream gradually changed. At first she was able to let out a little sound as the intruder approached. Soon the sound turned into a scream. Then she was able to fight him off. After about three months, she dreamed that she had a gun under her pillow, which she used to kill the abuser as he drew close. After that, the persecution dreams ceased.

It was like a tumor shrinking away. I was professionally convinced. When Nancy suggested that Mary and Marcia confront their father, I readily agreed. To help prepare them—and me—I decided to interview their father first. I was hoping, of course, that he would admit what he had done, which would allow him to apologize to his daughters and thus spare them a hostile scene that would leave more bad blood between them.

I phoned him, told him who I was, and asked if he would be willing to come in and talk to me for an hour. It would be important for his daughters' treatment, I said.

He put up no resistance. Playing the role of the good daddy, he insisted that he would do anything to help them. The appointment was made for the following week.

I guess I was expecting someone wearing a shabby rain-coat, needing a shave, and missing some teeth. Instead, he was a tall, nice-looking man, balding and perhaps fifteen pounds overweight. He appeared to be about sixty years old and wore a grey herringbone sports coat and a red knit tie.

I talked to him for a few minutes, building rapport. I asked him to give me an outline of his life. He said he could recall very little from his childhood but had a good memory of the last forty years. During our chat I learned that he had served in World War II under generals Patton and Clark. I am a history buff, and as we talked about the North African, Sicilian, and Italian campaigns he seemed to warm up a little.

At a break in the conversation, I swallowed hard, then told him that his daughters claimed he had sexually abused them as children. It would be very helpful for their treatment, I went on, as gently and professionally as I could, if we could find out if it actually happened. It would be safe, I said, to unburden himself. No one would tell the authorities, and he would be able to help right the wrong he was accused of and build a better, more honest relationship with his daughters, which he now seemed to want, since he was the one who had gotten them into Odyssey House and off drugs. (I am legally bound to report current cases of child abuse, but this happened years ago.)

He looked away from me while I spoke, and when I stopped, he began talking about the war again, as if he had not heard anything I had said. He had been a member of a burial detail, and he told me in gruesome detail how he had picked up parts of dead soldiers and tried to identify them, matching arms and legs with torsos and heads. He was the only member of the unit, he said proudly, who had come through the war intact. The others had either been killed or gone crazy.

He had not answered me, or had he?

I interrupted him and asked him again about having sex with his daughters. As before, he listened politely, then went back to the war. I noticed that he talked about his experiences without any emotion. It was as if he was talking about another person. The feelings had been drained from the memories.

It was obvious that I was not going to succeed. The man had strong defenses, which explained how he was able to tolerate life in the burial unit. I assumed his defense was dissociation. Was he perhaps, like his daughters, a multiple? The girls would say that when he "struck" he looked like a different person. Especially his eyes. They changed, his daughters said, just before he attacked.

I was fairly sure his daughters were telling the truth. After all, one corroborated the other. I had also gone through many abreactions with both of them, and no one could fake the intensity and pain I had witnessed. But if I had any doubts, his behavior now put them to rest. What had motivated him to abuse his children? According to the literature on pedophiles —which, like that on multiplicity, is surprisingly thin, perhaps because the subject is so uncomfortable—a majority have themselves been sexually abused or physically traumatized as children. They have low self-esteem, are fearful of the power of others, and are not able to obtain sexual, emotional, intellectual, or physical satisfaction from adult relationships. They choose to solve their own problems by having sex with children.

Of thirty-three sexual offenders incarcerated in a forensic ward of the Utah State Hospital, Dr. Eugene Bliss found that two thirds had spontaneous self-hypnotic episodes. He also found that six of the nine pedophiles in the group were multiples and the other three were possibly so. Normal inhibitions and prohibitions do not deter them, possibly because they dissociate or even get additional excitement by breaking a taboo. Afterwards, they may feel guilt and remorse, which sometimes compel them to commit another abuse to alleviate these bad feelings. It is a truly vicious cycle.*

The following week I told Mary and Marcia about my meeting with their father. I suspected that he was a multiple, which would explain how he could be so loving one moment and so loathsome the next. In my view, I said, a direct confrontation would not be very productive.

It was not what they wanted to hear. They hoped—fantasized, really—that some day their daddy would come to his senses and apologize, after which they could fully love him and he them, and this love would rescue them from their pain. (I am often struck by the quickness of children to forgive their abusive parents.)

In a rage, Mary decided to confront her father anyway. Marcia was less enthusiastic about a showdown but was unable to change her sister's mind. That evening both sisters left Odyssey House for Connecticut—and what would become Mary's Dunkirk.

In retrospect, I could see her mission had been doomed. The father was not cooperative, the confrontation was on his turf, Mary was not prepared, and I was not present. I began to think maybe my success with my patient Carmela had been beginner's luck.

---

* In *Out of the Shadows: Understanding Sexual Addiction,* Dr. Patrick Carnes argues that some people become addicted to sex. He writes that it is a four-step process: "1. Preoccupation—the trance or mood wherein the addicts' minds are completely engrossed with thoughts of sex. This mental state creates an obsessive search for sexual stimulation. 2. Ritualization—the addicts' own special routines that lead up to the sexual behavior. The ritual intensifies the preoccupation, adding arousal and excitement. 3. Compulsive sexual behavior—the actual sexual act, which is the end goal of the preoccupation and ritualization. Sexual addicts are unable to control or stop this behavior. And, 4. Despair—the feeling of utter hopelessness addicts have about their behavior and their powerlessness. The pain the addicts feel at the end of the cycle can be numbed or obscured by sexual preoccupation which re-engages the addiction cycle." Carnes recommends therapy based on the principles of Alcoholics Anonymous, and there are groups in major cities calling themselves Sexual Addicts Anonymous.

My next attempt at confrontation was with Susan. Therapy had made her much stronger, and she had graduated from the drug treatment program, which was no mean achievement. I felt that since her father had abused his other daughters, there was bound to be some sibling support for a confrontation.

Susan was reluctant, mostly because she was still frightened of her father, but at my urging she finally agreed. We spent many sessions discussing what she would say. Finally, it was time. Her father came to my office and categorically and angrily insisted that he had not abused anyone. Her mother, who was also present, flew into a rage at Susan for even suggesting it and accused her of trying to destroy the family. Most astonishing of all was the reaction of four of Susan's sisters, who we invited to the office a few days later. Even though each had also been abused, they lined up against Susan and defended and protected their rapist of a father. Even the sister who had earlier confirmed Susan's rape after Susan had abreacted it in my office now denied the event had taken place.

Dr. Halloran had warned me about such reactions. Incest is a family secret, and families have a huge investment in keeping it that way. An abusive father can lose his job and go to jail if he is discovered. A wife who turns him in or testifies against him will have to do without him, and for many of these women a bad husband is better than no husband. Wives of abusive men typically lack self-respect, perhaps because—as studies have shown—a majority of them were themselves sexually abused as children. In some peculiar way, they are marrying men like their fathers.

The young victims do not usually tell, either, often because of the same fear of abandonment. Abusive fathers work diligently to keep their families isolated from friends and neighbors, developing systems of reward and punishment to maintain a state of fear and secrecy. In standing by their father,

Susan's sisters were choosing safety and security over truth and the unknown.

Susan, like Mary, was crushed by the confrontation. Fortunately, one of the sisters broke the conspiracy of silence about a week later, calling Susan and apologizing for not defending her. Not surprisingly, it was the one who had earlier confirmed the rape. I guess she was ambivalent and kept changing her loyalties. Susan vowed never to speak to any other member of her family again—and to the best of my knowledge kept her vow.

The confrontation that haunted me the most was that of a patient named Martha, who had been abused not only by her father but also by her two elder brothers. Her parents were now dead, but the two brothers were alive. With Nancy's encouragement, I sought both of them out. One brother refused to have anything to do with me and told me not to bother him again. But the other one, Arthur, said he would be glad to come to my office the following week.

Arthur seemed like an agreeable man, about thirty-five years old, with a wife and four children back home in rural western Pennsylvania, where he scratched out a living as a carpenter. He looked like a fugitive from the sixties, with jeans and a down vest, a beard, and long, unruly black hair. I told him why we needed him. Repeating the promise that hadn't worked with the twins' father, I said that nothing would happen to him if he told the truth. On the other hand, it would be helpful for Martha to know for sure that what she remembered had actually happened and perhaps to get some explanation for it.

He listened impassively, remaining silent for a few moments after I stopped talking. Then he broke down sobbing and confessed everything. He said he had seen his father have sex with some of his sisters and brag to him about it afterwards, and that therefore he had thought it was all right for him to do it. One of the things a child learns from a parent is how to have a relationship. When a parent has sex with a child, the child concludes that in order to have a relationship one has to be sexual. Thus, the culture in the house supported such behavior, and all relationships became sexualized. Indeed, Arthur described how his father had sodomized him as well. He said their childhood had been a horror and he felt awful most of the time—except when he was in bed with his sisters. It seemed to me Arthur was as much a victim as a victimizer.

Arthur begged for Martha's forgiveness. This apparently heartfelt confession was exactly what she needed. It confirmed what had happened to her, so she no longer worried that she had made it all up. The apology also helped her come to view herself and her brother as covictims.

I suggested that Arthur seek therapy when he returned home. He thanked me and left.

Later I found out he never went home. He abandoned his wife and children and has not been seen since.

I can only speculate on why. Perhaps he was abusing his children, recognized that it was a compulsion that couldn't be stopped, and removed himself from the stimuli. He did fit the profile of an abuser, having been a victim of childhood abuse himself. Or perhaps he was afraid we would call the authorities and turn him in. Maybe he went off to find a fresh supply of young victims. Or to kill himself.

I thought a lot about Arthur over the next few months. Had I acted ethically? Morally? To save one life, had I destroyed another? Was I so concerned with my patients' problems that I failed to see the pain of others? Had I become Martha's advocate rather than her analyst? Therapists were supposed to be neutral, but I was enraged at abusers. Had I lost my professionalism?

Dr. Halloran had no doubts—or guilt—about Arthur or any of the others. There is a point where understanding ceases, she argued. Who cares if Hitler had a bad childhood? Nor should we have sympathy for a man who abuses a child—and may still be abusing one. "The only thing that you did wrong," Nancy told me, "was not to find a way to detain him and get a confession, so we could have him arrested and get him away from his children."

Later I found out a possible reason for Nancy's extreme attitude—*she* had been physically abused as a child. Her father had forced her to take icy showers, struck her, and tied her to her bed, all toward the end of making her a tougher person. Instead, he produced a woman in a constant rage, mostly at men. Little wonder she so relished confrontations with abusers and felt no remorse when lives were destroyed. She was using her patients—and mine—to get even for her own childhood. She wasn't just confronting her patients' fathers, she was confronting her own father, over and over again.

My thoughts on confrontation changed as a result of this discovery. I still believe it can be a valuable strategy, but I will allow a patient to attempt it only after I have interviewed the abuser and have assured myself that he is ready to admit his crime and apologize. If we can add an understanding of why it happened, what motivated the abuser, so much the better. Psychopathology is passed on from one generation to the next. Psychotherapy breaks the chain. It cannot redo the past, but it can place it in perspective.

If it seems an abuser will not cooperate, I believe it is almost always a mistake to try to confront him. I say "almost" because a few especially strong patients will derive benefit from an encounter with a stonewalling and unremorseful father. At least it puts to rest any fantasy that he will come around and they can be friends.

Instead of a face-to-face confrontation, I have successfully used hypnosis to create imaginary meetings that yield the same benefits without the risks. "See yourself walking down the street in your hometown to your house," I tell my patients. "Open the door and go in. See your father sitting in his chair in the living room. Walk over to him . . ." And so on.

It is a purer experience with hypnosis, since I can take my

patient back in time to the age when the trauma occurred. Patients filter real confrontations through decades of living, and of course their parents could also have changed in the intervening years.

Sometimes, too, I encourage patients to become involved in activities or organizations that will give them a sense of power over an aggressor, at least symbolically. For example, I have pushed incest victims, especially those who were lawyers, to become involved in the issue of children's rights. Others have become social workers or even therapists. I suggested that still others join feminist groups such as Women Against Pornography and combat the kiddie porn merchants. When windows are broken on Forty-second Street, it could partially be my fault. I do not feel bad about this.

In a sense, the strangest of my confrontations occurred when "60 Minutes," the immensely popular television news magazine, wanted to do a segment on multiple personality disorder and, through Densen-Gerber, contacted me. The more I thought about it, the more intriguing it became. Have a patient go on national television, switch from personality to personality in front of more than thirty million viewers and tell the world that she had been an incest victim. That would certainly get the secret out into the open. The program, I hoped, would also show the world what happens when you traumatize a child. Maybe some abusers would think twice.

I thought about it a while, concerned about a possible conflict of interest. I wanted the attention, there was no denying it, but not at the expense of my patients. I had to be sure, before I asked any of them to go on the program with me, that it was proper therapeutically. And I also had to be careful to present it to them in such a way that they could make their decision on the basis of what *they* wanted and not what *I* wanted.

After much soul searching I talked to Toby, Lauren, and

the twins about the program. They were all terrified. In fact, the twins said no right away. But the others said they would think about it.

In truth, I was terrified, too, at the prospect of being interviewed by the most ferocious questioner on television, Mike Wallace. If most of my own profession still didn't believe in multiple personality disorder, how would I ever convince this professional skeptic? I could see the sweat forming on my upper lip as he grilled me while the camera moved in for the classic "60 Minutes" close-up.

Wallace's producer, Ira Rosen, assured me that he had no intention of making a circus out of multiplicity or a fool out of me. Rather, he said, they wanted to put on a segment that would demonstrate that the disorder is real and that it can create vexing legal problems.

I invited Rosen to meet my patients and, like a male version of a protective lioness, watched him interact with the multiples. It went well. He was gentle and knowledgeable. I got a good feeling from him. So did Toby and Lauren, who consented to go on the air. They were still concerned, as was I, that the producer, in order to stimulate the ratings, would sensationalize their illness. And they wanted anonymity, which could be achieved by altering their appearances. Perhaps I was naive, but I could not believe that a television network would do anything to harm a psychiatric patient.

Early on the morning of the appointed day, the "60 Minutes" brigade started to troop in, turning my office—no, my entire apartment—upside down. In came a cameraman and his camera, two light people, two sound people, one makeup person, one or two others whose names and jobs I didn't catch, Ira Rosen and his assistant, Lauren, Toby, and my doorman, who couldn't believe "60 Minutes" had come to his building. When nearly all the equipment was ready, Mike Wallace entered, as if on cue. He was a short man, although he looked taller because of my anxiety. I noted that as soon as he entered the room he found the first available chair and sat down. One of the "60 Minutes" people whispered into my ear that he was insecure about his height and always looked for an empty chair. Sure enough, when we moved to another room for the interview, he did the same thing. It made us civilians feel better.

To say the taping went smoothly would be an understatement. They turned on the camera and kept it on for four and a half hours. After a while I didn't even notice it.

Mike gave Beth a chocolate-covered cookie, watched her devour it, and then asked to speak to Toby. When Toby came back, she puckered her face. Mike asked her what was wrong. She said that there was a strange taste in her mouth. He asked her if she remembered eating a cookie. Toby said yes, that is what it tasted like, but she didn't remember eating it. I could tell Mike believed her.

He also met Morgan and Anna but not Julia. She was too frightened. Then he met Lauren, Scarlett, and Jefferson. The mood became light, almost giddy. Scarlett, enjoying the attention, told Mike she thought he was cute, and he kidded her right back. The best was when Jefferson said he was attracted to him and wanted to know what he was doing later.

"I walked in a skeptic," Mike said as he left. "But I'm walking out a believer."

After the taping I kept Toby and Lauren in my office for another hour, debriefing them. I wanted them to share all their feelings about the show. Slowly it dawned on them that they had allowed themselves to switch from personality to personality in front of what would probably be a hefty portion of the country. And even though Toby was disguised, the act of publicly describing the hideous events of her childhood had been therapeutic. She had broken the hold of the pathologist who had raped her and threatened to put her in a jar of formaldehyde with the other specimens in his garage if she told anyone about it. She had broken the hold of her mother, who had tortured her countless times in countless ways. She had gone public, and she had survived.

Although they were concerned that the taping would be badly cut or edited, both Toby and Lauren realized that as adults they had made a choice, taken a risk. They could live with the results, they said. I felt elated. We had helped assemble an unbelievably valuable piece of videotape showing people with multiple personality switching and discussing their problem with Mike Wallace, no less. It would show the world that multiplicity exists, and further that even though it is a terrible affliction it can be managed and treated. Multiples talk, they work, they joke. We had showed that to the world, or at least the 33 million people who watch "60 Minutes." The episode would undoubtedly reach other multiples, who would now know that help was available. We had performed a public service and had a good time in the process.

If only "60 Minutes" hadn't screwed it up.

First of all, almost a year and a half went by before the episode got on the air. Even though the act of taping had been very beneficial for Toby and Lauren, the waiting, the wondering, and the worrying were not good for them or me. The reason for the delay, I was told, was that another network had heard that "60 Minutes" was preparing the episode and had scheduled a rerun of an old documentary on multiplicity. Apparently these people spy on each other. It was then that "60 Minutes" decided to allow some time to go by so the subject would seem fresh again.

When it finally got on the air, the segment was an anticlimax. It opened with Toby switching to Beth, then cut to me describing multiple personality disorder and what causes it. But the rest of the segment was devoted to the legal ramifications of the disorder. Mostly it focused on the case of Paul Miskamen, a born-again Christian from California who, on the night of August 13, 1977, took a stick and beat Bonnie, his wife of twenty-seven years, to death. After his arrest, he was given sodium amytal—a barbiturate more commonly known as truth serum—and another personality emerged, a drinker and gambler named Jack Kelly, who confessed to the crime. Miskamen said he was unaware of Kelly, and a California court believed him, acquitting him of murder by reason of insanity—multiple personality disorder. After fourteen months in Napa State Hospital, he was released. The "60 Minutes" episode contained a brief interview with Ralph Allison, who basically concurred with the diagnosis that Miskamen was a multiple but told Mike Wallace that it was possible Paul was "possessed." There was no talk about Jack Kelly being integrated, but he apparently had not been heard from since shortly after the murder.

The episode also mentioned the case of Kenneth Bianci, the so-called Hillside strangler who had killed nine people in Los Angeles in 1978. Allison had diagnosed him as a multiple, but Bianci later confessed to faking the disorder. And then there was Billy Milligan, who in 1977 was the first person ever found not guilty of a major crime by reason of insanity because of multiple personality.

Should someone be excused of a crime because he or she says another personality inside committed it? Clearly, this is a perplexing issue, especially since the psychiatric profession disagrees over multiplicity. But as far as Toby and Lauren were concerned, the emphasis of the "60 Minutes" segment was all wrong. They felt that multiple personality disorder had been given a bad name and that viewers would associate the illness with criminals. To a degree, I shared their view, although I still thought that anything publicizing multiple personality disorder would be helpful.

I would estimate that of the four and a half hours of tape recorded in my office, about three minutes got on the air. And poor Lauren, after working up all of her courage and submitting to the interview, ended up on the cutting room floor.

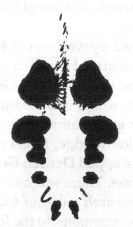

13

The Group

When I was young my mother used to tell me the tale of a Hasidic rabbi who was so wise that people lined up at his door for advice. Whenever people would complain about their troubles, the rabbi would take them out to see a tree in his backyard. He called it the trouble tree. Anyone could get rid of his troubles, he said, by hanging them on the tree. The only requirement was that he take someone else's troubles in return.

That is a function of group therapy. Lose your troubles—or at least put them into perspective—by listening to those of others.

We are all herd animals. We are born into a group. We live, work, and play in groups. Much of our behavior is determined by group approval or disapproval. We are successful as a species because we function so well in groups. We have been forming and using groups for therapeutic purposes for centuries, if not forever. Even though the Freudian revolution made us examine our unconscious motivations, we still seem to need societal and peer support for difficult tasks. Almost everything is easier if someone holds our hand. That is why I hired a supervisor to help guide me through the world of multiplicity. That is why Freud needed to bounce his theories off Fliess.

In cases of posttraumatic stress, group therapy is especially beneficial. The Israeli Army conducted a study in which soldiers who suffered battlefield fugues—say, after a buddy had been blown to bits in front of them—were hypnotized by Army physicians. They abreacted the trauma, put the soldiers into a group with other soldiers who had been through similar ordeals so they could talk about it, and then sent them back to the battlefield. This procedure, they found, prevented the fear from becoming a permanent affliction.

If it worked for soldiers traumatized by war, would group therapy also work for multiples traumatized by their child-hoods? In the spring of 1982 I suggested to Dr. Densen-Gerber that she allow me to form a group that would include some of the multiples I was seeing privately and others undergoing treatment at Odyssey House. To my knowledge, it had never been done before, but that had never stopped Densen-Gerber.

There was just one catch, she told me. There was no money to pay me. But I decided that the research value of such an unprecedented effort would more than compensate me for my time. So we made a deal: I would run the group at Odyssey House and in return be allowed to publish whatever data would result.

Although I was fairly certain the group therapy would ben-efit all the multiples we put in it, I had especially high hopes for Toby. At that point, I had been seeing her for almost four years. She had gone through many abreactions and made much prog-ress. The therapeutic work I had done with her alter Becky on the missing ring and Dr. Carter's death had seemed to be a breakthrough, at least at the time. And yet, after all of that, the case had seemed to stall again, and I wasn't sure why. I was anxious to get it moving.

I had once put Toby in a group with nonmultiple patients led by Pat Wellman. Although they all got along, their prob-lems—mostly involving dating, relationships, and marriage—were ultimately of little interest to Toby, and the problems Toby was concerned with—such as her confusion upon "awak-ening" to find herself in a different place—were alien to the rest of the group. I hoped a group of multiples would be different.

The group sessions would also give Toby another hour a week with me and, most important, would discourage her from assuming her favorite role, that of a victim completely without hope. She would be thrown in with people who were much sicker than she was, as well as people who were much healthier. The former would show her that things could be worse; the latter would inspire her to make them better. Thus, peer pressure would push her toward mental health. Or so I hoped.

Running a group therapy session for multiples was logistically daunting, to be sure. We started with only six patients—Mary, Marcia, Lauren, and Toby, plus two newly diagnosed multiples from Odyssey House. I never did allow myself to fully calculate the dozens of personalities and fragments of personalities that were gathering together in the boardroom on Eighteenth Street. That might have been the reason no one had formed a group for multiples before.

I was well trained in group treatment, having participated in a seventy-two-hour group marathon during my analytic training, taken numerous courses in group therapy, and spent much time at the Esalen Institute in California, where the modern encounter movement flowered in the 1960s. Even so, Densen-Gerber assigned Arlene Levine, the clinical supervisor at Odyssey House, to be my assistant and Candice, a fully integrated multiple who was a treatment counselor at the center, to help us. Densen-Gerber herself would attend sessions from time to time, when her schedule permitted. Her presence would have a twofold benefit. She would act as a check in case I missed something therapeutically, and she would keep Toby in a double bind. Toby had hated Densen-Gerber since the day we had met her in Westport, when she had accused me of coddling my patient. She had predicted that Toby would not get better if I persisted. Toby desperately wanted to prove

Densen-Gerber wrong, even if it meant getting better. A little more time with Densen-Gerber couldn't hurt.

Our group convened for what turned out to be a disappointing beginning. The hour started in the conventional way, with Judianne introducing herself and the rest of the staff and then asking everyone in the room to introduce themselves and describe their internal worlds and what they hoped to get out of the group. It turned out to be a time-consuming process, given the multitudes present.

Toby, who happened to be sitting next to Densen-Gerber, had the unfortunate task of going first. She told everybody her name and the names of all her internal people. She had joined the proceedings, she said, because she wanted to compare notes with other multiples and because her alters wanted to meet other internal people—especially Morgan, who was dying to talk to another teenager.

Lauren, sitting beside Toby, went next. She said she was really looking forward to the sessions—but she said it in a hollow tone that suggested she wasn't. Sure enough, it wasn't long before she began to whine about how hard it would be to come to the sessions. And although she told the group about her people, she also said that only Loverly was enthusiastic about the idea. Scarlett, Jefferson, and the rest of her internal alters couldn't care less.

Mary and Marcia, the twins, told the group a little about their history and rattled off their mirror-image internal personalities. Mary said she didn't really expect to get anything out of the group except a chance to see her sister, since she had been assigned to Eighteenth Street and Marcia was at the Mabon.

Marcia was only slightly more positive. She insisted that multiplicity was really not her main concern, not compared with the endless trials of living in Odyssey House, where it was, she claimed, difficult to make friends and follow all the rules. Madeline, one of Marcia's personalities, who was not an addict, had never agreed to be in the Odyssey House program and flew into a rage every time she took control of the body and realized she was essentially in a therapeutic prison.

Then the two new people, both of whom looked terrified, introduced themselves. The first, whose name was Helen, said she had entered Odyssey House in Detroit. A friend had brought her in after her seventh attempt to kick a heroin habit had failed. She had been in the program for a month when Densen-Gerber, who was on a visit to the center, interviewed her, diagnosed her as a multiple, and sent her to New York. That had been two weeks before. I could see Helen still did not understand what multiplicity was about. All she knew was that she occasionally "lost" chunks of time.

The second woman was named Alicia. She had entered an Odyssey House in Sydney, Australia, three months earlier and, after a diagnosis by Densen-Gerber, had followed the same path as Helen to New York. Alicia told us that she had been abused as a child and that people often called her by different names, which puzzled her. She did not understand anything about multiple personality disorder or, for that matter, why she had been told to report to the group.

So out of the six host personalities in the group, five were resistant—if indeed they knew enough about what was going on to be resistant. Only Toby seemed happy to be there.

Not an auspicious beginning, I admitted to myself, but then again, a big part of therapy is dealing with resistance. And that is exactly what we spent the rest of the first session trying to do. We—the therapists—ended up doing most of the talking, but I hoped that we could at least keep the group together long enough to allow them to bond to one another. Then maybe our experiment would have a chance.

The day before the second meeting, another problem emerged. Densen-Gerber told me that she was going to be out of town and that I would be in charge. I didn't like that much. There wasn't a rule book for running a multiples group. We were all setting out in a fragile boat, trying to cross an uncharted ocean. I had been confident because I felt we were a good crew. But now I felt as though the navigator was abandoning ship. I was also afraid this would affect the patients, who, like children, need a stable structure. And what about the other two therapists? Densen-Gerber was their boss. I was simply a consultant, a hired hand. Would they think I was violating their turf by taking over?

I soon realized that two groups were needed—one for the patients and another for the therapists. My experience watching the fights over desks and turf at Kean College had taught me that even—or perhaps especially—highly educated professionals are subject to vicious territorial squabbles. Freud knew about this, too. During his career, Freud fought with and lost many of the members of his inner circle—Jung, Adler, Ferenczi, Rank, and others.

I called my partners and discussed the situation. We agreed to meet for an hour before the group gathered to talk about the previous session and plan for the next one. And, perhaps surprisingly, we got along famously.

I wish things had gone as well with our patients. At the session the next day the two new multiples, Helen and Alicia, did not show up. I was told that they had both left the program the day after the last group meeting. They had gotten frightened and apparently done what multiples do, avoided reality. They were never heard from again.

In hindsight, it was obvious they had not had enough time to understand the diagnosis, much less accept it. They had detoxed, entered the program, been evaluated and sent to New York, and been put in with four people who said they had many other people living inside of them. And all of this had occurred within a few months.

I would like to think we learned our lesson, but we later made the same mistake with others. I remember a young woman from Louisiana who had become a multiple after being sexually abused by a Satanic cult to which her parents belonged. She entered an Odyssey House branch in Louisiana, was diagnosed as a multiple and sent to New York, where she enrolled in the group, just like Helen and Alicia. And just like Helen and Alicia, she became frightened and quickly left.

It happened a few more times before we learned that the icy waters of multiplicity are best entered gradually. Throw patients in, and they can go into shock.

The group sessions continued, and we learned to let go of our lofty expectations. We had hoped that the members would want to share experiences of what it was like to be a multiple. We thought they would want to trade horror stories from their abused childhoods, playing a can-you-top-this game of terror. We wanted to provide a forum in which they could let these secrets out. But we were wrong.

No abreactive work was done. The members seemed to feel that such serious episodes were too personal to be shared; thus they remained the province of private therapy. Mary and Marcia viewed the group as a place to talk about their problems in Odyssey House and visit with each other. They had very little, if any, interest in discussing their multiplicity, the abuse they had endured as children, their feelings toward their parents, or anything else that might remind them of the pain they had endured and worked so hard to neutralize. They were also very hesitant to switch in front of everyone. It was, they said, too embarrassing.

As for Lauren, she simply came less and less until she stopped coming altogether, so that our group was down to four. Even if the twins suddenly changed their minds, there weren't enough people left to get a good interaction going, given their resistance to the idea. I had new multiples in treatment, but I felt they were not ready to enter the group.

Without having any firm view of how to proceed, our only choice was to be flexible. We decided to give the group its head and let it go where it wanted to go. When the sessions seemed flat, even boring, we were forced to take a more active role than I had with other groups. We did a lot of teaching, trying to convince these alienated people that they could trust other human beings. We did a lot of hand holding. And to the uninitiated it might have seemed as if we did a lot of unusual things, too, although we at least hoped they would be more therapeutic than they seemed. We had a birthday party for Morgan—with a chocolate cake for Beth—because Morgan had never been given a birthday party before. When someone was sick, others in the group would call to find out if there was something they could do for them. We collectively sympathized when Mary's on-the-job performance in the Odyssey House kitchen was found wanting. She claimed she was really Jewish and that the only thing Jewish girls were taught to make was reservations, a wisecrack that got her busted all the way back to level one. Whenever someone abreacted—outside the group sessions, of course—we would encourage her to tell the others all about it, so everyone could share it.

At some point I realized that what we were really doing was running a support group for multiples, only without much discussion of multiplicity. We provided a second-chance family, a healthy nuclear unit these multiples had never known. We were a surrogate, sane, and sympathetic father and mother.

The group ran for two years before it was doomed by the turmoil that engulfed Odyssey House, a fallout from Densen-Gerber's troubles. No one will argue that it was a therapuetic breakthrough. Still, I think of it as a success, for Toby if not the others. It made her face multiplicity squarely. After all, how can one deny that it is real when you see other people switching right in front of you and conversely when you switch in front of them? In a funny sort of way, Toby now had friends who at least knew about her multiplicity and with whom she could talk about it. That was a major change in her life. When I went on vacation she could lean on her companions in the group and on Dr. Levine and Candice.

So, in fact, could I. Arlene and Candice even met the Dark Ones, something I found quite reassuring. And I knew that if I got into trouble with this case, I had two people who could back me up.

Whether it was the effects of group therapy or simply a delayed consequence of the abreaction of the ring, Toby was now showing signs of progress. It was most vivid in her alter Becky, though at first I misread the signs. Whenever I would access Becky she seemed a little dead. I don't know how else to describe it—not dead as in deceased, but she lacked the fire she had once had. She was calmer, subdued, much less passionate, and easier to talk to. After some initial worrying, I realized that Becky might be approaching a point at which she would be ready to merge.

I had not merged personalities before, although I had spent a good bit of time thinking about the process. My theory was that Becky, along with the other twins, had been created in response to the overwhelming grief felt by Toby and her original internal personalities after Dr. Carter's death. When this grief was resolved through Becky's abreaction over the ring, it seemed logical that Becky was no longer needed. Therefore, she could return to Beth. I took Becky's calmer, more obedient demeanor as an indication of this.

But what would a merger be like? Shuffling a deck of cards? Mixing two colors of paint? Combining two electronic files on a floppy disc?

There was still one major impediment—the wall erected by the Dark Ones to separate the five original personalities from their twins. It was as if the two groups shared the same two-family house but had never met. For Beth and Becky to merge, the wall would have to be surmounted or torn down.

The wall was in fact a defense mechanism to reduce internal confusion. I was trained not to tamper with a patient's defense mechanisms until I got a signal that the patient was strong enough to do without them. So I decided to bide my time. If my hunch about Becky being ready to merge was correct, it probably wouldn't take long.

One day in a private session a few months later, Toby

complained that there was an increasing amount of noise in her head—the chatter, I realized, of other personalities. She was not yet at the point where she was fully co-conscious—that is, where she could tell what the other personalities were doing all the time—but she was getting stronger, dissociating less and hearing more. She gave numerous examples. While shopping for a dress for her niece's bat mitzvah she had to pause and excuse herself from the salesperson in a boutique on Third Avenue while she had an internal debate with her people as to what to purchase. She also told me she often had similar discussions before she could tell waiters or waitresses what she wanted to order. In the past, her personalities would sometimes independently order the different courses.

What had happened, I suspected, was that the dissociative barriers had become semipermeable as her ego grew strong enough to handle the complications due to the other people living inside of her. After a number of years of treatment with me, she was finally beginning to face her disorder. She was taking the first halting steps toward merger, toward wholeness. Now is the time, I thought. I discussed the matter with Toby and came to the conclusion that the place to start was the wall. And I knew just the right people for the job.

14

ANNATHEA

"How can the wall be removed?" I asked the Dark Ones.

"We put it up," they replied. "We can take it down."

Quickly deciding not to inquire further, I said, "Do it."

"Don't you think you should warn the others?" they advised.

It was a good point. I had forgotten that what I thought was mere metaphor was to the internal personalities solid brick. I was about to order a major demolition without even consulting them.

I asked to speak to Anna and told her what we were going to try to do. Actually, she could see the wall off at the far end of their world, a red slab covered with ivy. She and the others would sometimes go up to it and wonder what was on the other side. The mystery had been resolved when the five other alters were discovered. Trying to keep a straight face and a serious tone in my voice, I asked Anna to warn all the others to stay clear while the wall came down.

The preparatory work done, I resummoned the Dark Ones and gave them the go-ahead.

They nodded. "Excuse us," they said, as the body before me stiffened.

Toby was sitting on the couch, in the way that she normally did when I was conversing with the Dark Ones. Her eyes were closed and her body relaxed. Then I noticed some trembling and facial grimacing that went on for a while. Were they using dynamite? A wrecker's ball? A bunch of alters with sledge hammers? Her eyes opened.

"We have done what you have asked. Is there anything else you require of us?"

"How did it go?"

"You don't have to ask. If we do something, it goes well. The wall is down. There is a lot of debris that we will clean up in due time."

"How did you destroy it?"

"You do not need to know that," they answered. "All you need to know is that the wall is down. We will finish the cleanup later."

"How are the others?" I asked, finally realizing that if there was this much debris I had better tend to my patients.

"They appear to be fine, but we haven't examined them. Do you require us to do that?"

"No, I'll do it myself. But I may wish to talk to you later."

With a rather formal "good evening" they left the body.

I tried to access Anna but instead got Morgan, who was quite angry.

"My God, what happened?" she said. "There was this loud rumble, then an explosion, then there was dust all over everything. I almost got hit by flying bricks. The whole place is filthy. And there are all these strange people running around. Who are they?"

I had told all the original personalities about their twins— and vice versa—during the course of our sessions. But, as Morgan's astonishment made clear, they hadn't believed me. Now, with the wall torn down, they had no choice. If the original personalities had been created horizontally, formed by Toby one at a time in response to different traumatic episodes, these twins had been the product of a vertical split that had happened after one particularly painful event, namely the death of Dr. Carter. The original personalities each now "saw" another entity that looked exactly like them.

"What did you do?" Morgan asked. "Beth and Julia ran into a cave to hide. Anna is lying facedown on the ground, and she hasn't moved."

I explained as best I could, noting that Anna was supposed to tell them what was going to happen. Morgan said Anna had in fact spread the word, but she did not tell them it would be this frightening.

One by one I talked to my ten little Indians, who acted like they had been vacationing in Hawaii on December 7, 1941. Beth and Julia would not come out of their cave until Morgan went in to get them. All three were furious with me.

When I asked about Anna, they told me that she was still lying on the ground.

Life without the wall was posing some challenges for the twins of the original personalities as well. Becky said she was finding it hard to adjust to having more space. And who was that other little person who looked like her, Becky wondered. I suggested that she go up and say hello, which Becky did. But Beth, who was usually quite extroverted, was too timid to respond. This suprised me. I had been fairly sure Becky was ready to merge, but Beth's shyness now indicated that she still had a way to go. Probably it was because I had abreacted the trauma of Dr. Carter's death in Becky, but not in Beth. I made a mental note that I would have to make sure I abreacted the trauma in both sets of twins, since both had experienced the pain. This was the reason, I also realized, that Toby's earlier spontaneous abreactions when she first entered treatment had kept repeating, without any therapeutic dividend. I was abreacting the trauma only in Toby, not in the other personalities. It was only half an abreaction.

In contrast to Becky, Laura, Julia's twin, was thoroughly enjoying the new surroundings. She was looking forward to having more land for her flowers and trees. And Megan, Morgan's twin, was excited by the prospect of having someone her own age to play with, as was Ka, Toby's twin.

But where was Thea, Anna's twin? Like Mr. Spock, had she gotten lost in space?

I asked everyone about Thea, but no one knew what had become of her. She had been there before the "big bang," as they called the demolition of the wall, but seemed to have vanished when it came down. After more fruitless searching, I summoned the Dark Ones and asked them to search for the missing personality.

A few minutes later, they returned with startling news: Thea was now part of Anna. There had been a spontaneous integration, an instantaneous merger of the two personalities, which was why Anna was "unconscious" and Thea was nowhere to be found.

The Dark Ones told me that the work I had done for the last few months with Thea had "weakened" her. When the wall came down she was exposed to Anna's more powerful "gravitational force" and was sucked in, just like that. The shock was too much for Anna, and she passed out.

I would have preferred a more conventional end to Thea, something that involved resolving her resistance and working through her traumas, just like the textbooks say. But it was not to be, and who was I to complain? She was gone.

The problem, though, was what to do about Anna, who somehow needed to be revived. At that moment I remembered an incident that had occurred while I was at Esalen during my Christmas break from college in 1974. After some intensive group therapy, a young man from the Midwest suddenly started to remember some very painful events from his childhood. These recollections were so overwhelming that he went into what appeared to be a psychotic state. He started to hallucinate, perspire, and tremble uncontrollably, as if he were having a seizure. The other members of the group, myself included, were quite shaken. I remember thinking that if it had happened in my office I would have considered having him hospitalized. But the group leader stayed calm. She had all of us gather around in a circle and place our hands on his head, chest, arms, legs, and stomach, while she stroked his brow. In about five minutes he was back to earth.

If it worked for her, why not for me?

I told the body before me to close its eyes and go into a deeper trance. Then I spoke through her to those inside, giving them instructions one by one. I told them that Anna was very sick and needed their help. They should sit around her in a circle and touch her. I asked Morgan to stroke her head.

I waited two or three minutes—it only seemed like hours. Then Morgan took control of the body. "Anna's eyes are open," she announced. "She is trying to stand up."

The crisis had passed. Soon Anna was strong enough to come out and talk for herself.

"I feel strange," she said, "like I'm bloated. Like my skin feels too tight for my body. And I have this funny feeling in my chest and hands. What happened to me?"

I explained to her as best as I could that I was fairly certain she had experienced a spontaneous integration and that she and her twin were now one. None of us had been ready for it. "It appears that you are both Anna and Thea."

"It's so strange. I seem to be seeing double, like my eyes are two telescopes. And it's like I'm thinking separate thoughts at the same time. How is that possible?"

She looked at me, perplexed.

"I think you're feeling this way because the process is not complete," I said, thinking out loud and fairly proud of my instant analysis. "I think you are only partially integrated. We should push it the rest of the way."

I already had an idea of how.

"Anything," she said. "Anything. I feel awful."

I put her into a trance and instructed her in the visual squash method that had failed so miserably with Beth a few years before. Thea in one hand . . . Anna in the other . . . bring them together . . . then into the stomach.

"Something shifted," Anna said. "I don't know how else to describe it. It just feels like something shifted. I feel different. I don't know how to explain it, but I feel Thea inside of me. I know it makes no sense, but I am me and I am her at the same time."

She paused for a moment.

"And something else is happening to me. It's my jaw. It's tight. I can't keep from clenching it."

I guessed that the feelings released by the integration were too strong for her to experience and some mechanism was converting them into a physical symptom, the tight jaw.

"Now focus your attention on your jaw," I told her, trying to help her unclench.

"Okay."

"Now clench it tighter. That's right, tighter still. Now open it. Okay, now clench it again. That's right, keep doing it."

She clenched her jaw, opened it slowly, and slammed her teeth together a few times. Then she let out a loud "Damn."

"I'm angry," she said. "I'm so angry. It's strange. I never feel this angry. It's wrong to be angry."

"Why can't you be angry?"

"It's wrong to be angry. Her [Toby's] mother was angry, and look what happened to us. We don't want to be like her. If you do evil to stamp out evil, you are just like the evil you are trying to stamp out."

"There's a difference between feeling angry and acting angry. Do you understand that?"

"No, not really."

"Look, Anna, I allow myself the freedom to think and feel anything I want. That's my right. But I can't necessarily act on what I feel. I may have the thought when I am in a bank that I would like to steal some money, but I can only be arrested if I really steal it. I might feel like killing someone, but that's not the same as actually killing someone. Your mother's crime was that she acted on what she felt."

I could see that she was thinking about what I had said. It was important for her, therapeutically, to understand the difference and let herself feel and release her anger. Anger is a natural response to injury. In this case I believed she was feeling rage from the abuse that had been festering inside her over the years. With the merger, some anger had been activiated. Now she needed to get it out of her system.

"Her mother. That terrible person. She did this to us. I hate her. I'd like to kill her."

"Okay. Do you see this pillow on the couch?"

"Yes."

"See your mother sitting on the pillow. Can you picture that?"

"This is stupid."

"Trust me, Anna. The integration has stirred up anger that you have been carrying inside you for years. We have to release it so that you can feel better. This is just a device to help you do it."

"I never get angry. We are not supposed to get angry."

"You have a right to get angry after all that has happened to you. Come on, humor me. Talk to the pillow."

It took more coaxing, but finally she consented. She visualized her mother on the pillow and cursed her for the sins committed during childhood. Even as she was indicting her mother I noticed that her words lacked passion. There was no feeling attached to them. She was still dissociating from the emotional content of her anger. She was still too frightened to really let go.

Then I noticed that both hands were clenched. The rage was all in her fists. So I would let her fists do her talking.

"Hit the pillow," I commanded.

She looked at me like it was the stupidest thing she had ever heard.

"Just hit the pillow. First with one fist, then the other. While you are talking."

She continued to look at me as if she thought I had gone off my rocker.

"Don't think about it, Anna. Just do it."

Methodically, like a drummer on a galley beating out the

time for the slaves with the oars, she started to hit the pillow, slowly at first—left fist, right fist, left fist, right fist—talking to the pillow all the time. Then the pace accelerated, her voice rose, and calm, controlled, intellectual Anna started to get good and angry, at long last.

"I hate you . . . I hate you!" she said as she slammed away.

I decided to charge her up even more, so we could get it all out.

"Hit her harder," I shouted, raising my voice. "She deserves it. She deserves it for the scalding. She deserves it for the stabbing. She deserves it for the beatings. Hit her again . . . again . . . again . . . again."

I was yelling now, my voice as angry as I could make it, trying to show her how to be angry and timing my instructions to correspond to her rhythm as she punched.

Her ferocity kept climbing. She slammed the pillow. I shouted. She shouted. She slammed it again. The sweat ran down her face. Her eyes flashed. It was wonderful.

After I don't know how long, she started to lose strength, and soon her hands were flailing weakly. She was worn out. After a few more moments she collapsed facedown on the pillow, exhausted, sobbing.

"Mommy. I hate you. I hate you. I hate you."

She paused.

"I love you."

The last sentence was very soft, almost a whisper. I knew it was over.

She sobbed a few more minutes, her face in the pillow. Then she lifted her head and looked at me.

"I think I need a new name," she said. "What do you think of Annathea?"

15

Merger

"I'm depressed and unhappy. It's hopeless. I keep coming in here, week after week, year after year, taking my turn like a good girl, talking to you with the hope that something will change. I talk and talk, but nothing changes. You are no help to me. I'm unhappy most of the time—I'm miserable. I can't even remember when I was happy last. There's no point in continuing this—I have to get away. I've tried to stay here and work things out, but it's no use. So I am going now. There's nothing else for me to do. Even if there was, I have no energy to do it. I just lie around all day, thinking about how awful my life is. Everything is. There's no one of my intellect to talk to anymore. Anyway, the others have each other and don't need me anymore. I've thought it all over, and it's never going to get any better. It's really hopeless."

Annathea was complaining, as usual. In the six months since Anna had been integrated with her twin, she had spent almost all of her therapeutic time complaining. I was getting tired of it. I was having a hard time remembering that an adult's complaining is the way an adult cries.

"I thought you liked having nothing to do so you could just think. You told me a long time ago that you were so busy you couldn't find enough time to think, and that you had so many things to think through."

"I've had the time. I've thought them through. Suddenly, it's all very simple. I understand everything now."

"You understand everything?"

"Sure. What's at the end of outer space?"

"I don't know."

"No one knows. That's the answer to all my questions about life and the universe. No one knows. So there really isn't any point in thinking about any of that anymore. I chose some system that would make me feel more comfortable. I chose God. I trust in God and have decided to devote my life to him. Someday, I'll enter a convent."

"Come, on, Annathea," I said, thinking to myself how much Anna dominated the new, fused personality. "You're a reasonable, logical, intelligent person. You know this is impossible. What would happen to the others if you went into a convent? You know what I think? I think you are just throwing a pity party for yourself."

She glared at me and said she didn't care about the others. She knew I was right—and she knew I knew she knew—but she wouldn't be budged from her self-sorrow.

"What am I to do? The others don't need me anymore. Toby reads stories to Beth when you are away. Beth plays with Becky, so she doesn't need me to take care of her. I have no job and nothing to do. I always thought that when that happened I would be able to enter the convent. But I guess you're right, I can't. I'll never be able to. God would never accept me. Maybe that's why I am so miserable, I have been secretly cursing God for my fate. He will punish me. I just want to die."

"What about your soul?" I asked, trying to instill a little religious guilt that might act as a brake if she indeed tried to commit suicide—and thus kill everybody. "I thought you were a Catholic. As I understand that religion, killing yourself is a mortal sin. Baptized or not, your soul goes to hell."

She just stared at me again. She knew that I was right. But she was still stuck. With her back against the wall, there was nothing she could do but attack me. It was all my fault. I had made her problems worse. There used to be four people inside. Now there were eight, which made it more crowded, more confusing, and more noisy. My therapy had made things worse, not better, and she was sorry that she had ever talked to me.

We had been going around and around like this for weeks. I had tried everything I could think of—arguing, reasoning, cajoling, kidding—but nothing helped. What was making things even worse was that her hopelessness was contagious. Even I was beginning to feel it. I had to keep reminding myself that I was simply feeling what she was feeling. Still, if these induced feelings, as they call them in analytic school, were an accurate measure, Annathea was very depressed.

Clearly, she had reason to be. The arrival of the twins had given the other alters new friends to play with, so they did not need Annathea as much. And now that the alter Thea had spontaneously merged with Anna, she did not have a twin of her own to talk to or share her feelings with. On top of that, I had been gradually convincing Toby to take over more and more of Annathea's functions, such as reading Beth stories and making decisions for the group. These were the sort of things Annathea used to do, and they had acted like a psychological aspirin that eased the depression she had suffered all her life. One of the functions of the Annathea personality, as I understood it, was to be the repository of depressed, hopeless feelings. Anna avoided feelings by managing the others' lives and, when she had any time left over, by endless philosophical rumination. When the former was taken away, the depression blossomed. It was like "weekend neurosis," a malady that strikes when its victims have a block of free time and nothing to do.

Depressives have the knack for twisting everything you say to them, negating any positive suggestion and proving conclusively that everything is hopeless. I knew the case was going well, yet Annathea was so convinced that it wasn't that she was making me feel defeated. At times like these the advice of my old supervisor, Arnold, was particularly valuable. Don't fight resistance, he used to teach. Join it, go with it, lead it, and thus change it.

"Look," I said to Annathea, "you're probably right. It might be hopeless. The more we work, the more we are successful, the less you have to do. I can see your point. I can understand why you might contemplate killing yourself."

I paused for a moment, watching her relax. She liked being agreed with. I had thrown her off her track. It was time to press the advantage.

"But how can you kill yourself without killing the others? If one dies, you all die. Then you would be a murderer."

I paused to let it sink in.

"Look, if you're really intent on killing yourself, I have another idea: Why not just merge with Toby? At least then you wouldn't be murdering the others. And besides, your death would have meaning."

"What meaning?"

"By merging with Toby, you would give her all of your knowledge, experiences, and strength. That will make it much easier for her to get over her problems. Think of it, your knowledge merged with Toby's—what a combination."

Although she and her twin had spontaneously merged, Annathea, like all the other personalities, was extemely resistant to the concept of integration. To them, merger equaled death, and none of them—not even Annathea for all her talk, really—wanted to die. The other personalities would constantly point out that Thea was no more. I argued that she was part of Anna, but to them the Thea in Annathea was more of a myth, since they could not see or talk to Thea anymore. Even Anna, though she could sense Thea inside her, felt that Thea was but a minor component of her personality. I was, more often than I liked, accused by all of them of homicide.

In a sense, they were right. Merger was a death of sorts. The individuality of each personality definitely was lost. But the personality did not die. Red and blue make purple. Of course, when you look at something purple, you no longer see blue or red, yet in a sense the colors are still there.

I would argue that the advantages of merger far outweighed the disadvantages of maintaining their autonomy. Instead of being consigned to the internal world most of the time, they would all be outside, in reality, in a position to partake of life's pleasures. However, some of the personalities responded that they felt safe inside and did not have to confront life's displeasures. Although under the current system they did not have free or equal access to time outside, it was a small price to pay for safety. I was asking them to give up some of their individual freedom for the greater good of having a unified group.

I tried one more time with Annathea. She said she wanted to die, that much was clear. But if merger was death, why not merge instead? The logic was irrefutable. All I had to do was put her into what seemed an inescapable double bind. Then, if she still didn't agree to merge, she would have to recognize that her wish to die was in fact just more of her complaining and a continuation of her pity party. Once she recognized that, she would have to give it up and start working therapeutically again. So she had two options, work to get better or merge. Either way, I would win—and so, of course, would she, though she still did not see it that way.

"What about my soul?" Annathea said, trying to wriggle off the hook of my logic.

"Your soul?"

"Yes, my soul. Let's assume you're right. Since I want to die anyway, I might as well merge. But what happens to my soul when I die? I'm a Catholic, and before I die I need to receive the last rites of the church. But to receive the last rites I have to be baptized, which I never was. I want to be baptized, I want to finally be a legitimate, baptized Catholic. After that, I will die, or, to use your term, merge."

I had not anticipated this problem. How was I to get her baptized? I could just see myself walking into St. Patrick's

Cathedral and asking for a priest. "Good afternoon, Father. I am Dr. Robert Mayer, psychotherapist. Let me introduce you to my patient, Annathea. She is an alter personality of Toby, who suffers from multiple personality disorder. Now Annathea is an unbaptized Catholic who is about ready to merge with a host personality. But before she does, she wants to be baptized so she can receive extreme unction. She views merger as death and is concerned about her soul. She does not want to die without receiving the last rites of the Church. However, there is one small problem, your eminence. The host personality, Toby, is Jewish, as are all the other internal personalities. They do not want to be baptized because they feel it is against their religion. Can you be of any help to us?"

It may seem funny, but it wasn't to Annathea. The problem had to be solved, or the case would stay stuck. If each of a multiple personality's personalities has a separate soul, then it might be possible to merge the personalities only and not the souls. But perhaps a multiple has one soul that has split and would also be merged. If that was the case and Annathea was baptized, would her Catholic soul merge with Toby's Jewish soul, or would it create a religious conflict?

Fortunately, I remembered that one of my classmates in analytic school was an ordained Catholic priest who was studying psychotherapy to help him with pastoral counseling. We had shared some classes and had occasionally talked over coffee. I hadn't seen him in years, but we had once been quite friendly. I phoned him and explained the situation, hoping he would take me seriously.

There was a long silence on the other end. Finally, he said that he did not know the answers, nor did he have the authority to come up with them on his own. He would have to talk to his superior, the bishop.

About a week later he got back to me. The bishop, it turned out, did not know the answers either and had to talk to his superior. It was the same story with the archbishop, who was writing to Rome. My friend felt that it might take years for a reply (though his off-the-record opinion was that a baptism would cover the entire body, not just one personality). As for whether a multiple had one soul or several, it would take awhile for that to be determined as well.

I couldn't afford to wait, and neither could my patient. But until there was a ruling I was afraid there was no way Toby, a nonpracticing Jew who nonetheless felt strongly about her religious heritage, would let herself be taken into the bosom of the Church. Thus I could not grant Annathea's request, even though I feared that not doing so would actually make a complete merger impossible.

I phoned my friend the priest and asked him whether, as a personal favor, he could just sprinkle some holy water over Annathea and let it go at that. He got upset—as I probably should have expected—although he did allow that this was an extraordinary circumstance and that, in his view, God would understand and love Annathea even if she weren't baptized. Well then, I said, taking a slightly different tack, couldn't he just tell this to Annathea? Fortunately, he agreed. I gave her his phone number, and she immediately arranged an appointment.

Two weeks later, Annathea came to my office in an upbeat mood. Her spiritual conference had gone well. "He said he was sure that God would understand and love me anyway," she reported. "I feel better. Now I'm willing to be merged with Toby."

I asked her to fill me in on the details of her conversation with the priest, trying to stretch the discussion until the session was over. In truth, although Annathea was ready for merger, I was not. I had spent so much time thinking about how to overcome the religious hurdle that I had neglected to consider exactly how the integration would be accomplished. I needed time to think about it. My only other experience with merging had been with Thea, and that had happened automatically, or at least without my participation.

Actually, I shouldn't have been concerned. Once again my

patient, Annathea, took the lead, reporting the following dream fragment at her next session: "I was walking along the edge of a pit. It was narrow and dangerous, sort of like walking on the edge of a curb, trying to keep your balance and not fall into the street, only this was much higher. You couldn't see the bottom of the pit. I had to be very careful because I thought I might fall in. It was very hard to keep my balance. At one point, I started to fall, and then I woke up."

That was all there was, but that was the point to her dream. I didn't know exactly how to bring about the merger, but I was fairly certain it would be a lengthy process. Now Annathea had made the decision, and that, she seemed to be saying, was that. She told me she was feeling weary, with very little energy. In fact, she didn't want to talk anymore because she was so exhausted. All she wanted to do then was to go back inside. The next-to-last words she said to me were to tell Beth that she was sorry that she had to abandon her. With her last words, she thanked me for all that I had done for her and said good-bye.

I felt all this was a little premature, not to mention overly dramatic. But when the next session came and I asked to talk to Annathea, Morgan came out instead.

"What happened to Annathea?" she asked me. "She came inside after the last session, lay down on the ground in the midst of a grove of birch trees, and has been there ever since. She won't talk to anyone, she's not even moving, she just lies there like a rag doll. We've all gone over and tried to rouse her, but she won't say anything. She just lies there. What did you do to her?"

I tried as best I could to explain that Annathea was in the process of merging, but Morgan was convinced that she was dying, if she wasn't dead already. Nothing I did could allay her fears or the fears of all the others. But although everybody was quite convinced that I was killing Annathea, they didn't seem angry about it. Rather, they just seemed sad, and I noticed that I was feeling that way, too. I felt like I was losing someone as well.

Although she was now officially both Anna and Thea, I still related to her as Anna, since I had never really gotten to know Thea and since Anna's traits seemed to dominate the combined personality. Anna and I had come a long way together. Although she was a complainer and whiner, she had a fine mind and I enjoyed talking to her. More than that, she was also extremely helpful to me. She was my main contact and had introduced me to all the other alters. She had read to Beth when I was away, controlled Becky's shoplifting, stopped Toby's suicide attempts, and always found the Dark Ones when they were needed. She was a force for order, stability, and logic, inside as well as outside. I had hoped that she would be the last to merge—although I had to admit this might be more a reflection of my own needs than my patient's.

At the next session, Toby told me that Annathea was still lying on the ground, with the others standing around her as if on a death watch. Toby, whose turn it was for therapy, told me her latest dream: She was walking down a street in a city reminiscent of New York, when it started to rain. She hurried home to her apartment in a red brick building. Once inside she looked out the window and saw that the rain was getting heavier and heavier. Then she noticed that the apartment was starting to leak. Water was seeping through the walls and the ceiling. She frantically ran around with buckets trying to catch the water but could not keep up with it. Then she tried to dry the plaster walls with rags, but it was like going up a down escalator. Then she just gave up and sat down in a chair and watched as the rain dissolved the walls around her. She awoke feeling very frightened.

Amazing. Walls were literally dissolving. As she approached integration, she seemed to be running out of energy. She said she was beginning to have real difficulty in getting to her office and paying attention to her work. If Toby couldn't earn a paycheck, who would? Beth? Morgan? I asked myself.

Although the previous merger had been more or less spontaneous, I decided that in this instance I would intervene to hasten the process. First I put Toby into a trance. Then I sent her inside and put Annathea into a trance. "Okay, both of you. Just relax and listen to me as I talk.

"Toby. You are lying on your back at the bottom of a pit. It is not a bad pit, it is a nice comfortable pit. Think of the dream you told me about the rain and the apartment walls dissolving. See the walls dissolving. Watch yourself try to stop them from dissolving. It is very hard. Let yourself think that you don't have to stop it, let it happen, go with it. Watch your walls dissolving, they are getting wet, little by little, they are dissolving, like the waves on the shore that lap up and dissolve a sand castle, the walls are going, going, going.

"Annathea, see yourself walking along the edge of the pit that you have been dreaming about. You are trying to keep your balance. Notice how difficult it is to keep your balance. It is getting more and more difficult. Stop for a moment and look down into the pit. At the bottom you will see Toby. She is waiting to catch you. You will not hurt yourself because Toby will catch you. It is safe. That's right. Let yourself fall toward Toby. Float down gently like you have a parachute on. That's it, feel yourself floating down. Easy. Slowly. Gently. Down, down, down.

"At the bottom of the pit is Toby. Look at her. You can see her more clearly now. Her arms are open. She is waiting for you. She is waiting to receive you. Let yourself go.

"Toby. Look up and see Annathea. She is floating toward you. You feel happy. Your companion is coming down toward you. Open your arms to receive her. Feel her with you. Put your arms around her.

"Now both of you, hug each other. Think of the rain forming little streams, the little streams run down the mountain and become bigger streams. They merge with other streams and become rivers, the rivers merge with other rivers and run out to the sea, where they become part of the ocean. That's right. Just let it happen."

I noticed that the body before me had become very still. I let it rest a few moments, then brought Morgan out.

"Geez. What happened? We were all sitting around Annathea, holding her hand and putting cold washcloths on her brow, when she just disappeared. Poof. Just like that she was gone. What happened? Where did she go? Did she die?"

"No," I said. "She has merged with Toby. She went outside to be with Toby. There is nothing to worry about."

"Where is she?"

"She is with Toby."

"Where is Toby?"

"Outside."

"She can't be outside. I'm outside."

Good point, I thought.

"I guess she went to the place where Toby usually goes when she is inside. You know, her secret garden. Look, both Toby and Annathea are tired, and you will have to take the body home. Can you do that?"

"I guess so."

"Do you know how to get home?"

"What, do you think I'm stupid?"

"Sorry." I said. "Now go right home—no stopping or partying."

"Can I stay out and watch the Mets on television tonight?"

"It's okay with me. But perhaps you had better check with the others to make sure none of them wants some time out tonight."

Completing the process of integration took us about a week. For the first couple of days the merged personality was quite ill—she couldn't go to work or even talk to me during our sessions. Morgan called in sick for her and brought the body in for therapy. I used the hour to check in with the remaining alters and reassure them. Their structure and routine had changed, and they were all frightened. Losing Annathea, who had been the eldest, was for them almost like having a parent die. Beth was particularly inconsolable. Deep down I think even she sensed that the process now under way was not about to stop. The remaining personalities faced an unappealing choice: They could either merge—or "die," as they still thought of it—or watch all the others merge and risk being the last one left—which, given their fear of abandonment, probably seemed a worse fate.

After about a week, the "new" person brought herself into my office. Tobyannathea was a mouthful, so I decided simply to call her Toby. She had barely settled onto the couch before crying out in anger, first at me and then at her mother. And then, just as suddenly, she calmed down. Her major complaint, like Anna when she merged with Thea, involved her eyes. Like a pair of binoculars slowly being adjusted, they were only beginning to come into focus. When the process was over, she would need a new prescription.

Morgan and Megan were the next two alters to merge. In this case, however, a bout with measles led to the integration. First Megan relived the episode, which had occurred when she was ten and made her feel as though she were about to die. Realizing that she had endured only half of the trauma, in the next session I abreacted the rest of the episode with Morgan. Then, at the next session, Megan reported a dream in which a huge black creature was running after her. When she looked back at it, she said, she saw it had no face, only a big black hole that seemed like it was about to engulf her. I couldn't have written a better dream.

As I had with Toby and Annathea, I put both twins into a trance and had Megan reexperience her dream, but with a difference: This time, I gave her the suggestion that the big black creature was Morgan, and I instructed her to let it engulf her. Meanwhile, I told Morgan that she was running after Megan. To make sure they were together, I used my reinforcement from before—having them visualize a trickle of water coming down a mountain, joining other streams of water to make a river that joined other rivers and eventually ran to the sea.

The new, improved Morgan, like my last merged alter, was quite ill for about a week, during which time she rested inside. As before, the other personalities were concerned about the strange goings-on, so I spent the next few sessions calming them. Also as before, Morgan emerged from the integration with her twin in an angry mood, which was directed first at me and then at her mother.

After the merger there was a period of calm, and I was able to reestablish a normal therapeutic schedule with the remaining unmerged personalities—Julia, Laura, Beth, Becky, and Ka. I would try to ease their fears that they, too, would "die," waiting until one of them gave me a signal that another act in this drama was about to occur.

As it turned out, the next merger was that of Toby and her twin, Ka. I didn't know Ka very well, but she had told me about her role. Toby's mother had been so domineering that Toby hadn't developed much of a sense of self. She was what my profession used to call an "as if" personality. She would assume whatever role she thought the people around her wanted her to assume. To compensate, she had birthed a personality she called Ka, which is ancient Egyptian for "soul," to fulfill her feelings of independence and sovereignty. Ka described the episode that had led to her creation during a session in my office:

"I am at the dinner table and that woman served me applesauce. She knows I don't like applesauce. She served it to me to torture me. I'm not going to eat it. She yells at me. She knows I don't like it, and she yells a lot. I am mad and yell back, 'You don't own me, I hate you. You can't make me do anything. Hit me and I will show you.' I shouldn't have done that. She is bigger than me. I don't care—let her hit me—I won't cry. She goes to the drawer and takes out a wooden spoon. I get up from the table and try to run away from her. She gets up and runs after me. She is bigger, and I can't escape her. She catches me and starts hitting me on the arm. She holds me and hits me. It hurts! I hate her. But I am not going to let her control me.

"Next thing I know she brings me to the basement. It's dark there. All the way down the stairs she keeps hitting me. I sit down on the stairs and tell myself, 'Don't make any noise. If you cry, the thing in the furnace with the scary red eyes will come and eat you up. It will hear you if you make any noise.' Then she turns off the light and shut the door. That makes it even darker. I have to be quiet. I am my own person, she does not own me, my name is Ka. I am my own person. I have to be quiet. My arm hurts bad where she hit me."

As the abreaction reached its climax, the release of all the feelings and experiences allowed Ka to merge with Toby. As in past integrations, Toby became ill and Morgan, now strengthened with the addition of Megan, took charge of the body, a task she relished. When I checked in with Toby from time to time during the week, she again reported that she was seeing —and thinking—double. She had to change her eyeglass prescription one more time. (I figured by the time I was done integrating her she would have a drawerful of useless glasses to remind her of the ordeal.)

While all this was going on, Beth was increasingly miserable. So I took advantage of her misery to abreact the sadness of Dr. Carter's death and merge her with Becky, who had been ready, willing, and able to integrate with her twin for months. However, the new personality, which I continued to call Beth, was still miserable. She missed Annathea terribly, and my time with her during our sessions was largely spent listening to tearful recollections of her lost friend. She didn't even want me to read to her. Nothing I said seemed to help. She was convinced that Anna was dead. I tried to explain to this five-year-old that Anna was with Thea and Toby, but Beth just could not grasp the concept.

About this time I realized that I was being stupid. Why was I trying to console Beth? If I were to resolve her grief and make her happy, she would have no motivation to change. Why not use the grief to elicit a change? At the next session, I gave it a try. I brought Beth out and suggested that if she really missed Annathea so much maybe she could go to her and be with her.

I could see that it appealed to her. But how, she asked, could she do this? I told her all she had to do was trust me and do what I told her. I would bring Anna to her. Rather than wait for a dream or an abreaction to pave the way, I decided to make the most of this unexpected opportunity and manipulate a merger. I accessed the Dark Ones and asked them about the trauma that first had caused Toby to produce Beth.

They paused, looking through her cerebral "files," then reported the following story: "Toby was quite young, playing on the kitchen floor, and, for apparently no reason, her mother scalded her with boiling water. She called for Anna to come and take the pain, but Anna refused. So she had to create Beth. After that, Beth would be a companion when Toby was sent to the cellar for punishment."

I couldn't get much more out of the Dark Ones, but I decided it really didn't matter. I felt that I could start the abreaction and fill in the blanks as it went on. At least I knew what to look for. I also knew by now that the trauma was contained in both personalities and had to be abreacted in both personalities. I started with Toby. I explained what we were going to do and got her agreement. Then I hypnotized her and took her back in time. It took a few minutes, but finally I saw her expression and posture change.

I asked her where she was.

She replied that she was in the kitchen, on the floor. Then she started to whimper.

"What's happening, Toby?"

"I am a little baby, playing on the floor. It is black and white . . . pretty floor . . . Mommy is big. I look up at her. She makes sounds at me—I don't know what they mean. I make sounds back." Then a pause. "It hurts! There was a loud sound, then it hurts, it hurts too much, and then she comes to be my friend"—this is where Beth was born—"and that made it hurt less. She took away some of the hurt. She just was my friend, and it didn't hurt as much. She understands my sounds."

"What are the sounds?" I asked her.

"Ma. Beh. Mil." I assumed this child was trying to say mother, baby, and milk. Beth, the new personality, could understand Toby, since she was the same age. Beth told me later she had stopped growing when she was five—the age when Toby was raped—as a way of avoiding "that dirty thing," which was what she called sex.

"Does your new friend have a name?" I asked.

"I don't know."

"Keep making the sounds."

She did. It sounded to me like baby talk. She suddenly let out a scream and her memory went blank. I figured the rest of the memory of the grotesque incident would reside in Beth.

I let Toby go back inside with instructions to simply rest in the trance and called Beth out. I then hypnotized her and brought her back to the same afternoon, the same kitchen floor. As I suspected, it was Beth's earliest memory.

I told her to just report the scalding without any feelings, which can sometimes be done in a hypnotic state. I needed the data for the abreaction. Again I heard about the same grisly scene on the black and white tile floor.

"Why did you go out of the gate?" I said, referring to the exit from Toby's insulated internal world.

"To be with her, to talk to the other baby."

"Did it hurt when you went out?"

"Yes, there was terrible pain in my arms and back."

"Did you cry?"

"Not at first, but then, yes, I screamed."

"Did anyone help try to ease the pain?"

"Yes, the big lady put cold water on it. I went up high in the sky. It got cold and then it got black again. Then there was this fuzzy thing all over my face."

That made sense. The fuzzy thing was probably gauze.

Someone had tended to her burns—it could have been her sister or a doctor or even her mother, it really didn't matter. What did matter was the trauma that had caused the creation of another personality.

Having gotten the details made my work simpler. I just kept them in a trance and told them to experience the episode again, but this time with more feelings. I accentuated and amplified the awful details, trying to make sure that I had wrung out every last drop of emotion. I had them endure the pain, cry and scream. It always upset me when I did this, but I knew of no other way. I once read an autobiography of a surgeon who used to apologize to the worlds within worlds when he cut into tissue. That was how I felt. I could almost feel the pain myself. Performing these abreactions also made me angry. How could anyone intentionally scald a small child? That was a mystery I have never understood. I would have given anything to have a talk with this monster of a mother.

The session was draining for all of us. I gave each of them posthypnotic instructions to go into a trance when they got home and rest throughout the night. As usual, Morgan took care of the body and enjoyed her additional time out.

I always scheduled Toby at the end of my day so I would not have to face another patient. After her first painful abreactions I had taken walks or gone to my health club. But now I had built up calluses. Even to scalding hot water.

The abreaction must have worked, because at our next session Toby told me a dream that indicated she was ready to integrate with Beth. In her dream, she was walking up to a house, looked in the window, and saw another person inside. She realized that there was someone in the house who did not belong there.

I quickly accessed Beth, who also had a dream to tell me: "I am in a place, in a house. There are lights all over the place, but I am by myself and I am afraid. I need to find somebody."

What a cooperative patient Toby had become, I thought. Quite different from the beginning. Instead of resisting, she was helping me, to the point of providing the symbolism with which I could bring about the integration process.

I went through the usual drill. Hypnotic trance . . . put Beth in the house . . . took Toby to the house . . . walked her inside . . . had her look at Beth . . . hug her . . . take her by the hand . . . and walk out of the house.

I felt empty. I could not resist asking my still hypnotized patient to raise an index finger if Beth was indeed with Toby. Sure enough, her finger rose. Then I noticed the fingers on her other hand were quivering. Is that you, Anna? The index finger on the right hand rose. Is that you, Ka? The index finger on her left hand rose. I assumed the others were in there, too. I felt better—and more than a little astonished.

The game of musical chairs continued as Laura merged with her twin, Julia. That left only Julia, Morgan, and of course Toby. My position was that either of them could be integrated into Toby in any order. It was up to them.

Actually, I knew that it would happen quickly. Neither wanted to be left alone inside.

Morgan, the bravest, was the first to go. It was easy for both of us. She had no traumas to work through. There was no bloodcurdling abreaction. She was a functional personality. Once a person has the machinery to create alters, he or she can then create them to handle not only trauma but also tasks the host personality cannot perform. Convivial Morgan was Toby's sociable side. She was created to have fun, to be happy, to go to parties, which Toby especially dreaded. But after all the mergers Toby was now stronger and braver and able to be somewhat sociable on her own. I attributed that to my multiples group, which had taught her how to interact more comfortably with people. Now she no longer needed Morgan.

A simple ceremony and poof, another finger wiggled. Even the recovery period was shorter than usual, about three days.

———

Julia's integration was another story. She was quite timid, to say the least. Brave for Julia would be to let me escort her from my office to my living room to look at my plants. But she was in a bind—she my have been frightened to merge, but she was also frightened to be alone. I tried to calm her fears about life outside. I even had Toby write her a letter telling her how wonderful it was. Julia preferred the safety of her internal world, but in the end her loneliness was too much. After about a month she finally said to me, "I think I'm ready."

I learned from the Dark Ones that Toby had been a weak, sickly child, who had suffered from asthma and numerous allergies. Nevertheless, her mother had required her to do the gardening, including mowing the lawn and tending to the rosebushes—chores for which her new alter ego, Julia, who was remarkably free of allergies, had been created to do. Julia also had tremendous stamina, so she could work for long periods in the heat of a midsummer's day.

One day, while she was tending the roses, a swarm of bees descended on Julia and started stinging her. She ran, screaming, toward the house, but her mother, who was standing by the door, slammed it in her face and locked it, allowing the bees to engulf her daughter.

After abreacting this incident, Julia was totally drained. She lay on my couch barely moving, able to breathe only in short bursts.

"Am I dying?"

"No, Julia, you are reliving all of that pain and the fact that you are going to join Beth, Becky, Anna, Thea, Morgan, Megan, Ka, and Toby."

It was like talking Turkish to an Armenian.

"I'm dying," Julia said. "Please, hold my hand."

I moved my chair close to the couch and took her hand in mine. She held it tightly.

"I want to thank you for all that you have done for us," she said weakly. "I know that it was hard . . . that we were difficult and you didn't get paid a lot for it. I am sorry we caused you so much trouble."

"Don't be silly," I said. "Just rest."

"How are your plants?"

She often asked about my house plants and gave me suggestions on how to care for them. Her favorite was an aloe, which she claimed had medicinal qualities. You could break off a leaf, squeeze out the oil, and use it to heal certain skin ailments.

"They are doing fine. Would you like to see them?"

"Yes, but I don't think I can make it." Then she paused. "I just want you to know before I die that I love you."

I felt my chest tighten and my eyes start to water. We sat there for a while, Julia breathing slowly on the couch, me sitting beside her, holding her hand. Neither one of us talked. My mind was filled with mournful images from my past. My grandmother's coffin. My grandfather's coffin. My Aunt Hilda's coffin. My Aunt Rose's coffin. My Aunt Mary's coffin. My father's coffin. Shoveling the dirt onto his grave. The sickness and sadness and death of people that I loved. I wanted to forget, to dissociate, but I knew that I had to stay there for Julia, waiting for her to talk again, cursing a profession that forces you to dredge up thoughts that people would prefer to leave buried.

When Julia spoke again, her voice was barely audible. "I don't want to suffer anymore. Please help me die. Do me that one last favor, okay?"

"Okay," I said. "Go back inside. Bring Toby out, and I will do what you asked."

Julia said good-bye, and I felt her hand go limp. Toby was now in charge of the body, although it was still inert. I told her to visualize Julia in her left hand and herself in her right hand. Then I asked her to bring her two hands together and press them into her stomach. I felt the tears on my cheeks.

"Julia, if you are there wiggle the left pinky on Toby's hand."

The finger wiggled.

I breathed deeply, for what seemed like the first time in hours. The last little Indian had merged.

As Fritz Perls said: "To suffer one's death and to be reborn is not easy."

16

One Patient Indivisible

 My patient Lauren's case paralleled Toby's in form if not content. She had an initial period of resistance, then a turning point after which the quality of our sessions changed. While Toby constantly demanded that I nourish her pain away, Lauren always seemed to be enmeshed in a crisis. It shifted her attention from the proper focus of our therapy—her childhood traumas, her multiplicity, and her guilt over the damage that might have been done to her child while she neglected her. Thinking about and trying to solve these external dilemmas threatened to become her new addiction, replacing cocaine and heroin and clicking in whenever her therapy got too tough.

But like Toby, Lauren passed through this rough period and was now starting the process of integration. There were three reasons the case turned around. Like Toby, Lauren needed time to discard preconceived notions of how I was supposed to behave and to learn to trust me. The second reason was her mothering instinct, which was finally released after she quit drugs and saw clearly the jeopardy they had put her daughter in. She had allowed her to be abused by her husband, and her clear, drug-free knowledge of this was a powerful motivation for her to continue therapy. The third reason for her improvement was the therapy itself. The regularity of our sessions gave her stability and strength. The fact that someone was trying to help rather than hurt her was healing.

Once they began to cooperate with me, both women were propelled by the classical clinical procedure of abreaction. Like countless others, they had proved Freud right. At the end of the last century, he realized that unhappy incidents buried in the memory would fester and create symptoms. "We must presume rather that the psychical trauma—or more precisely the memory of the trauma—acts like a foreign body which long after its entry must continue to be regarded as an agent that is still at work," he wrote. Later on, he boiled down his new theory into five telling words: "Hysterics suffer mainly from reminiscences."

But it was after they both began abreacting that the similarities between the two patients ceased. Toby resolved her traumas and gradually merged her alters into the original personality who had first come into my office. As this happened, she became stronger, more self-assured, more creative, and more energetic. It was wonderful to watch her new, true self emerge, especially since, to her great surprise, she had lost no one in the transition. No alter had to die. Toby simply grew into a fully developed, emotionally mature individual, able to experience all of her former personalities as we experience all the various aspects of our own personalities. After she integrated, she had a dream that she was a perfectly formed crystal with many facets. Thanks to Beth, she now enjoyed playing with children in the park. Thanks to Morgan, she followed the Mets. Thanks to Julia, she could accept and give love. Thanks to Ka, she felt a sense of autonomy.

Lauren was slightly behind Toby but probably driven by her progress. Lauren watched her in my multiplicity group, and there was a healthy competition between them. She abreacted the trauma of having to clean her father the killer's bloody clothes. She abreacted the fear that she was going to be turned over to dark, sinister people to pay for her father's indiscretions. It all seemed to be going smoothly.

Then Lauren abreacted an early anal rape by her father—and his brother—and in the process we uncovered a number of new personalities or, more accurately, fragments of personalities. Some were named L1, L2, L3, L4, L5; others began with Lo, Lor, and Lori and were also numbered. There also was an assortment of twenty-some La's. I started to lose count after about fifty. These personality fragments were of various ages, and each seemed to contain the memory and pain from a single traumatic event. It was a different filing system than Toby had used, with major events in the major personalities and the smaller ones in the fragments. The bits of personalities were not as fully rounded as her main alters, since they had not been "out" in the world enough to develop.

Upon investigation, I found that the fragments were Lauren's convoluted way of preserving her love for her father. By creating a fragment for each incident, Lauren was able to keep the dreadful experiences separate, not letting herself or any part of her know just how many times she had been raped. If she had, her anger would certainly have overflowed and she would have had to hate her father. She couldn't let that happen, though, because she needed her father to protect her from her mother, who also physically and psychologically abused her. So her father would be a rapist one day and a loving parent the next.

From a therapeutic standpoint, the fragments were much easier to deal with than the fully formed personalities. Each was simply a container of pain. Abreact the trauma, and the container was drained. It was just a matter of time.

I was encouraged. Mergers were occurring. True, the major personalities were not yet coalescing, but that didn't bother me. The fragments had to go first, and one by one they went. Moreover, Lauren was getting glowing reports at Odyssey House, where she had reached the top—level four. This is the stage at which residents are encouraged to get jobs and meet people outside the therapeutic community. In that way they begin to wean themselves from Odyssey House.

This is harder than it sounds. Because of the stress and anxiety of facing the world straight, many level fours leave the program just before graduation and go back to drugs. Others break rules and are busted to a lower level, thus delaying their moment of truth. Some find a way to postpone separation permanently by getting a job with the program. Odyssey House is hardly a pleasant place, but it is safe and secure, emotionally and physically. It set out to be—and mostly was—a moral, honest, and open community. Everyone knew the rules, and if anyone, resident or staff, violated them, he or she would be confronted in a prescribed, formal manner—and tried by a jury of peers. It was an attempt to create a perfect family and thereby to "reparent" the residents. It was quite a contrast to a world that is often terrifying and sometimes downright demonic.

Like many other level fours, Lauren had difficulty meeting outsiders. She eventually started to date after encouragement from the Odyssey House staff and me. We wanted Lauren to confront her fears because in so doing she would see that she could succeed—and thus would be encouraged to confront additional fears. We were all happy at her progress and congratulated ourselves on our therapeutic skills.

Unfortunately, we all underestimated how frightened she really was. Our expectations for Lauren were too high, given her history and the fact that she had a child to care for with no money or skills—well, no skills that we could advise her to turn into money. After three dates with three different men, Lauren fell in love with the fourth. He was a newly divorced electrician from West Virginia who had custody of a seven-year-old son and had just moved to New Jersey to find work.

A few weeks after they met at a club in New Jersey where she was tending bar, she announced to the staff that she was going to move out of Odyssey House and move in with him. Dating was one thing, but this was another. I talked about the dangers of getting so deeply involved so quickly. I told her that she needed time to adjust to life outside Odyssey House before she could begin the adjustment of living with someone. I also told her that I was worried he might only be interested in her because he needed a mother for his child. Basically, I tried everything I knew to discourage her. The staffers at Eighteenth Street tried their best, too. They put Lauren in a confrontation group of her peers, who tried reasoning with her and, when that didn't work, progressed to screams and threats. Their logic was hardly a match for her love, her insecurity, and her loneliness. I knew it was a lost cause. Lauren would not be deterred. At the end of the confrontation, she announced that her mind was made up and she was moving out. Spring had come after a long, hard winter, and she was in love. Her new beau promised her security, companionship, and a steady paycheck. She would even have the money to complete her therapy.

Unfortunately, it didn't work out that way. Lauren moved to New Jersey, but with her daughter and his son and the new marriage she had very little time for therapy. Nor did she feel much of a need for it, given her new domestic bliss. She managed to see me about once a week, which was much less than I would have liked but much more than she thought necessary. Obviously the treatment of her multiplicity was no longer a priority.

I wondered how I would ever fully integrate this case. It is such a difficult process, so draining emotionally and financially, so time-consuming. Toby needed to see me every day for the week or so it took to merge just one alter. I used to think that we were being obsessive about this until I learned that other therapists often hospitalized their patients after an integration because the process created so much stress and chaos.

Lauren and I spent months talking about all this. At first she didn't understand what she was really doing. She trotted out the obvious excuses. It was so difficult to get in to see me with both children to watch. She believed we were making progress and edging toward some sort of partial unity. She insisted that she—Lauren—was now able to feel Peg's anger, and a few sessions later she reported that Peg was gone.

A few months after that experience of unity she had a homosexual experience, which, of course, she did not tell the electrician about. She said that instead of going away and letting Honey, her homosexual personality, have the experience, she was present the whole time. (My guess is that she was bisexual but needed her two homosexual personalities, Jefferson and Honey, to act it out because making love to a woman was repugnant to her main personality.) At the next session she reported that Honey, like Peg, was now gone.

I was skeptical. It just didn't feel right. When I tried with hypnosis to speak to her supposedly integrated personalities, no one answered me. But it certainly wasn't the way Toby had merged. There were no bloodcurdling abreactions, no double vision or double thinking, no dramas of death and rebirth during which I was the attending physician, nurse, undertaker, midwife, and minister. Just Lauren reporting in her rather matter-of-fact manner that she could feel Peg's rage and that Honey was no longer at home didn't seem right. Were these spontaneous integrations really true? There were some encouraging signs because Lauren was functioning well. Her relationship was stable, she had stayed off drugs, and she was extremely cooperative with me, except on the issue of coming into the office more frequently.

Maybe it was me, I thought. Maybe I had too rigid a view of how patients were supposed to act during this phase of their treatment. Maybe I hadn't taken into consideration important character differences between Lauren and Toby. I had often felt that Toby would suck me dry if I let her. Lauren was much less demanding and far more independent. Had I forgotten Erickson's admonition so quickly? All patients are different, he had said again and again. Avoid theories and treat individuals.

Still, no matter how hard I tried to rationalize it, my therapeutic self-helper told me something wasn't right. If Lauren was so independent, why was she so quick to link up with a man? Chance? Psychoanalysts, like insurance underwriters, do not believe in chance.

My doubts grew greater when Lauren started to cancel some of the few sessions she was willing to schedule. She blamed missed trains, a sick child, a husband who needed the car, or some other factor. Her attendance at my multiples group also lessened. When I questioned her about her absences, she continued to blame circumstances. But slowly I shaved away at Lauren's excuses. Why couldn't a relative have taken care of the children? Why couldn't she have rescheduled her appointment and taken a later train? Gradually, Lauren began to realize what was going on.

One day it came to a head. She had missed two appointments in a row and had been late for the previous three. I decided to confront it directly. She was in the process of telling me about yet another missed train when I cut her short.

"Couldn't you drive in to the city?"

"No," she replied. "My husband needed the car."

"I realize that it was difficult for you to get in, but it seems to me that there were other solutions you didn't try. For example, when you talked to me on the phone you could have asked me if I had a later appointment."

"That wouldn't have worked. I had to be home when the children got out of school."

"Well, if it were really impossible for you to get in to see me, why couldn't we have had the session on the telephone? You remember we have had phone sessions in the past."

That got her. She sat back, looking thoughtful. "You're right."

"I think, Lauren, that it is not a question of the train but your resistance to treatment. Therapy must be dragging up things that are very uncomfortable for you to face, and your system is trying to avoid them."

"No, that's not it, Dr. Mayer. I don't know how to tell you

this." She paused. "Look, I just don't want to lose my internal people."

"But you have already merged Peg, Jefferson, Scarlett, and some others. Aren't you happy with that?"

"They haven't merged," she said sheepishly. "They're still with me."

I was more confused than surprised. "What about the fragments? Are they still there?"

"No. They're gone. They merged. I'm talking about the major personalities. It's them I don't want to lose."

It was my fault that Lauren had lied. I had committed a therapeutic blunder. I had an expectation she couldn't fulfill. I wanted her to merge, and, not wanting to disappoint me, she chose to tell me what I wanted to hear. The irony is that on some level Lauren had let me abuse her. She had put my needs over hers, just as she had with her first husband when at his urging she let other men sleep with her. We had the material here for many sessions, if only she would remain in therapy—but she wouldn't.

Lauren argued that her system was stable. She had co-consciousness, which meant she could hear and converse with her internal personalities. Sometimes she would chair meetings where they would decide what to do and then pick one personality to do it. Sometimes she functioned alone, and the others did not bother her unless she got into trouble. Then one of them would take over the body and help her out. Later, they might have another internal meeting to talk about it. Somehow or other this system had worked, at least so far. If, as Lauren insisted, she was doing better than she ever had, why should she press her luck and attempt to go further? Why undergo more pain? Anyway, the other personalities did not want to die.

So Lauren chose to make a political settlement among her personalities rather than fully integrate. I had come across other multiples who claimed to have established equilibrium. Some were democracies, where every personality had a vote. Others were benevolent dictatorships.

Marlene, a thirty-five-year-old from upstate New York, started with seven personalities born of the same sad forces as those of Toby and Lauren. During one particularly hideous episode Marlene's father actually nailed her hands to a wooden cross as punishment for sleeping with him. She had also been abused by her mother, who had inserted implements into her vagina that had destroyed any possibility for her to have children.

Marlene was a highly motivated patient, driving two hours each way three times a week to see me. Her treatment went surprisingly quickly, in part because she had seen several therapists before me who, though unable to treat the multiplicity, had helped with other problems. After a short period of resistance, the trust between us grew. Soon there were abreactions and mergers. Then, just when Marlene was down to her last extra personality, an eleven-year-old named Peggy Sue, she abruptly stopped therapy. She was happy, she said. Why go any further?

One of the chief reasons she stopped therapy, it turned out, was her husband, Martin, whom she had met just before we started treatment. He had been supportive up until now, encouraging each integration, so I asked him to come in and talk to me about his change of heart. At the interview he told me very frankly that he was not in favor of Marlene continuing therapy if it meant the loss of Peggy Sue. It seemed that he dearly loved the eleven-year-old. She was the daughter he had never had but always wanted. He enjoyed taking her to amusement parks and to the beach. To his credit, or so he said, he never made love to her, telling her to "skedaddle" when he and her "mother," as Peggy Sue called Marlene, were preparing for bed.

Marlene told me that she was afraid that if she integrated and lost Peggy Sue she would also lose Martin. So she stopped.

Her solution to the problems of having two people in one body was a benevolent dictatorship. Marlene was generally in charge of the body and made the major decisions. If there were disagreements, she and Peggy Sue would negotiate. Sometimes Peggy Sue would come out and do the things an eleven-year-old likes to do. When Peggy Sue was out, Marlene had no knowledge of what went on; strangely, when Marlene was out Peggy Sue was aware of what had happened. In any event, Marlene was in control about 90 percent of the time, so it didn't really matter. Given the risks her last merger entailed and the slim benefit, I could understand her reluctance to fully integrate.

Shirley, who was about twenty-seven when I met her, was about five feet tall, slender and quite attractive. She had four personalities, one of whom was a professional masochist who worked in the same sort of establishment as the twins, Marcia and Mary, but of course played the other role. She would let herself be abused by men for a fee. This alter had been born during a peculiar parochial school experience in which she had physically and sexually been assaulted by a nun. The same sadistic sister would force her to do penance for various religious infractions by kneeling for hours barelegged on rice.

Just when we were getting closer in therapy to uncovering these memories, a customer fell in love with Shirley and started to hire her privately. He convinced her to leave the business and move in with him. Eventually they were married. Obviously, he did not want the masochistic personality to integrate, so he was opposed to any therapy that would result in a complete merger. Like a "good girl," she obeyed and stopped our sessions with one personality left to merge.

Charles was one of the few male multiples I worked with. He was forty-five years old and had five alter personalities he had managed to keep a secret from his wife of twenty-five years. She thought his sudden mood swings and occasional temper tantrums were due to his long-standing alcoholism. His AA sponsor, who happened to be a former patient of mine and knew of my interest in multiplicity, had a feeling about what was really going on and referred Charles to me.

His mother and father had belonged to some sort of satanic cult, and as a baby Charles had been taken to bizarre rituals where animals were slaughtered and children were ritualistically drenched in blood. Then the participants would have orgies, often including the children.

After meeting his other personalities, I formulated a treatment plan and Charles made a series of appointments. He worked with me for a couple of months but then stopped, blaming a shortage of time and money.

In an effort to keep him in therapy I tried to enlist the support of his wife, Robin. After talking to her, it became clear that she was on the other side. Indeed, Robin was relieved to know that her husband's problem was not alcohol, since in her mind that would have been worse than multiplicity. She was also worried about how much therapy would cost, since they had a daughter in college and were not well off. She also enjoyed one aspect of her husband's multiplicity: "I get laid by six people every time we have sex," she told me.

Robin talked to her friends constantly about Charles's problem and also began trying to form a support group for spouses of multiples. She also considered selling her story to Hollywood. (To my knowledge, she has not succeeded at either.) All in all, I'd have to say she adjusted to his multiplicity—perhaps better than he did.

I once treated a multiple named Essie who, of all things, lived with another multiple, Michele. Both women had host personalities who were lesbians, but they each also had male personalities as well as children inside them. Somehow they managed to form a complete closed system. They needed no one. They could be homosexual lovers. They could be heterosexual lovers. They could be mother and daughter. They could be father and son. They could be childhood playmates. They could be pedophiles. Or they could be any combination of the above. It was truly a "perfect" relationship, if one considers endless variety as perfection.

The case was difficult. They each needed therapy, but I couldn't treat them both, since that would risk even more complications. So I referred Michele to another therapist. She worked with her for a while but soon stopped treatment and tried to talk Estelle into following suit. She knew that if Estelle merged she would lose her relationship. And eventually my patient did stop therapy, although not before she reached co-consciousness. That allowed her to attain a political peace with her alters similar to Lauren's.

Of course, patients have other reasons to stop therapy, many others, besides the fear of what it will do to their personal lives. Therapy is expensive, especially for a multiple, and a complete merger of all personalities and fragments is not always cost-effective. Therapy takes time. Therapy is painful. Past memories and past feelings have to be relived and reexperienced. For the child abuse victim, this is especially trying. So remaining in therapy until the end may be a lot to ask someone to go through for the promise but by no means the certainty of a better life. It reminds me of religions that ask followers to give up all earthly pleasures for the promise of a blissful hereafter.

A multiple's internal world is a place of safety, a place where alter personalities can retreat from the often nasty reality of reality. The internal world also offers companionship; it is a good place for multiples to amuse themselves when they are lonely or bored. If you have an internal world, you do not have to invest in the work the real world requires, nor do you risk the disappointments. All the patients I helped to achieve merger commented on this. Toby was sad after her last personality integrated and the Dark Ones destroyed the internal world. There was no longer a place for her to escape to. When she complained about how hard life was, which was often, she would always lament the loss of her Shangri-La.

Are we purportedly healthy people really that different?

How many of us drift into the fantasy rather than confront the alternative? How many of us watch soap operas rather than face life's drama? How many of us hide behind alcohol or drugs? Could I really blame Lauren for not wanting to sail out into the unknown? Should I blame her for playing Cinderella and clinging to Prince Charming?

I thought about all this after Lauren stopped therapy. I had to admit I was conflicted. My perfectionist side felt that merger —complete merger—was the only proper therapeutic solution. That part of me could not conceive that someone would want to stop short of this goal. What kind of life could she lead if she had to have an internal meeting every time she faced a decision? If the inside of her head resembled the French Chamber of Deputies during the 1930s? Who uses the body when? Who's out? Who's in? Each day would be a parliamentary struggle, an endless debate, a total conflict.

I know I have an overly rigid way of looking at things. It is a reflection of my own unbending character. I like to be thorough. I like to do something as well as I can, and I am obsessive about completing tasks. But what if my patient lacked the psychological resources to complete the process? What about those patients who may have been too damaged? The anxiety multiples endure coping with their pasts—pasts from which they have been fleeing for years—can be too much. Psychotherapy can only build on what is there. It cannot create. The public—our patients—thinks we practice a science, but any therapist will tell you it is at best an art. And mostly we just practice.

A patient's decision to quit isn't necessarily final. Some people go on to graduate school directly from college and do not stop until they have a Ph.D. Others rest along the way, taking decades to earn a doctorate.

After years of gazing through my existential telescope at the problem of patients who quit, I think I have finally seen a glimmer of light. As someone hired by patients to do a professional job, I try to tell them that merger and only merger is the best solution. Nothing is lost, and the entire personality will function better. However, I do not force this view on my patients. And if, after discharging my professional responsibility by telling patients what I think, I cannot get them to agree, then I help them reach whatever goal they set. If what they want is a partial solution, such as co-consciousness, which allows the alters to conduct internal debates that lead to group decisions—in effect, a rational, organized government—so be it. And if in the future the government is overthrown and the system breaks down, therapy can always be resumed.

If Lauren ever decided she wanted to complete the task of personal unity, she would always know where to find me.

17

Epilogues

Toby's final integration was complete, and the glue binding her personality together seemed to be holding. In a way, she was only starting therapy. She still had trouble with relationships, still was too sensitive, still acted as though she needed a savior, and still was overweight, which was one of her ways of insulating herself from the world. In other words, she was mildly neurotic.

Toby was also a little anxious about leaving me and being on her own. In session after session she complained about her loneliness. She missed her "people," and she missed the security and sense of independence that multiplicity had given her. In the past, if life had disappointed her it did not matter. She could always retreat to the comfort of her internal garden. Now it was gone. Half jokingly, I would offer to ask the Dark Ones to restore it, but she always refused. She knew the disadvantages of multiplicity far outweighed the advantages.

Gradually, Toby began focusing her energy outward rather than inward, and in so doing started to activate her true self. She slimmed down and paid more attention to her appearance. She found her old friendships were not adequate, having been developed by a different person in a different time, so she went out and cultivated a whole new group of friends. Amazingly, they even included two or three men.

Toby had been a paper pusher at an educational publishing house, a job that was secure but emotionally and intellectually unrewarding. She had talent as a painter, but it was exceedingly difficult to make a living painting. As part of her new life she quit publishing and got a job as an illustrator, allowing herself to express her creativity. It was nice to see her enjoy her work for a change. It was gratifying to watch her fantasies give way. Toby had finally started to grow up.

At the beginning of her second year after her integration, Toby took a big step away from me and reduced her sessions to once a month. Like most such actions, it came after a major event led to a new insight. One evening, out of nowhere, she started drifting into one of her old memory cycles. She became anxious and frightened without knowing what was causing it. She had the same old sensation that something was trying to force its way up to consciousness, but she didn't know what it was. She just knew that she felt frightened.

She came in to see me the next day. I was worried that she might be unconsciously recreating an old problem just to remain in therapy. Years ago Densen-Gerber had warned me that sometimes patients who are getting ready to leave therapy will manufacture a crisis—or even a new personality, in the case of a multiple—in order to hang on to a therapist. I was not looking forward to another of Toby's abreactions—not now, not after I had presided over so many of them. What could I do? Toby's new problem had to be solved. Her fears had to be eased.

I suggested she go into a trance, so that we could get directly at the memory. Surprisingly, she refused. "I have to learn to do it myself," she said. Then she threw me back an Odyssey House line I had used with her many times. "If I let you do it, it's like giving a man a fish rather than teaching him how to fish. If you give him a fish, he eats a meal. If you teach him to fish, he eats for the rest of his life."

I loved her response. I wanted to applaud, or at least tell

her I approved, but I realized that in so doing I would be giving her permission to do whatever it was she was about to do anyway and thus reinforcing an adult-child relationship that she needed—and seemed about ready—to break. So, like a good analyst, I said nothing.

She asked me how she could put herself into a trance. Again, I decided not to answer, forcing her to figure it out for herself.

At first she was angry at me for not helping her, but about three or four minutes later she caught on, realizing that this was a problem that she needed to solve for herself. Remembering all the times I had instructed her to simply lie on the couch and tell me whatever came into her mind, she set out to be her own therapist. Just like the cases in the textbooks, she let her mind wander, trying to remember and isolate the moment she had first started to feel the anxiety and fear. She traced it back to a dinner during which a friend had spilled a small container of milk she had been pouring into her coffee. We both knew she was on the right track.

At this point she started to feel uncomfortable. In the past, her first impulse had been to avoid this feeling. Her second would have been to ask me for help. This time, though, she tolerated the feelings and then let her mind free-associate, jumping off from the milk. Soon her memory burst forth. It was, perhaps predictably, another of her childhood horrors. Toby was at the dinner table and had accidentally spilled a glass of milk on the floor. Her mother, apparently out of control with rage, screamed, "Milk is expensive, we will not waste it," and to prove her point brutally punished Toby for her clumsiness by making her lap the milk up off the floor like a dog. Halfway through this chore Toby threw up. But that did not deter the mother, who insisted that she lap that up as well.

Toby thought about this episode for a few moments. She let herself feel the old feelings—the pain, the disgust—performing her own abreaction. She also analyzed why the memory had popped up now rather than earlier in treatment. Her conclusion was that it was a memory shared by all the personalities and had only become accessible once she was fully integrated.

I continued to say nothing, for one of the few times in the years I had treated her. I was thinking back to Beth's hysterical reaction years ago when we had been in Connecticut and Densen-Gerber had offered her milk with her cookies. Another mystery solved.

At the end of the session I thought it was appropriate to reward Toby, so for the first time in my professional career I gave a patient a hug. It was something a classical analyst would frown on. Thinking back on it, perhaps I should have done it sooner. Far from being sexually suggestive, Toby was really asking for the kind of physical comfort a father might give a child, and on some occasions it could reasonably have been granted. We primates do comfort one another by touching.

At the next session, Toby said that while she appreciated the hug, she had had a strange reaction to it. It didn't do what she expected it would do, which was to make her feel wonderful. At first that had disturbed her. She had thought about it for days at a time and finally concluded that the hug had been from the wrong person. The right person would have been Dr. Carter. Similarly, the lap that Beth had demanded to sit on was his, not mine. He had soothed her as a child, and she had assumed I was a reincarnation of him and could do the same. But in thinking about the last session Toby fully realized that I was not some version of Dr. Carter but Dr. Mayer, her therapist. She had broken the transference. Toby had separated from me. She had individuated. She was well on her way to autonomy.

At the end of 1986 she ceased regular therapy, telling me she would come in when and if she needed it. She has returned every six months or so for what she calls "psychological tune-ups," but that is all. The glue is still holding.

———

The Dark Ones, at my urging, stayed around for the first year to make sure things were really all right with Toby. Every few sessions I would put Toby into a trance, call them out, and check in with them. But they made no secret of their impatience to leave. They would tell me—in their mystically obtuse way, of course—that they had other work to do. Finally, to their relief, I told them that as far as I was concerned Toby was fine and we had no more use for them or the internal world, which they proceeded to destroy. They told me they would be available if they were ever needed again. And they also advised me to develop my spiritual side, so I would be more accessible to my own Dark Ones. Then they bade me a good evening, lay down on the couch, closed their eyes, and went wherever Dark Ones go.

Thinking about this later, I wondered whether the Dark Ones were Toby's way of discharging her anger and disappointment at me for not giving her what she wanted, which was more attention than I thought she needed. She would not have dared express it herself for fear of losing her relationship with me altogether. But I will never know for sure, since she would never allow me to analyze the Dark Ones.

Evidently, they had a hold on both of us. In 1987, when Toby came in for her yearly tune-up, she told me that whenever she passes a church she feels compelled to enter and light a candle. Very often she gives in to the urge. I asked her for whom she lit the candle. One of the archangels, she replied. I didn't bother to ask which one. I knew it was Michael.

After a two-year investigation, Judianne Densen-Gerber maintained her innocence but agreed to repay some personal expenses charged to Odyssey House, under a 1982 agreement with the New York State Attorney General reported in the New York *Times*.

Densen-Gerber eventually left Odyssey House and went into private practice. I see her from time to time at professional meetings, where she always inquires about Toby, Susan, Lauren, and the rest.

She has found other causes. One of the first voices to bring attention to the problem of sexual abuse of children, she inveighed against the pro-incest and pro-transgenerational sex lobbies, including groups like Nambla, the North American Man-Boy Love Association. She had become aware of the problem years before, when addicted young boys started turning up at Odyssey House, claiming they had escaped from men who had kept them addicted and used them as sex slaves and boy prostitutes.

Toby, Lauren, Susan, and I will always be grateful to her— as should all of those who were rescued from the oblivion of drugs at Odyssey House.

As a treatment center, Odyssey House is still in business, but staff members, realizing that the times and patient populations have changed, have rethought the Odyssey House philosophy. When Densen-Gerber started the program, the average resident was a hard-core addict with a conscienceless personality. Today the addicts are less antisocial and more passive, and drugs are their way of medicating themselves to blunt psychological pain. As a result, the techniques of humiliation designed to break addicts down no longer work with the new residents, who have weaker egos and feel more guilt. The program still operates on the principle of behavior modification, with rewards and punishments aplenty, but the atmosphere is less harsh, more humane, and more tailored to the individual needs of the residents. Instrumental in bringing these changes about was Arlene Levine, who is now chief of clinical services.

Mary and Marcia, the twins, left the program a year or two after the confrontation with their father. Mary went into private therapy and gradually became fully integrated. She has since started a new life in charge of production at a furniture factory in the South. She says she loves the responsibility.

Marcia, on the other hand, headed for northern California. A year later, she reentered another drug program. She also sought treatment for multiplicity and was eventually fully integrated. She is now working as a counselor at a women's shelter in the Midwest.

Thus the twins not only kicked their habits and unified their personalities, they also accomplished another difficult task that all twins face: their psychological separation from one another. Recently I heard that their father had died of cancer and their mother had died soon after of a heart attack. I doubt either were mourned.

After her disappointing confrontation with her father, my patient Susan plummeted into what I considered a state of potentially suicidal depression. She could not understand why he would not admit to what he had done, especially since there even were witnesses. Worse, she was terribly wounded that her mother and all but one of her sisters—including the elder sister who had cleaned her up after the abuse and the younger sisters whom Susan had unsuccessfully tried to protect—denied what had happened, called her a liar, and banished her from the family.

It took a year on my couch to resolve these issues. After months of languishing, her energy returned and her depression, which in her case was a combination of loss and anger turned inward, became converted to pure anger. She left those who had abandoned her, ceased all contact with her family, went back to college, and obtained a degree in social work. She is now working as a therapist in Southern California.

Susan still sends me postcards from time to time. In the last one, she told me she had married and was expecting her first child.

Lauren continued to see me for a while, but only sporadically. She would make appointments when she had a specific problem, most of which involved her husband or her children. For a while her daughter was exhibiting possible signs of multiplicity, such as imaginary playmates that stay around too long, as well as displaying alarmingly seductive mannerisms, which is a signal that a child has been sexually abused. I strongly suggested that both begin some type of therapy in her hometown.

Lauren comes in only every year or so, mostly for marital crises, not multiplicity. She tells me, when I ask, that her "people" are still there, but that they come out only when she needs them. They do not disrupt her life. Apparently the political solution she worked out years ago is still stable. Still, I feel that someday Lauren will complete the task of integration, though perhaps this is just my idealism.

I still teach college, write technical papers, and sit in the same analytic chair—which is still comfortable although no longer new—while I listen to patients. I still struggle with my countertransferences. I still struggle with the central paradox of my profession: that the best way to help people is not to help them, but to help them help themselves. I must content myself to, as Toby puts it, teach them to fish.

But my chance encounter almost ten years ago with Toby altered my professional and personal life in a way no one could have predicted. Toby opened many new worlds to me. I was forced to think about things I would have preferred not to think about—drug addiction, child molestation, rape, many people living in one body, and mysticism. I had to learn to allow myself to have feelings that were far more intense than I had ever experienced, but at the same time to be able to keep myself at least partially dissociated from them in order to work with her. I was forced to stretch intellectually as well as emotionally.

It also made me take a fresh look at my practice and my patients, especially those who were not progressing in therapy. Had they been physically or sexually abused as children and not been able to tell me about it because they had dissociated the experiences? Had I missed the clues? Had I assumed it was an Oedipal issue? The answer in some cases was unfortunately yes. I found that I had missed a number of cases of childhood abuse. When I started to treat them accordingly, cases that were stuck started to move forward.

I have learned to have respect for multiples and the ingenious way in which they deal with their catastrophes and survive. Creating other people who live in your body—it sounds so pathological, yet the ability to dissociate, to enter a hypnoid state, and to create a new personality to share pain can be an asset as well as a liability. Without it, some of my patients might have become psychotic. Some might have committed murder or suicide.

An ability to dissociate is necessary for day-to-day functioning as well as survival of childhood trauma. None of us could function without it. We are exposed to so many stimuli every moment from the inside as well as the outside. The ability to dissociate is also the ability to focus, to choose which stimuli to respond to. Without that ability we would be nonfunctional. Some people dissociate better than others, but with a little training we might be able to control pain or get through a boring meeting without dozing off. How wonderful life would be if you could look at the speaker, smile attentively, and go someplace else in your mind. What about listening to a stutterer? You could dissociate between stammers and hear a normal conversation. What about going to the dentist? The potential is unlimited.

When I first heard the details of Toby's brutal childhood, I was appalled. It is one thing to read about it in a technical book and quite another to have a patient reexperiencing an anal rape in front of you. As a therapist I was supposedly an expert in man's inhumanity, but there was a part of me that was too naive and idealistic. I found it hard to accept the rape of a two-year-old. I was also a victim of my countertransference, my feelings toward the patient that were based in my own past experiences rather than what was happening at the moment. I was too much the patient's defender. I was trying to make her childhood better, trying to fix it, trying to be her white knight. I felt her pain; I enjoyed her victories, just as I took delight when the neighbor who had raped Carmela as a child went to jail.

As I got used to working with multiples, my idealistic anger found another target—my fellow professionals. When I began treating Toby, a great many therapists, like Freud before them, still refused to acknowledge that multiplicity existed. Patients would tell them they had been raped by their father when they were five years old, and the therapist would think they were lying to cover up their true feelings—that these five-year-olds really wanted to sleep with their fathers. Patients would abreact these rapes in the office, and these skeptical therapists would accuse them of faking.

The average multiple is in therapy nearly seven years with three different therapists before the proper diagnosis is made. Who knows how many multiples have left treatment or never been properly diagnosed? Studies show that almost all child abusers were abused children, so the chain of abuse continues.

I came to regard aspects of Freud, my old hero, with disdain. I couldn't believe that anyone interested in treating the victims of childhood abuse would write: "Almost all my women patients told me that they had been seduced by their father. I was driven to recognize in the end that these reports were untrue and so came to understand that the hysterical symptoms are derived from phantasies and not from real occurrences."

Freud refused to believe what his patients told him. He was

intellectually dishonest. Is it possible that the originator and first investigator of the concept of countertransference denied that he himself suffered from it? In a recently published letter Freud wrote in 1897 to his friend, colleague, confessor, and "analyst," Wilhelm Fliess, he related a dream in which he was feeling "overly affectionate" toward his daughter Mathilda. It came about the time Freud was shifting from the seduction theory, in which the parent sexually abused the child, to the Oedipal theory, in which the child has incestuous feelings toward the parent.

Was Freud intellectually honest with his feelings? Did he change his theory into one he was more comfortable with in order to deny his own incestuous desires? How many therapists are still doing this, missing the point—that their patients have been abused—and then wondering why they don't get better?

I saw Freud's legacy every day in my profession. Once a patient of mine, Roberta, a social worker in the psychiatric ward of a New Jersey hospital, called me to discuss a woman who had recently been admitted to her ward. Given the patient's behavior—she was carving her arms and saying that someone else named Sally was doing it—my patient thought she might be a multiple. After hearing the symptoms, I agreed. The problem was that the psychiatrists at the hospital were missing it, and the patient was not getting the proper treatment. Not comfortable with telling her supervisor how to do his job, Roberta asked me what she should do. Like Dorothy in Oz, who naively thinks that if one can find and talk to the man in charge everything will be all right, I advised her to tell the attending psychiatrist that she thought the patient was possibly suffering from multiple personality disorder. He might not be familiar with it.

She did, but he chewed her out, telling her that multiple personality disorder was so exceedingly rare the chances were one in ten thousand that this patient was a multiple. The psychiatrist refused to confer with me or even invite me to come to the hospital and work the patient up myself.

The patient, who had been diagnosed as schizophrenic and put on antipsychotic medication, kept getting worse. The psychiatrist then changed the medication five times, with no success. At a staff conference it was decided to give the patient electric shock therapy. The patient got worse still and became very angry. Then they put her in a "rubber" isolation room, which also didn't help.

Finally, they stopped all medication and the patient eventually was returned to the condition in which she had first sought treatment at the hospital. The staff decided the treatment had been a success. After all, she had improved from the time she was in the rubber room. The patient was then discharged. Before she left, Roberta suggested she seek help from someone like me. But the patient by now would have nothing to do with the psychiatric profession. I suspect that she will never trust another therapist, and who would blame her?

I have heard too many variations on this theme to believe that much has changed. After Toby's "60 Minutes" episode aired, for instance, I got a call from a Canadian named Allyn Pearson. He told me that he thought that his wife, Nancy, was a multiple. She had been in treatment with a psychiatrist in Canada for the past four years but was not getting better. He was, in fact, convinced she was getting worse. Her psychiatrist had her on all sorts of drugs, but the only person they were helping was the pharmacist. Nancy had also been hospitalized several times.

I told him that since she was in treatment, it was unprofessional of me to butt in; however, if their psychiatrist would call me, I would be glad to consult with him. Like the psychiatrist in New Jersey, I erroneously assumed he was a reasonable professional who only needed to be made aware of what to look for.

The doctor never called, and I put it out of my mind. Two weeks later Allyn called me again and said he had begged the doctor to call but he had refused. The doctor told him there was no such thing as multiple personality disorder and that he knew what he was doing. Allyn asked me if I would phone him. I figured that he wasn't about to listen to me anyway, so I suggested that Allyn take his wife for a consultation with another doctor in Canada who was familiar with multiplicity. I gave him a couple of names I had obtained from the International Society for the Study of Multiple Personality Disorder in Chicago.

One of them saw Mrs. Pearson, quickly diagnosed her as a multiple, and started her in therapy. Within a few months she was off all medication and progressing rapidly. Several months after that, three of her eight alter personalities had been integrated.

About a month after his wife had started with her new therapist, Allyn called to thank me. He also told me that before they had hooked up with me they were so desperate that they had entered into a mutual suicide pact. The pact had ten days left to go when they saw Toby and me on television. Allyn felt I had saved both their lives.

How many more are out there without a sympathetic or enlightened analyst? Richard Kluft, of the Temple University School of Medicine and the Institute of the Pennsylvania Hospital, surveyed a number of patients who had been hospitalized and diagnosed as borderline, which is a catchall phrase for people who are on the border between psychosis and neurosis and very difficult to treat. He found that 80 percent had been sexually abused as children, a fact missed by all the physicians working with them. How many patients who go to therapists year after year without results—and keep going because there is no other option—are misdiagnosed because the analyst refuses to ask the right questions or believe the answer?

In the fall of 1984 I convinced my training institute, the American Institute for Psychoanalysis and Psychotherapy, to let me teach a course in Multiple Personality and Dissociated States. The classes were not very well attended in the four years they were offered. My guess is that young therapists—and older ones who advise their students on what courses to take—think the disorder is simply too rare to turn up in private practice.

After discussing this problem with a few like-minded colleagues, including Arlene Levine, we decided to organize a conference that would bring the word to the profession that multiplicity was more common than generally realized.

We cast about for money for this project and found there wasn't any. No organization we contacted would touch it (Freud's legacy lives). With no other option, Dr. Levine and I reached into our pockets and came up with the $12,000 we needed for mailing lists, stamps, printing, audiovisual technicians and equipment and a hotel. We hoped that enough people would attend—at sixty dollars a head—to defray most of the costs. We invited Kluft to be the keynote speaker and also began preparing speeches of our own.

It took about a year of planning, but somehow or other it all came together on November 15, 1986. The Georgian Ballroom of the Penta Hotel in New York City was jammed with two hundred professionals, each with one or more multiples in treatment, thus demonstrating that the disorder is not that rare. They craved information as desert travelers crave water. Most of them were like myself when I first started with Toby. They were alone in the trenches, enduring the abreactions of their clients and the displeasure of their colleagues and not quite believing that what they were seeing was real. The conference, aside from giving them a methodology of treatment, validated their clinical experiences and put them in touch with others. Other than financially, the session was a smashing success.

Acting on requests made from some of those in attendance, I started running training workshops in the treatment of multiple personality disorder and the use of hypnosis. I have also responded to dozens of requests for consultations to confirm diagnoses and set up treatment plans for patients suspected of multiplicity. I estimate that more than a hundred patients were diagnosed properly and started along the proper therapeutic course due to the conference.

Way begets way, as Robert Frost said. Other organizations invited me to speak, and I did. Responding to requests made to me at the conference, I started to run teaching groups for treating multiple personality disorder in my office. Dr. Levine and I formed a study group for multiple personality disorder and became the clearinghouse for information and training in the New York area. I am contacted once or twice a month either by a therapist who suspects a patient is a multiple or by a patient.

Invariably I start with the basics. I tell them that multiple personality disorder is real. I tell them it is caused by trauma in childhood.

And above all, I tell them that, if it is diagnosed properly, if a therapist is trained or at least has an open mind, and if the patient is motivated, it can successfully be treated.

Glossary

Abreaction: The process of bringing forgotten feelings, memories, or ideas into consciousness.

Affect: Emotion, feeling, or mood. Sometimes thought as one of the three mental functions, along with cognition and volition.

Alter personality (or alter): A separate identity with a substantial emotional range and an extensive history of its own.

Amnestic barrier: A wall in the mind preventing one personality from being aware of the experiences of other personalities.

Co-consciousness: When alters are aware of the thoughts, feelings, and behavior of the other personalities.

Co-presence: The influence of one personality on another, for example, when an alter struggles to gain control of the body from another alter or even the host personality.

Countertransference: Feelings the therapist has toward a patient, based on the therapist's own life.

Dissociation: An unconscious defense mechanism in which a group of mental processes or activities, such as memories, thoughts, and/or feelings, "splits off" from the main stream of consciousness and functions as a separate unit. This is the basic defense mechanism in multiple personality disorder. It is also a feature of ordinary psychological functioning; forgetting is dissociation in its simplest form.

Fugue state: A state in which a person forgets who he or she is.

Fusion: The joining of two or more alter personalities into a single personality. Also called integration or merger.

Host: The personality that was born and then created other personalities in order to help it cope with severe trauma. This may or may not be the personality that is active in the world or enters treatment.

Hysteria: An archaic term for a group of psychiatric disorders characterized by amnesia, paralysis, hallucinations, somnambulism, and dissociation.

Incest: Sexual relations between parent and child or between siblings.

Inner self-helper: An alter personality that is rational, sort of like a very well balanced conscience. It differs from the other alter personalities in that it wasn't created to handle pain or trauma.

Pedophile: An adult who is sexually attracted to children.

Personality fragment: A part of a personality that is not fully developed and lacks the emotional range and extensive history of an alter personality.

Psychoanalysis: Conceived by Freud, a method that seeks out the roots of human behavior in unconscious motivation and conflict. Can also refer to a specific psychotherapeutic technique in which the analyst is passive in order to elicit material from the patient's unconscious.

Psychiatrist: A medical doctor who specializes in diagnosing and treating mental disorders.

Psychologist: A person, usually with a master's degree or doctorate, who through a course of training has made a specialized study of the science of psychology.

Regression: The reestablishment of older patterns of behavior.

Repression: The process by which a patient delegates to the unconscious feelings of shame, guilt, or embarrassment.

Resistance: Words or actions of a patient that hinder psychoanalytic treatment by blocking access to his or her unconscious.

Schizophrenia: A severe psychiatric ailment characterized by disordered thought, hallucinations, and the loss of a sense of reality. The term literally means "splitting in the mind" and was originally chosen because the disorder appeared to reflect a cleavage between the emotions and thinking.

Switch: An alter personality who controls the mechanism that determines who has control of the body.

Transference: Feelings a patient has for the therapist that are based on feelings for someone else in the patient's life.

For Further Reading

Allison, Ralph. *Minds in Many Pieces: The Making of a Very Special Doctor* (New York: Rawson, Wade Publishers, 1980).

Braun, Bennett G. (editor). *Treatment of Multiple Personality* (Washington, D.C.: American Psychiatric Press, 1986).

Carnes, Patrick. *Out of the Shadows: Understanding Sexual Addiction* (Minneapolis: CompCare Publications, 1983).

Crabtree, Adam. *Multiple Man: Explorations in Possession and Multiple Personality* (New York: Praeger, 1985).

Crewdson, John. *By Silence Betrayed: Sexual Abuse of Children in America* (Boston: Little, Brown, 1988).

Densen-Gerber, Judianne. *We Mainline Dreams: The Odyssey House Story* (Garden City, New York: Doubleday, 1973).

Ellenberger, Henri F. *The Discovery of the Unconscious: The History and Evolution of Dynamic Psychiatry* (New York: Basic Books, 1970).

Erickson, Milton H., and Sidney Rosen (editor). *My Voice Will Go with You: The Teaching Tales of Milton H. Erickson, M.D.* (New York: Norton, 1982).

Fiore, E. *The Unquiet Dead: A Psychologist Treats Spirit Possession—Detecting and Removing Earthbound Spirits* (Garden City, New York: Doubleday, 1987).

Haley, Jay. *Uncommon Therapy: The Psychiatric Techniques of Milton H. Erickson, M.D.* (New York: Norton, 1973).

Kluft, Richard P. (editor). *Childhood Antecedents of Multiple Personality* (Washington, D.C.: American Psychiatric Press, 1985).

Masson, Jeffrey M. *The Assault on Truth: Freud's Suppression of the Seduction Theory* (Toronto: Farrar, Straus & Giroux, 1984).

Masterson, James F. *The Real Self: A Developmental, Self, and Object Relations Approach* (New York: Brunner/Mazel, 1985).

Miller, Alice. *For Your Own Good: Hidden Cruelty in Child-Rearing and the Roots of Violence* (translated by Hildegarde and Hunter Hannum; New York: Farrar, Straus & Giroux, 1983).

Veith, Ilza. *Hysteria, The History of a Disease* (Chicago: University of Chicago Press, 1965).

Zeig, Jeffrey K. *A Teaching Seminar with Milton H. Erickson, M.D.* (New York: Brunner/Mazel, 1980).